Encountering the Indian
Contemporary European Images of India

Encountering the Indian

Contemporary European Images of India

Edited By

Vibha Maurya

ARYAN BOOKS INTERNATIONAL
NEW DELHI

Encountering the Indian
Contemporary European Images of India

ISBN-81-7305-162-3

Published in 1999 by :

ARYAN BOOKS INTERNATIONAL
Pooja Apartments, 4B, Ansari Road, Darya Ganj
New Delhi - 110 002 (India)

In association with
DEPARTMENT OF GERMANIC AND ROMANCE STUDIES
University of Delhi, Delhi

Computer Typesetting at Welcome Computers, New Delhi
Printed in India at B.B.N. Printers, New Delhi

Preface

Tales of European encounters with America, Asia and Africa have been narrated by Europeans over and over again since the end of the fifteenth century. Columbus in Guanahani, Vasco da Gama in Calicut, Prospero and Caliban, John Smith and Pocahontas or Marco Polo and Kublai Khan, all of them present a discourse, which is epitomised in an engraving *America* by Jan Van Der Straet, showing a clothed and armed European meeting a naked American.

However, the process of the dissolution of colonies and formation of independent states has generated new debates and constructed new discourses. A change may be perceived in the concerns of the people of the former colonies and their ideas of the hegemony of external forces. Therefore, the contemporary period seems to have marked a shift in the representation of India in European discourses as well.

Encountering the Indian (Contemporary European Images of India) is a collection of articles and contributions from different disciplines and different parts of the world and come after several years of debates around the construction of image of the Indian Other in contemporary Europe. This volume brings together varied experiences and views bound in a common frame of reference and makes an attempt to reread those cultural texts, which emerged during India's freedom struggle or after the dismantling of the empire. The texts included, are drawn from literary and sociological fields, travelogues and electronic media including films and documentaries. Image is not viewed here in its meaning of representing an object/person as an optical reflection. It may also serve as a theme, motif or symbol and is free from any notable consistency. European Indian images are unstable and anamorphic, therefore seems to consolidate the image of the European self.

This volume would not have been brought out without the support of the colleagues of the Department of Germanic and Romance Studies, University of Delhi. I would like to thank Shaswati Mazumdar for her advice in conceptualising the theme and Jyoti Sabharwal, Vijaya Venkatraman and C. Devika for helping me in editing and proof-reading the articles.

Contents

VIBHA MAURYA

Introduction

In its connotations perhaps no single word has been so loaded with emotion, even with passion, as has the term 'Orient'. Depending on the thinkers involved, or even the phases of their thought, the word has evoked fascination, repulsion and dread. It has been associated with the most diverse images. Each time that portion of the world called 'the Orient' has expanded or contracted, changing its fauna and flora, reason has given way to bias, antipathy or fear. Even when the images appeared to be neutral, the ubiquity of solar myth made the concept of 'the Orient' again applicable to all lands outside our own, and it became the passkey to the creations of all the heaven in turn.

The Oriental Renaissance, Raymond Schhwab

The entire twentieth century has been witness to a profound pondering over the issue of Orienalist discourses and a radical review of the same are being brought out in an assertive manner by those who were the object of the Orientalist Studies so far, i.e. the Orientals themselves. The rereading of Orientalist texts and their reinterpretation have served to draw attention not only to some of the representational problems, dwelt upon as 'signs of the other', but also have served to expose the Orientalist politics of representation. It is so because the Other is not just another subject, but is identifiable as the colonial or ex-colonial Other linked with expansion in the sense of imperial power.

A major scholarly work entitled *The Oriental Renaissance,*[1] published in 1950 was written by the 'integral humanist' Raymond Schwab, who has tried to retell the nineteenth century history of European Oriental Studies and particularly of India. The European experience of the Orient—influences of the Orient in the West and the impact of it on the vast body of European literature—constitute the underlying theme of Schwab's text. As against the classical Renaissance wherein a European was shown to be firmly 'grounded on the self sufficient terrain of Latin and Greek cultures', the Oriental Renaissance opened up before them a 'different' world. Schwab suggested that the eighteenth century 'rediscovery' of

Sanskrit and other ancient languages had perhaps the same relationship with European romanticism as the classical texts had with the Renaissance.[2] Thus the European awareness about the Orient, in his view, was of a productive nature as is reflected in the writings of the Romantic and Pre-romantic periods. Schwab, therefore, brought a major change in the way the Orient should be looked at or studied. The concerns, thus, of the Romantics were very different from their classical predecessors. Schwab is also responsible for initiating an informed debate on the notions of civilization and barbarism, primitive and advanced, origin and end, etc. In this process he attempts to show that the Western image of the Orient has progressed from being a primitive to a 'real' one. In our view, thus Schwab's study indicates one of the first shifts which is perceived in the West's understanding of traditions and its pre-textual dependence on the 'fable' and 'fabulousness' of the Orient. This marked shift in the construction of Oriental images by Europe has also been manifested in varied approaches adopted towards the study of the Orient (anthropological, scientific, textreading, etc.), which in turn thrust on the Europeans a new, more strange and complex image.

For a long time the Orient as a geographical entity only comprised of Judea, Persian, Arabic or Chinese spaces because India looked quite inaccessible to the Europeans. The eighteenth century arrival in India of Anquetil Duperon and William Jones marked an important 'Discovery'. The reading of the *Avestan* and Sanskrit scriptures helped in constructing such an image of India which would be able to enter universal configurations. Therefore, Schwab explains that: A 'cultivated' man would not necessarily have included India in his considerations of the cosmos. Judea would have been included because of biblical traditions, Persia because of wars and its traditions of magic, Arabia because of its conquests and physicians(...), China seemingly because of the missions. The Indic world alone remained behind its wall. And then, in a single wave it poured forth. One came to know more and more what to think about it, and subsequently one no longer knew what to think about it.[3]

Thus, the duality of the Indian image and its instability led to more complexities and more efforts at decipherment. Each passing phase experienced a new construction of images based on their own ideals of indigenous past.

The object of our concern in the present issue is to look at these shifts and to enquire whether or not any real transformation in the European understanding of India actually takes place in the contemporary period (i.e. from the beginning of the twentieth century).

Images in our view, are located historically in a particular living context therefore, do not wander around freely. Images are also created through an interaction between the people and are not restricted to their primary meaning, i.e. representation of a person or thing as an optical reflection (e.g. statues, paintings, etc.), nor are they limited to literary images of objects or persons as depicted in a particular work/text. Thus, images can function as theme or symbol or even motif. We have used this word 'image' in a broad sense which is free from any notable consistency. We find it important to emphasise the inconsistent and diverse aspect of it as it is to a great extent conditioned by its analogical usage all along Orientalist history. Oriental images, as will be seen in the following pages, were neither stable nor singular all along the contemporary period as well because the objective has been more intended to consolidate European images, show their splendour (to go native might even be a means of reflecting our own national splendour[4]) than to represent any 'real' experience or 'idea' of the Orient.

Edward Said's important study *Orientalism (1978)* has viewed the European Studies of the East as essentially 'a Western style of dominating, restructuring and having authority over the Orient'.[5] The fact that there does exist a link between the 'knowledge of the East and history of colonial power' has helped in demythifying a number of earlier beliefs and has contributed in opening up a new area of academic inquiry. The central focus of the entire Saidian discussion has been a variety of texts produced over several centuries in the West and the codification of knowledge about non-metropolitan spaces and cultures, i.e. all those areas which were under colonial control. While it is true that Said throws into disarray such understandings as the one Schwab had that the Orient, however 'foreign' it may look is a complement to the occident and vice-versa.[6] Nevertheless his assertion of a single, unified Western discourse on the Orient over about two millennia creates a serious impediment in understanding these discourses because overlooking historical processes and not locating hegemonic voices in concrete historical conjunctures results in perpetuating those very images and signs which were intended to be demythified.

Various discourses on India since the Enlightenment have tended to represent India as 'eternally ancient'. This was done by attributing to her several essentialist constructs like the Indian mind which is inherently irrational, mythical, therefore incapable of thinking in rational, practical and 'semiotic' terms. Similarly its caste system or its idea of divinity and power of religion are some other features which distinguished India in representational discourses of Europe from the rest of the world. These precisely formed the basis of imperial knowledge on India in the earlier period.

Dissolution of colonial empires and establishment of independent states from 1946 onwards was achieved after a long drawn battle of resistance of an explicitly nationalist nature. End of colonial rule, no doubt, generated new debates and created new concerns. A clear rift occurred between the ideas of Western hegemony and popular public perception about the same in former colonies. Therefore, the post-World War II and the post-independence era seem to have marked a shift in the representation of India in European discourse as well. While major strains of earlier representation continue, the more recent images have incorporated emphases of a different kind. On the one hand prevalent images are of misery and poverty and on the other of mystic/exotic spaces, of erotic pleasures and of total renunciation of worldliness.

We have attempted in this volume to reread and reinterpret those cultural texts which have emerged in the period of independence movements in the colonies and eventual dismantling of empire. We understand that major cultural texts and discourses in Europe include representation of India in literary and sociological texts, travelogues, as also the electronic media including films, TV documentaries, etc.

We begin by taking a critical view of the so called 'discovery of signs of the Other' embedded in the claim to superiority of European cultures. Shashi Raina's essay 'Edward John Thompson: Grasping the Colony' dwells upon the question of Imperial power and knowledge in the context of British colonial rule of India. Thompson, as a prototype of those Britishers who 'straddled two middle but anti-thetical positions-between that fringe of Indian nationalists and British radicals... who saw British empire as historically oppressive and exploitative but were often taken in by the legitimacy discourse of imperialism', therefore justified colonialism as an altruistic project aimed at elevating the primitives. Shashi Raina, by citing extensive examples from the texts of colonial fiction and juxtaposing them with the reflections of missionaries like EJ Thompson in the first half of the twentieth century, has convincingly shown the divided sensitivity of some of the Britishers of that time. Thompson's sincere efforts to bring about a 'classical liberal compromise' within the framework of empire were not the expressions of momentary or passing altruistic fancy. Shashi Raina argues that Thompson's association with the Indian people, history and living ethos involved him so much that he lived through a 'painful duality'. On the one hand he acknowledged the right of the Indian people to their own destiny and on the other, a felt need for the perpetuation of empire was perceived very strongly. Admittedly he propagated a more benevolent and democratic relationship. Shashi Raina, while noting Thompson's striking blindness to economic realities, concludes that from a position of neutrality he attempted a rapprochement between the coloniser and the colonized, that is where perhaps he is different from EM Forster.

Forster's *A Passage to India (1924)* could not conceive a friendship between Feilding and Aziz, till India's independence, but in a more liberal English framework at a later period, a privileged positioning of an Englishman did allow the friendship and even synthesis between the native and the English. In the essay 'The English Curator and the Buddhist Doctor: Charles Fábri's Identities in India' Margit Köves discusses Fábri's concerns of cross-cultural friendship and love (inspired, obviously by Forster's above-mentioned novel) in a new imperial context. Through a case study of Fábri's novel *Indian Flamengo* (1945), Margit Köves has drawn our attention to the fact that even in changed situation-at the time of transfer of power-a person (Fábri) of multiple identities and liberal thought ascribes 'agency of emancipation' only to the Indian middle class, therefore, the alliances could take place only between the privileged classes (middle class English educated Padma and John with special status). Thus, Charles Fábri, though more radical in his pronouncements vis a vis the colonial subject does not speak from a position of neutrality. In the course of discussion on Fábri's autobiographical text, situated in Lahore and written during the period between the second World War and partition, Margit Köves raises a series of important issues related to the question of identity, race, culture and nationhood: 'the period between the war and the partition lends significance to the narrator's identity and to issues of 'race' and culture which acquired new relevance after the holocaust. A number of solutions in the novel betray Fábri's multiple identities as a polyglot, assimilated Jewish Hungarian, a liberal Englishman and a Buddhist convert'. Charles Fábri's prescription for independent India consisted of the transfer of culture into nationhood with Hindustani language, Buddhist religion and educated middle class and women's creativity as a prerequisite condition. Obviously during his stay in India Fábri's interaction with one type of Indian gave way to the formulation of a very European self-definition which attributed reason and sensibility to the privileged ones and violence and racism to labourers and villagers. Converting to Buddhism for him was more appropriate as Buddhist ethics according to him conformed to the above qualities.

The manner in which the two writers articulated the liberal concerns about the colonial Other does not in any way signify that they sought to subvert the imperialist project, nevertheless, they did trouble the empire by raising the issue of the people's right to freedom. Therefore, while it is correct to assert the links between knowledge of the East and colonial history, to ignore other practical effects of the encounters, the external pressures, faced by the European writers would be incorrect.

Voluminous writings produced by the French fiction writers, journalists, travellers, etc., in the last few decades of our century serve as an examaple of these very 'practical effects, accommodation and pressures'. 'India Mirrored in Contemporary French Writings' by Radha Sharma focuses on the 'fertile imagining' of French writers of our days whose unstable and monological images of India only help in creating a series of contradictory representations. Central to this critique of French texts 'is not the discourse—Orientalist or otherwise—of Indologists but rather that of contemporary French writing whose readers are drawn from the lay public.... The texts examined include literary as well as popular writing, cover fiction, mainly novels, as well as non-fiction such as travel accounts and essays.' While discussing the duality of Indian images- 'country of monsters' and 'cradle of wisdom'- Radha Sharma emphasises the point of 'eternal' India of antiquity as an antithesis of European modernity. Extensive quotations from the French texts of most recent years are used to discuss not only the Eurocentric attitudinal problems but the 'incapacity of French writers today to apprehend and depict India in her indisputable modernity and modernization'.

This informative article covers almost all the important fictional and non-fictional writings of the last three decades and deals with the discourses of an iconic, peregrinic, eternal and miserable India. Radha Sharma while concluding the essay shows that the French Indian Other is rooted not so much in the perception of distance as of time.

The question of the construction of the image of the 'Other' and the projection of this constructed image assumes significance as it reveals the manner in which it is constructed. Chitra Harshavardhan draws our attention to the politics of translation and preparation of anthologies of short stories by Indian women writers in German. In her article 'Bridging Differences? Translation Anthologies: Constructing the Other' Chitra Harshavardhan not only discusses at length the reasons for a renewed interest in translation anthologies the world over but also shows how they are becoming a 'site for the clash of cultures' and how they can expose the power relations involved. Analysing two translation anthologies of Indian women writers in German it is shown how the reader-consumers influenced the selection of short stories which resulted in creating two diverse images of 'modern Indian women'. Chitra Harshavardhan argues that construction of such predetermined identity and creating a prototype of an 'Indian women', modern or otherwise, not only emphasizes the 'otherness' of Indian women, viz., the German/European one but also underlines the traditional/modern dichotomy. The discussion on the process of selection, preparation and translation of the short stories in this article clearly reflects the attitude, understanding or the agenda of the anthologists and translators. Therefore, they present only a selective or partial vision of 'reality'. That's why a homogeneous and national culture is shown to be privileging of urban over rural. It is concluded that the commercial interests as well as consolidation of 'traditional'

India (through 'Indian women') are the basis for the production of these translation anthologies.

The recurrence of older Eurocentric narrative of the 'timeless' India and inability to articulate the critical theory of reality are central to the discussion of Mira Nair's two films *Salaam Bombay* and *Mississippi Masala*. Ranjani Mazumdar in her essay 'Orientalism Redefined: Studies of *Salaam Bombay* and *Mississippi Masala*' defines these films as being largely a 'national' experience with transnational focus aimed at the Western spectator. She goes on to examine critically issues of migration, inequality, race, sexuality which are seemed to be raised in the films but which in the ultimate analysis serve as 'cultural commodities' produced on the 'Third World'. Therefore, a reinterpretation of the films, after taking the Indian points of view into consideration will help in exposing the 'tensions arising from the imaging of otherness and self taking place across the West and the Third World'. Commentators of the West have in a way overlooked the politics of power and have acclaimed it as being a realist depiction of the barbaric exotic East, incapable of enough sensitivity towards the major social problems of the time. The films have also perpetuated the motifs of the East's incapability to settle its own problems therefore a 'modernising force' (from the West, obviously) has to step in. A sort of pleasure is sought to be viewed out of the depiction of the reality of the marginalized existence. A forthright critique by Ranjani Mazumdar proves that unlike nineteenth century Orientalist/colonialist ideologues, who comfortably distanced themselves from the 'area in question'- the twentieth century's onlookers are the Westernised Third World elite. These discourses have the advantage of being taken as a legitimate voice but which are completely devoid of any critical analysis of social problems and people's struggle. Films like *Salaam Bombay* and *Mississippi Masala* end up being a 'sentimentalist and harmless piece of international libertarianism'. However, the Western critics promote them as real alternative to the Third World parallel/critical cinema.

German Indology and debates around studies on India have been the focus of attention for centuries in both the countries which led to overshadowing discussion on representation of India in other forms of artistic creation like films and documentaries, etc. Incipient stages of Indian film industry, in the 1930s, saw a major exchange of expertise and ideas between pre-independence India and Germany between the wars. 'Franz Osten—From Munich Cinema to Bombay Talkies' by Gerhard Koch highlights the contribution made by this German cinematographer not only to the Indian film industry but to the world cinema. Strangely enough the history of Indo-German cultural relations has completely overlooked this contribution. High points of this relation can be defined in terms of sixteen directional ventures by Franz Osten, which include the silent era film on the life of Buddha *The Light of India* and the masterpiece *Achut Kanya* produced by Bombay Talkies in 1936. Great Indian directors like V. Shantaram, Mohun Bhavanani, Himanshu Ray, etc., worked in close co-operation with Franz Osten. Thus Osten played an important role in developing both silent as well as sound films' industry in Bombay. In a detailed and descriptive article based on major research, Gerhard Koch has shown various stages of cinematic and commercial developments of Bombay Talkies. The essay also analyses the success story of many of Osten's films which were not only more realistic but also marked an edge over others because of their superior technical quality, editing and sound recording. Osten's stay in India from 1935 to 1939 turned out to be most experimental and creative period of his life. Just after the outbreak of Second World War the British in India made him abruptly cut short his work and return to Germany. Though different in style and focus, this essay has touched upon an important aspect of German concerns of India. European public got to see, perhaps for the first time, a new treatment of Indian theme and different images of the Indians, particularly of women.

Cinema, if discussed as part of 'cultural industry' must include both commercial and entertaining components. However, in this process a total mythification and misrepresentation of India/Indians occur. Brigitte Schulze, in her essay 'Subjected Non-Subjects: Indians of German Cinema and TV Screens' though has argued for the 'necessity of misrepresentation' but has justified it in the context of complexities of market calculations, targeted viewers and predetermined notions of India. Analysing German cinema and TV from the beginning of the twentieth century she has shown how 'Indians' are used as icons of cinematic meanings. Brigitte Schulze examines the perpetuation of mythical discourses on India in cinema/TV and shows that they are determined by the public. However, the public is a very much mediated one, therefore the vicious circle viewer-media-viewer only leads to the undermining of real subject matter. She start by giving the analysis of 1996 elections coverage on German TV wherein the most prominent candidate for the German Delhi correspondent was Phoolan Devi whose actual election campaign was covered less and clippings from Shekhar Kapoor's film were projected more. Thus, a complete Phoolan Devi myth was recreated, which in the final analysis only focused on the barbaric and uncivilized Indian existence as opposed to the 'civilized German other'. The essay also discusses the so-called 'awareness' of German viewer about India and shows that it is largely based on the 'habitual consumption' of TV programmes, therefore, any debate on the issue of India is generated and opinion formed from a great distance (which, obviously was not the case with German Indologists or India enthusiasts of the earlier period). Brigitte Schulze concludes that any major/decisive shift in Germany's representation of India has not taken place because the commercial and competitive orientation of cinematic industry determines the construction of images and their representation. Therefore, the perpetuation of old stereotype images is inevitable.

Politics of publications and awards are also central to the Spanish Orientalist discourse of the present century. In Spain, the second half of our century has witnessed a major 'boom' in the production of literature concerning India. In my essay on 'Oriental Images in Contemporary Spanish Writings and Politics of Publication' I discuss the representation of India in Spanish writings in the backdrop of growing commercialization of publishing industry and suggest if certain aspects of this writing could be defined as Neo-Orientalist elements of pop-variety. Indology, historically by not being a discipline of any great consequence for Spanish scholarship, did create a void which was strongly perceived by renowned philosophers and philologists. Therefore, India as an 'erudite', 'civilized' space was and continues to be central to the Spanish discussions on India. However, I argue that the commercial concerns of publication does influence the books of pop variety both of literary or semi-literary genre.

The present volume, though it does not pretend to be an all encompassing study of India's images, has made an attempt to present a contemporary view of India and to examine the shifts in the construction of her images. Finally we can perhaps say that even if there is no fundamental change or shift in India's European images, nevertheless, the European preference of Indians has certainly undergone a dramatic change. If during the pre-independence times a 'Westernised Indian' was preferred over the one who was steeped in tradition, religion, superstition, rituals, etc., today the situation seems to have reversed. The perception about and understanding of an 'authentic Indian' is just the opposite, the focus is on rescuing this 'authentic Indian' from the modernist drives and contemporary tendencies in order to preserve the ancient rituals and traditions.

NOTES

1. Raymond Schwab, *The Oriental Renaissance*, Trans. By Gene Patterson-Black and Victor Reinking, New York, 1984, p. 3.
2. Raymond Schwab, op.cit. (Foreword by Edward Said), 1984, pp. viii, ix.
3. Raymond Schwab, op.cit. p. 7.
4. Nigel Leask, *British Romantic Writers and the East,* Cambridge, (Indian edition, 1993), p. 9.
5. See Edward Said, *Orientalism,* London, 1978.
6. Raymond Schwab, op.cit. 2.
7. See Ronald Inden, *Imagining India,* Oxford, 1990.

REFERENCES

Juan Goytisolo, *Cronicas Saracinas,* Barcelona, 1982.

Francis Barker, Peter Hulm et al, *The Politics of Theory,* Colchester, 1983.

Aijaz Ahmed, *In Theory: Classes, Nations, Literatures,* London, 1992.

Aime Cesaire, *Discourse on Colonialism,* New York, 1972.

Theodore Ziolkowski, *Disenchanted Images: A Literary Iconology,* Princeton New Jersey, 1977.

SHASHI RAINA

Edward John Thompson: Grasping the Colony

Edward John Thompson (1886-1946) started out as a rather typical John Bull who accepted unquestioningly the reality and desirability of an empire spread over vast spaces of Asia, Africa and the Middle East, wherein, the colonized peoples paid tribute to mighty Britannia. Some awareness of the inherent and unacceptable iniquitous content of imperial connections began to dawn upon Thompson as a result of direct interaction with India-a captive-country-to which he came as an educational missionary. The homage of an old sweepress holding his feet and the awestruck dumbness of the villagers on being accosted, instead of making Thompson feel vastly superior filled him rather with irritation and anger. The flexing of the State muscles in the Amritsar Massacre in 1919 brought an increasing recognition of the need for better racial understanding. Thompson's attitude towards the corrosive impasse between Britain and India was to undergo many alterations during the two decades of his endeavour to cause mutual friendliness between the colony and the imperial power. While his writings led to the restricted view that rapport of any sort was possible only between individuals, the last days of his involvement with the British-Indian situation yielded the recognition and the acknowledgment that any amity within a context of colonial relationships was bound to be false and brittle.

During the days of his active intervention, mainly through his writings during 1924-40, the period under examination here, Thompson, without aligning himself either with those who seemed excessively imperialist (Carthill or Mason) or with those others who rejected altogether the notion and validity of empire, straddles two middle but antithetical positions-between that fringe of Indian nationalists and British radicals wholly critical of the empire, and those British liberals and socialists (Digby, Hyndman, Agatha Harrison, Fenner-Brockway) who saw the British empire as historically oppressive and exploitative, but were often taken in by the legitimating discourse of imperialism. A polemical conviction in the superiority of British/Western civilization posited colonialism as an altruistic project calculated to elevate the primitive black and brown races towards enlightenment.

Thompson's quality of effort is characterized by a felt sincerity and can be seen as an attempt at a classic liberal compromise within the overall paradigm of empire. The quality of his engagement and intervention requires to be set apart from that of other liberals like E.M. Forster, in that Thompson's endeavours were not the expression of a passing, momentary, or merely aestheticized fancy. Thompson spent years acclimatizing himself with the history and living ethos of the people of India, something that became truly a lifetime involvement.

A recally briefly of some divergent stances towards colonialism and towards the justificatory rhetoric attending upon it may help to put Thompson's positions and contributions in perspective.

II

Located strategically within the Indian Civil Service, Philip Mason[1] spent two most crucial decades (1928-47) in India. There were years of the most consequential turbulence in Indo-British relations, climaxing into Indian Independence from colonial British rule in 1947. From that experience Mason drew his two-volume account of the Empire, titled *The Men Who Ruled India,* published under the pseudonym Philip Woodruff. Basing himself, rather pretentiously, on Plato's discourses, Mason designated the ruling British elite as the 'guardians' of the 'child-like, change-less and half-evil India'. Overwhelmed by the self-sacrificing character of the imperial enterprise, Mason eulogized the civil servants as "a corps of men specially selected, brought up in a vigour of bodily hardship to which no people have subjected their ruling class, trained by cold baths, cricket and the history of Greece and Rome, a separate race from those they ruled, aloof, superior to bribery, discouraged from marriage until they were middle-aged and then subject to long separations" (I. 15). Thus, denial and a harsh, altruistic regimen prepared these angels of selfless goodwill for a heroic and virtuous destiny: 'When they were eight years old, the children from whom the rulers were to be chosen were taken from home for three quarters of every year, taught not to mention their mothers' or their Christian names, brought up in the tradition of Sparta which Plato had admired. And the children grew up to be true guardians' (I. 16). Just to underline the doggedness of Mason's conviction, all this was published in 1953, six full years after the emergence of India as an independent nation!

This faith in being the chosen, of being ordained to administer, to control and rule other peoples, to bring to them the unique advantages of Western experience, of course constituted the 'white man's burden,' an awful destiny shared, along with England, by the marauders from France, Spain, Portugal, Holland and Germany, as they set about to carve out empires in the interests of individual and collective good life. Bold postures of martyrdom were being struck across Asia, Africa and other conquered territories. The imperialist ideology, driven by solid economic motives and bouyed up by legitimations from Old Testament Puritanism and Social Darwinism, went from strength to strength. Lord Curzon was to perorate:

> Remember that the Almighty has placed your hand on the greatest of His ploughs, in whose furrows the nations of the future are germinating and taking shape, to drive the blade a little forward in your time, and to feel that somewhere among those millions, you have left a little justice or happiness or prosperity, a sense of manliness or moral dignity, a spring of patriotism, a dawn of intellectual enlightenment, or a stirring of duty where it did not before exist—that is enough, that is the Englishman's justification in India (Raleigh, 389-90).

Quite a mouthful of paternalism there, informed by an Orientalist construction of Indians and other conquered non-white peoples, as primitive, dark and inferior in every way. Sir Lepel Griffin,[2] for example rejected as ludicrous any suggestion that the Indians 'are intellectually or morally our equals, and that to them have been confined by fortune those secrets of government which in the modern world are the inheritance of the Anglo-Saxon race alone' (quoted in Parry, 18). Indeed, what could be more explicitly stated as a racist text?

In the same vein, Al Carthill[3] was quite convinced that Indians could only be grateful for the happy 'paradise' created by the colonial rulers; in return, Britain only expected 'the increasing wealth and prosperity of this market for her valuable reward, and the consciousness that she was ruling and benefitting three millions of the human race' (42). That larger than life British hero of World War II, Winston Churchill, had no difficulty in identifying Indians as lower breeds; in 1931 he was to pronounce that 'to transfer..... responsibility to this highly artificial and restricted oligarchy of Indian politicians would be a retrograde act. It would be a shameful act. It would be an act of cowardice, desertion and dishonour'. More to the point, 'it would bring grave material evils....upon Great Britain; but it would bring upon Great Britain a moral shame which would challenge for ever the reputation of the British Empire as a valiant and benignant force in the history of mankind' (V. 4986). A contemporary comment on the imperialist hoax appears quite pertinent: 'They, (the colonizers) converted their history of chance encounters and good luck into a morality play, interpreted storm clouds, rains and bird songs as signs of a secret providence urging them on to fulfil their colonial destiny, and came to regard the money gathered here as grace' (Bhalla, 5).

Fortunately, such untroubled homage to imperialism, especially as late as the twentieth century, could hardly establish itself as normative. Clear-eyed social thinkers and historians, in gradually increasing numbers, had begun to be disturbed by the problematic subjugation of an alien country and people, as well as by the dehumanizing effects of the imperial enterprise upon the indigenous psyche. Benjamin Disraeli,[4] a scion of the Tories, had early questioned the paternalistic discourse of colonialism spawned as a charitable institution to nurture the inadequate black, brown or yellow races; he was succinctly to demystify the notion of a mission by saying quite simply that 'that East is a Career' (*Tancred*, I. 182). This refreshingly honest perspective, is also reflected in Sir Roper Lethbridge's disarming comment in 1913: 'Indian is still by a long way the largest employer of British labour in the world' (quoted in K.T. Paul, 210). John Stuart Mill specifically characterized imperialist expansion as, 'a vast system of outdoor relief for the British upper classes' (quoted in Green, 3). Yet not everyone was fit for such work; the policemen, George Orwell's Burmese sojourn, convinced him that 'imperialism was an evil thing.... As for the job I was doing I hated it more bitterly than I can perhaps make clear. In a job like that you see the dirty work of Empire at close quarters' (*Shooting an Elephant,* 15). The American, Louis Fischer[5] pointed out the historical linkage between suppressing alien peoples and the growing aggressive tendencies within Europe; imperialism was simply a 'negative law.' 'It is might without right ... the blood brother or perhaps the father of fascism' (8). Despite ingenious legitimations offered by ideologues of imperialism from time to time, the reality and growing strength of Indian unrest was to force even a Valentine Chirol[6] towards the end of the nineteenth century to comment on 'the human and not unnatural impartience of subject races fretting under an alien rule which, however well-intentioned, must often be irksome and must sometimes appear to be harsh and arbitrary'(2) T.G.P. Spear, himself a historian, was to critique liberal historians at a starting point of enquiry: 'Their taste for moralizing found outlets in criticizing the methods by which that power was attained but it never occurred to them to question the desirability of the power being there at all' (408).

Another strand of opinion regarding the dominance of British interests in India expressed itself as a sustained critique of British economic policies; this included a number of Liberals, early Socialists, Labourites and Communists. In 1886 H.M. Hyndman[7] squarely accused Britain of bankrupting India: 'firmly convinced that in India we are working upto a hideous economic catastrophe beside which the great Irish Famine of 1847 will seem merely child's play' (vi). Questioning facts and figures adduced by George Hamilton, Secretary of State for India, which sought to establish that British colonial presence was not tantamount to economic exploitation, William Digby aruged (1901) 'without going outside the covers of your own office productions, I establish, as I think beyond all peradventure, the great, the dismal, the awful retrogression, not only in material prosperity but also in other important respects of the country you govern' (xiii). To this S.E. Stokes, promoting Gandhi's khadi campaign (1922) added: 'the policy of sending our raw products to England to be returned to us as a manufactured article at a vastly increased cost is progressively draining the country of the little wealth that has been left in it' (3). Fenner Brockway[8] extended the indictment (1930) to include the neglect of literacy and the fact of poverty due to 'lack of proper organization of agriculture and industry,' 'iniquitous land system' and 'capitalism....introducing inhumanities' (38). Finding it 'scandalous' that impoverished Indians should 'provide princely salaries for British Governors and generals,' he warned that 'the families of the British ruling classes must give up the hope of India providing secure and well-paid posts for their sons in perpetuity'(51).

Among Indian commentators, as is well known, Dadabhai Naoroji[9] and Gopal Krishna Gokhale[10] had protested firmly against the drain of wealth from India and had demanded stringent measures to reverse the trend. Even Gandhi, the apostle of peaceful and non-violent action, was obliged to justify the burning of foreign cloth; in the Foreword to Stokes' book, he was to write: 'destruction is as useful and necessary as construction for any organic growth.' Rajni Palme Dutt's[11] celebrated *India Today* (1940) was to analyze searchingly, the destructive results of British colonial occupation; he was to comment on 'the gigantic internal problems, social strains and conflicts which have accumulated through centuries of foreign domination and arrested development' (2).

III

The multiple facets of the imperialist situation found their inevitable reflection in journalism and literature.

These writings varied from those of Rudyard Kipling, Maid Diver, Flora Annie Steele, G.H. Henty celebrating the heydays of the Empires' glory; to those of Edward Candler, E.M. Forster, Leonard Woolf, George Orwell, Edward John Thomson, Christine Weston, who in their expressions of self-questioning with regard to stipulations about the supposed intrinsic merits and possible demerits of colonialist relationships, encompass a spectacle of great historical interest. While none of the authors, cited above, might be regarded as acknowledgedly occupying a stature of first-order recognition, their significance for our purpose does not lie so much in their literary/aesthetic standing as in their ability to portray with directness the rough and tumble of the colonial situation during their times. The currents of those times are more reliably deciphered in their work; as Hugh Ridley states in an expressive metaphor, the 'needle of a seismograph to record tremors' has no need 'to be held in illustrious hands' (12). Whether their stay in India took on the colouring of manly adventure—Kipling, Henty—or sought to come to terms with an alien land and environment, their offerings suggest how far imperialism had penetrated their lives, thoughts and cultural orientations, conditioning their imaginations in differing ways and degrees. One extreme expression might be the following invocation from Kipling[12] to Englishmen desirous of a deified martyrdom:

> Take up the White Man's burden—
> Send forth the best ye breed—
> Go, bind your sons to exile
> To serve your captive's need;
>
> To wait in heavy harness
> On fluttered folk and wild—
> Your new-caught sullen peoples,
> Half-devil and half-child.
>
> Take up the White Man's burden—
> Have done with childish day
> The lightly proferred laurel,
> The easy, ungrudged praise.
>
> Comes now, to serve your manhood
> Through all the thankless years,
> Cold-edged with dear-bought wisdom,
> The judgment of your peers!
>
> (XXXIII. 241-2)

With an increasingly industrializing Europe no longer available as a site for heroic deeds writers were inclined to move Eastward in search of exotic locales in which to place their tales of action and adventure. Henty's stories of adventure, Kipling's construction of lion-hearted male prowess, Rider Haggard's fantasies vis-a-vis dark Africa, and to an extent Joseph Conrad's tales imaged Oriental spaces and topographies as battlegrounds, wherein Englishmen might prove their mettle. Such an agenda did not involve interacting with the peoples that inhabited these exotic spaces. Even the staid *History of India* by James Mill, who had himself never visited India, contributed to constructing that strong, dominant paternalistic role for adventure-starved, future rulers of India as the *History* became staple diet for all aspirants to Civil Service in India. Virgin and primitive territory became an essential backdrop against which English/western machismo performed exploits of valour. Susanne Howe reads this genre of writing as constituting at the time 'an escape from the dead-end social problems of the English novel; for while there was impasse in England, there seemed hope in the far-off colonies where personal courage and endeavour may still be valid' (8). Thus, people like Violet Jacob, who lived with her soldier-husband in India during 1895-1900, were enchanted by the vast and picturesque beauty of India whose wildness refreshed a mind jaded by the crowds in England: 'I could wander for ever about this Indian country. With all its drawbacks it is the most congenial environment to me that I have ever been in' (61).

One must note, however, that self-criticism was not entirely lacking as to the wider context of Empire within which the new writing took place. George Bernard Shaw, for example, was to ridicule the Englishman's supreme belief that 'every Englishman is born with a certain miraculous power that makes him master of the world.' Thus, smug in the righteousness of his moral and religious duty,' 'you will never find Englishmen in the wrong' (186-7).

With growing dissatisfaction among newly educated classes and urbanized working people in England, a newer generation of writers came to question previous perceptions and assumptions. The novel could no longer rest content in portraying an unfamiliar and potentially Edenic world for the valorous; inevitably, current issues became material for scrutiny and debate, veering increasingly toward considerations of the political question as well By late nineteenth century, 'the British-India encounter became a battle expressed as a political struggle and experienced as a psychological crisis' (Parry, 2). Was it acceptable that any land or people should come under alien and colonial control? How seriously could the argument about the burden to civilize be taken? There were those who thought that the present impasse, in the Indo-British situation, had resulted from the English people's refusal or failure to connect socially with the natives; within that diagnosis, a heavy part of the blame was to be laid on English women as, supposedly, they remained aloof and snobbish. This, of course, was not the only time when the ills of history were to be laid at the doors of women as a class, since, even now such convictions permeate the world.

Writers like E.M. Forster, J.R. Ackerley and the early Edward Thompson of *Atonement* and *The Other Side of the Medal* had the belief that by transcending the social divide the Empire could be put on the non-antagonistic footing. This sort of attempt is evident in Forster's *The Hill of Devi* in the way in which his early visit to the Raja of Dewas is handled, as the differing social and cultural environment evokes reactions of wonder and novelty into which considerations of value-laid judgments do not enter. Pleasure at the encounter is sought to be evoked by discarding the habitual superiorities of the colonial perspective. Forgotten promises and lack of punctuality evoke not derision but a warm amusement. The delayed banquet is passed off tolerantly: 'I have forgotten the time it was meant to be and the time it was' (Forster, 21). Amusement is evoked at the ostensibly typical noisy and confused Indian farewell accorded Forster, at the time of leaving Dewas and conversely, also at the tight-lippedness of 'absolutely English' American fellow traveller, forcing the servants to ride the foot-board of the train (34). A yet, more forceful vignette, depicting this stance of mutual accommodation is enacted at the inept but enthusiastic participation in the Dussehra celebration; it 'was enjoyable. The first time I adored a pen, an inkpot, a waste paper basket and a piece of foolscap, under the direction of my clerk, and administered both to them and him a sacrament of coconut.... One hasn't to say anything, still less to feel. Just wave incense and sprinkle water and dab with red powder anything you like' (139).

A similar spirit of cheerful suspension of any over-particular critique and a forward-looking hope echoes through Ackerley's *Hindoo Holiday,* along with tone of ridicule for British airs. Ackerley finds amusement in the Political Agent's scolding of the Prince (89), and the British tourist Mrs. Montgomery's grandiloquent announcement, proving an inbuilt sense of racial superiority. 'You'll never understand the dark and tortuous minds of the natives and if you do I shan't like you—you won't be healthy' (23-4). Yet, the shadow of the future is visible in the incident when an Indian cultivator refuses to help a British woman to her horse, 'I'm not your slave, miss' (11).

Edward Thompson's *Atonement,* though cognizant of the dark shadows of the 1857 event and the 1919 Amritsar massacre, still reposes faith in a human structure of apology and forgiveness; atonement, it seems to him, constituted largely by a British acknowledgement of wrongs done to India rather than by any resolve to up and leave the colony, might produce the answer to the Indo-British conflict.

Yet, while Forster, Ackerley and Thompson and others may be credited with having to some extent transcended any debilitating or abrasive racial bias, the ground situation was far from idyllic. It was increasingly more difficult to hold on to faith in the gospel of an ordained mission; gathering self-doubt could not but lead to a more critical examination of the past, the present and the possible future or lack of future of the Indo-British connection. Comment and opinion take in rejection/reaffirmation of past history, awareness of the present turmoil as leading either to despondent or hopeful perspectives on the future, a modification or rejection of the concept of colonial/imperial destiny, and recognition or denial of the rights of individuals/nations to freedom and self-government. All this made for anguished introspection. Ray Sinclair's words (in *The Singer Passes*) about being caught in a traffic jam succinctly captures the dilemma: 'We're really stuck... We can't go forward. We won't go backwards. Rather like the English in India! (Maud Diver, 202). The sense of an impasse, that has grown beyond human mending and that may be resolved only through the mechanical power of passing time, pervades Edmund Candler's *Abdication* (1992). E.M. Forster's *Passage to India* (1924) and Edward Thompson's *A Farewell to India* (1931). With the closure of the heroic/imperial phase, of bravado and adventure, the protagonists of such novels as mentioned above are disturbed and introspective, having 'a very human, puzzled, rueful quality' (Susanne Howe, 22).

Although, Riley in Candler's novel speculates that 'if only they met us and knew us.... it would be all right (8), Forster already suggests the awareness that such hope is vain so long as the Indo-British relationship is one shaped by a vitiating colonialism. Well-intentioned individuals like Adela Quested and Mrs. Moore do not succeed; they land severally in fantasy of one sort or another—a rape or a more comforting but entirely mystical epiphany. Either situation points to the inadequacy of any sustained connection with real people within the contexts and contradictions of history. Fielding and Aziz, however much they will, cannot come together at the depicted time and place. Thompson's surrender in 1931 was to take the form of reading in the present the dark designs of a malignant Father Time: 'I think the age from time to time, in one land or another, gets sick of certain people and gets rid of them... They're doing it now, with the English, all over the world and most of all in India' (*A Farewell to India*, 117).

These writers exhibit a painful daulity; on the one hand, there is the sensitivity to acknowledge, in whatever shape or degree, the right of colonized peoples to their own destiny; on the other, there remains the strongly felt need for the perpetuation of the British connection, admittedly, along a more benevolent and democratic axis, all that, of course, guided by a progressive and democratic Great Britain. In M.E. Chamberlain's words, 'so long as belief in the superiority of Western forms of government remained intact and popular belief in progress and the 'backwardness' of non-European people was pervasive, even good liberals and socialist could—and did—persuade themselves that, although the acquisition of empire was usually a reprehensible business, the good government of an empire was a noble duty' (190). Hugh Ridley underscores similar tendencies among French and German writers as well. Speaking especially of Pierre Loti—and others—he comments that their 'criticism of France did not involve scepticism about French expansionism' (18).

There is also another strain available in comments of the period—the emotional wrench at the parting from India to which many English people felt they really belonged. Thompson's Alden, necessarily shipped back to England after collapsing in the colony, threatens to return 'home' dead or alive. Jon and Rumer Godden who eschew politics as Indian freedom draws near, reiterate: 'we never felt we were foreigners, not India's own; we felt at home, safely held in her large warm embrace, content as we never were to be content in our own country (viii).

On the other hand, Leonard Woolf and George Orwell—and others lesser known—were to reject without equivocation the idea of empire-building altogether. His experience as a civil servant in Ceylon made Woolf 'for the first time dimly perceive the problems of an imperialist .... and the awareness brought my first doubts whether I wanted to rule others, to be an imperialist and proconsul' (I:202). Orwell saw all unequal relationships as doomed to end in mutual hatred: 'All I knew was that I was struck between my hatred of the Empire I served and my rage against the evil-spirited little beasts who tried to make my life impossible... Feelings like these are the normal by-product of imperialism' (15-16). The debate as to the nature of colonialism continues as newer forms replace older ones, and as, in our own day, some of those newer forms seem highly seductive to enlightened segments of urban populations among developing countries.

Nor has there been any serious re-assessment or rejection of these values among British creative writers after India gained independence in 1947. John Masters and Paul Scott have both been involved in a post-colonial recapitulation of the days of British rule in India. Masters, it might be said, inherited the colonial impulse from his forefathers who had been for five generations connected with India. Masters himself was in active service at the time of Indian independence. Joining the Indian British army in 1934, he promptly fell in love with his Gurkha soldiers, participating in their joys and sorrows. It was his intention not to romanticize India: 'I did not think of India as quaint, picturesque, exploited, inscrutable or otherworldly. I thought India was ugly, beautiful, smelly, predictable, and as material as the West' (Bugles and a Tiger, 87). But, his sense of possessiveness remained the dominant discourse in what he was to write; India he saw as 'my lusty, disinterest mistress' whose conquest challenged his maleness: 'To hell with justification..... I was in love with India, and she'd have the hell of a job getting rid of me' (329-30). The defeated Englishman, unable to adjust to a shattered post-war Britain, adopted the younger and lustier America where, as a professional writer, he wrote of his affair with India. Master's novels are saturated with nostalgia; his reluctance to accept the historical fact of India's hardwon political independence would suggest that somewhere at heart he remained an imperialist.

While Masters' fiction, spans more than a century of British annexation of India, Paul Scott, in his dozen-odd, India-related novels, confines himself to the last five years of the Raj, from the Quit India Movement of 1942 to 1947, the year of India independence. His work here, shows a clearly growing awareness of the inevitability of the end of British domination, obliging him to experience, in Patrick Swinden's phrase, a 'loss of Paradise' (6), suggesting that the whole colonial enterprise for somebody like him might have been in the nature of a search for a chimera, an illusion that forever eludes. His British characters, especially in *The Raj Quartet,* in their several ways confront this reality via shades of resignation, anger, a reluctant acceptance, or a guarded welcome. India, seems a touchstone which helps them define their own identities, their social, cultural and moral orientations, their duties and professions, their doubts and beliefs. The complex and multiple emotion contributes to enacting a rich representation of the India of the last days of empire. Not surprisingly, an elegiac quality permeates this work, as though a dirge were sung to a lost glory.

IV

Most European colonial fiction, of the first half of the twentieth century showed a similar involvement with the historical process of the dismantling/collapse of colonialism. Often, the responses have been subjective and introspective, with the authors having to walk the thin line between 'the distortion of history into the raw materials of literature or the debasement of literature into the mere documentation of history' (M.M. Mahood, 3). This overlap between history and literature, between fact and imaginative reconstruction characterizes much of the production of these decades, and is a genre pervasive in Edward John Thompson. It is also a mode of expression suited, in a tragic sort of way, to projecting the requirements of a divided sensibility. Continuously preoccupied with the emerging critique of empire and the growing dissensions of opinion, Thompson came to employ varied discourses—history, biography, letters, fiction, drama, poetry, expository exhortation, in an attempt to diffuse contention or to assimilate it.

Thompson's beginnings were as an apolitical educational missionary in Bengal during 1910-16 and 1920-3, years in which he rather relished his foray among a different people, place and literature. His rude passage into political awareness may be said to have been occasioned by the gruesome massacre of unarmed Indians by Dyer at Jallianwala Bagh in Amritsar (1919). Unable to shake off the enormity of the event and, consequentially, the accountability of the British, Thompson's first liberal intervention took the form of a new reading—new British reading, that is—of the uprising of 1857. *The Other Side of the Medal,* was to be an attempt to offer amelioration and atonement to the wounded Indians by acknowledging hitherto unacknowledged culpabilities of the British during the 1857 event; the evidence of objectivity was depended upon by the author to evoke a softening of Indian sentiments so that a 'struggle,' especially an 'embittered one' (21) could be avoided. Alas, however, times did not permit such uncomplicated answers to a tangled and abrasive colonial history; acknowledgement of guilt and the willingness to atone through noble confession did not seem enough. That sort of liberal Christian hope seemed inadequate to the demands of the Indo-British situation.

Thompson's three subsequent visits to India in 1932, 1936, and 1939 in various official and semi-official capacities deepened his commitment even as his optimism shaded into anger, frustration and an eventual resignation. Meanwhile, he taught Bengali at Oxford and wrote to and for national dailies on various India-related issues and events. He also retained/developed close personal contacts with several influential British Indian officials and Indian nationalist leaders, attempting throughout to intervene at crucial historical moments. An Englishman with a liberal bent, considerable empathy and a decent and humane attitude, Thompson's was a sincerely meant effort to mediate between opposed realities. Colonial history, however, has remained a harsh and unforgiving experience and fact, something that was to oblige Thompson, however reluctantly, to acknowledge the weight of the chief argument against colonialism—the right of peoples to be free to control/shape there own spaces/destinies.

Thompson's oeuvre, can then be seen as Thompson's often agonized attempts at contributing towards a rapprochement between the colonizer and the colonized, from a standard of neutrality which he proposed to himself. Benita Parry, characterizes these attempts as 'the incantations of a principled Englishman to the spirit of racial and international harmony rather than a coherent political analysis' (167). It remains a sad fact that the pervasive subjectivity of his perceptions and his false consciousness as to the nature and purpose of empire, flattered his notion of a mission. Civil and social developments within the empire were routinely seen as selfless projects aimed at the ennoblement of India. There is, when all is said and done, meagre questioning of the British ruling class ideology in the 'civilizing mission', the 'white man's burden', of legitimations of exploitation based on the notion of 'doing one's job', or the total, impersonal pragmatism of Britain's supposedly sacred duty in India.

One should also note Thompson's striking blindness to the economic realities of Empire, a fact that Englishmen in late nineteenth century had done much to expose. True enough that Thompson's overall fidelity to the noble mission idea does not negate the sincerity of Thompson's desire to 'connect' what he called the 'unbragging India' with the 'unbragging Britain,' the problem lay in the fact that Thompson seems unable—more than unwilling, perhaps, to recognize that his own assumed neutrality was not as ideologically neuter as he might have persuaded himself, or the larger fact that within a colonial context such neutrality was, on either side, a theoretical and practical impossibility. Put more bluntly, the politics of his supposedly idealized perspective, disallow him to detach his narratives from silent presuppositions about the history he seeks to disinfect.

Unlike Woolf, Orwell, Robert Wallace, Henry Beveridge, Chartres Malony and a host of others, Thompson was reluctant to admit the exploitative character of the British colonial enterprise. In spite of his anxiety to avoid taking sides, his endeavour remains precariously perched on the hegemonizing myth of British benevolence. While accepting the charge in regard to the looting of wealth by servants of the East India Company, Thompson insists that selfless service to India by officers of the Crown after direct takeover more than compensated for the earlier aberrations. The critical failure here is underlined by Sumit Sarkar: 'The entire drain of wealth-economic exploitation discourse central to Indian nationalism from Naoroji onwards, and one to which Indophile Englishmen had also contributed, seems to have passed him by' (118).

Thompson was also unable to read correctly, the emergent social and emotional fervour, which led to the construction of new and more aggressive symbols both to express and to further a growing nationalist upsurge—Sivaji, Kali Charkha, Khadi the Gandhi cap—powerful weapons in the armoury of aggressive nationalism' (Arthur Mayhew, 219-20). Thompson's failure here, for example, is in sharp contrast to Frantz Fanon's evaluation of the veil adopted by women in Algeria during the anti-colonial struggle there as a cultural expression of nationalist politics, even when the donning of the veil could not ordinarily have been interpreted as constituting an element of progressive history. Parry defines that assertiveness as 'a means of defending corporate identity against calculated assaults to alter or reform them' (173).[13]

Another way of saying this is, that Thompson's liberalism—the desire to be 'one with the people' (Jenny Sharpe, 5)—skirted the problematics of empire as an aspect of British class rule. That fact must explain Thompson's inability to cognize critically the positive response of the Lancashire Mill workers to Gandhi in the face of Gandhi's call for a boycott of British textiles. Thompson's early mediations into aspects of Indian cultural life, likewise, lay themselves open to the charge of an orientalist projection of a knowledge of Indian texts as simultaneously a knowledge of Indian realities. His sociological accounts of sati (*Suttee*), his plays dealing with Rajput history and Rajput 'values' and his *History of India* remain ideological discourses; however well-meant, these constitute representations of an alien reality to an alien people in an alien space, coloured by the paternalist assumption that his knowledge of it is better than their own. This may have been, to whatever extent, the context that roused Tagore's—and more specifically—some Tagoreans' anger at Thompson's analysis of Tagore's writings in *Rabindranath Tagore: His Life and Works.* (This is without underplaying the role of the cult of unquestioning homage to Tagore's greatness whose latest victim is Kushwant Singh today for daring to undervalue the poet.) Truly, his own comment at the time of the award of the Nobel Prize to Tagore is most apposite here: 'All mastes, boys, servants did homage. I could have done it myself almost; but I am an Englishman and have a stern contempt for the fools who pretend they are easterners' (quoted by E.P. Thompson, 114-15). For some reason, Thompson seemed not to remember that reality when expounding with authority on matters Indian. As we know, attempts to claim privileged expertize on the cultural history of the country were to be increasingly resisted by the burgeoning Indian intelligentsia.

Often, Thompson's naivete was his armour. In *An Indian Day,* for instance, aware of 'the pulse of wild excitement and hatred' (199) beating in India, Thompson can still root for the efficient sahibs who 'get the job done', and who 'carry his ideals out' (180). It is quite late in the day that Thompson shows some awareness that the 'job' being done and the 'ideal' being carried out may not, after all, be beyond taint. Which is when amity and mutual noblesse later shade into an incomprehensible atmosphere of resentment and hatred in response to a figure like the revolutionary Dinabandhu Tarkachuramani[14] of *A Farewell To India.* Within the trilogy, if Alden the liberal seems almost to give up his attempts at amity, it is not so much because he has developed any fundamental self-questioning regarding the reality of empire as owing to the realization that there is, after all, no job 'raggeder' than that of the

Englishman in India (*A Farewell to India*, 283). Thompson's letter to Horace Alexander[15] reads in a similar vein: 'I have ceased to think Indian politics worth while; there is no place for me in any of the established camps' (30 June 1938). His shift from politics to 'other aspects of Indian efforts' (*Ibid.*) such as persuading the Rhodes Trust to institute scholarships, fellowships, visitorships and so on for eminent Indians, and prevailing upon the Oxford University Press to bring out Oxford books of verse in various Indian languages was a project directed at helping sustain 'their self-respect' by being told 'that their intellectual effort was not an isolated and unknown thing but recognized as part of the Empire's life' (quoted in Parry, 171). No longer could the intense and frequently exasperated affection of Thompson 'in his semi-autobiographical novels' (Mary Lago, 322) cope with the complexities of the historical situation.

The famous Indo-Anglian writer and critic Mulk Raj Anand described *An Indian Day* as 'a rich and overcharged Russian novel', (26). Thompson found greater possibilities of expressing the complexities in his novel, yet critically pressing and vital moments demanded more overt response. I believe that in any attempt to fully understand Thompson's interventions into a profound and problematic historical and cultural interface, a combined testing of his historical/political writing needs to be made against his imaginative writing. *The Other Side of the Medal*, *The History of India* and *The Rise and Fulfilment of British Rule in India* (the last with G.T. Garratt) comprised Thompson's attempt at writing 'objective' history as distinct from what he thought to have been less than objective British accounts, an endeavour that made him seem to have a 'slight embarrassed or defiant air' (Spear, 414).

Yet, as the complexities of the historical situation seem to defy analysis, Thompson was to take the position that expository writing could not carry or express the burden of manifold meaning, and that 'truth' could have 'integrity' only when it was explored in the creative/imaginative mode (*A Letter From India*, 30). The inference here is inescapable that somewhere Thompson developed a perception as to the inadequate objectivity of his expository writing. Yet, two things need to be noted: one, that this perception follows upon Thompson's historiographical endeavours, and, two, that it does not remain a definitive or conclusive perception in Thompson on the question of the confluence of form and integrity, since he does return to the historiographical mode during and *after* his creative offerings. The important and laudable fact here is that the problematics generated by the fact of empire are sought to be looked at through diverse strategies of enactment in order to achieve fullness of comprehension. Thus suitable points of entry are made available for profitable assessment: are Thompson's failures those of empirical insufficiency, or are they, after all, located in ideological predilection, claims to 'objectivity' notwithstanding.

What sets Thompson apart from British commentators who took clearly defined positions on empire, one way or another, is the fact that he endeavours to examine the merits and demerits of each side with a view to evolving the modalities of a rapprochement. The problem that must be addressed is whether the colonial impasse permitted divided loyalities, however honestly felt, to furnish syntheses that would at once draw consent and leave empire intact. One is impressed, of course, by the strenuousness of Thompson's commitment to the cause as he visualised it; his affair with India outlasted his sojourn at Bankura. His post-Amritsar plea for atonement for the excesses of the past in common with a large number of liberal thinkers, differed from the rest, to the extent that he dedicated himself punishingly to the Indian situation at the cost of a poetical promise and career.

Nor were important Indians slow in acknowledging that fact. Refuting the charge that he ever thought of Thompson as 'an enemy of my people,' the Nobel Laureate Rabindranath Tagore with whom he had an enduring relationship, wrote to him: 'while not agreeing to all you have said or written on India, I have never questioned your sincerity or your love or affection for our people' (6 Feb. 1934). Jawahar Lal Nehru, one of the major architects of the nationalist movement and later the first Prime Minister of independent India was to write thus to his daughter, of Thompson's qualities and intentions: 'in his own way he is perfectly straight and honest and keen on doing the right thing.' Although, Nehru continues, 'not a very great person, but at any rate one who refused to behave as an automaton and who could decide for himself in spite of all the pressure that was brought to bear on him' (VIII. 805). Nehru's commendations were not, of course uncritical or unqualified; he wrote to Krishna Menon (2. Dec. 1939)[16] to say that he did not think Thompson sharp enough 'to grasp the situation here,' being prone to forming 'impressions.... likely to be superficial' (X. 262). Perhaps what Orwell said of himself in regard to these contexts applies to Thompson's dogged attempts to interpret India as well; Orwell was to say that he wished 'to make political writing into an art. My starting point is always a feeling of partisanship, a sense of injustice... I write because there is some lie that I want to expose, some fact to which I want to draw attention, and my initial concern is to get a hearing'. (II.9)

Probably, one of the last pieces of critical writing by Thompson, was the preface that he wrote for the second revised edition of his

Rabindranath Tagore (which came out posthunously in 1948). On the frontpiece of the book is a long quote from George Tyrell.

One may desire to show that the cause for which he has lived and laboured all the best years of his life is not so preposterous, intellectually and morally, as of late it has been made to appear...; that he has not been duped by the sophistries and puerilities of its approved controversialists, but has rested on graver and worthier reasons, however ill-defined and ill-expressed that even if his defence of it should have failed, he has not failed in courage or candour or sincerity.... Thompson seems to have positioned it as his own epitaph.

Edward Thompson's expository and imaginative writings have to be examined from the stand point of the histories of which he was or made himself, a part. The attempt has to be made at totalizing the contours of a significant liberal attempt, at comprehending and controlling extremely problematic issues and contradictions. A conflict of loyalties and perceptions occasioned in Thompson by his desire to maintain a seemingly objective poise between the virtues of British presence and 'genuine' Indian aspirations created within him a troublesome binary. The resultant knottedness, often uncritical regressions, constructions, reconstructions, recapitulations and retractions make a close reading of Thompson's oeuvre a highly instructive enterprise. The periodic shifts in his epistemological drive as depicted in the twists and turns of his fiction and in his polemics, together offer a very rewarding interface with a time that was to be of the highest formative value both for England and India.

NOTES

1. Philip Mason (1906-) served in I.C.S. from 1928 to 1947 in various distinguished positions. He has written several books and essays on race relations under the pseudonym of Philip Woodruff, of which *The Men Who Ruled India* in two volumes is the best known. He also wrote some novels like *The Island of Chamba* and *The Wild Sweet Witch* about India.
2. Sir Lepel Griffin (1839-1908) served as an ICS officer in India. He joined in 1859, and moved up to become Agent to the Governor General in Central India during 1881-9. He was greatly interested in various Indian issues, commenting on them in his writings. The given quote comes from an article on 'Indian Princes at Home' that he wrote for *Fortnightly Review*, Vol. XXXIV, 1883: 495.

3. Al Carthill was the nom de plume of B.C.H. Calcraft-Kennedy (1871-1935), a member of the ICS who joined in 1889 and served in India in various senior capacities till his retirement in 1926. He wrote several books under this pen-name. *The Lost Dominion* (1924) asserting Britain's right to retain its domination of India, is one of his better known books.
4. Benjamin Disraeli, First Earl of Beaconsfield (1804-81) started life as a solicitor, but found more success as a novelist. After repeated attempts he was elected as a member of the British Parliament for Maidstone in 1837. As a leader of the 'Young England' group of the Tory party, he was in and out of power several times. He finally succeeded to Prime Ministership in 1874. It was his idea to confer on Queen Victoria the new title of Empress of India in 1876.
5. Louis Fischer (1896-) was an American journalist who was deeply involved with problems of imperialism. Though chiefly interested in Russian politics he was attracted by Gandhi's methods of fighting for freedom, and wrote some articles about them and about India.
6. Valentine Chirol (1852-1927) was an expert on imperial and far-eastern affairs of the British foreign office and served on several Royal Commissions. He frequently visited India and wrote extensively on connected problems in an official capacity.
7. Henry Mayers Hyndman (1842-1921), was a Socialist leader and founded Democratic Federation in 1881. He later resigned from the British Socialist party to form a National Socialist Party. He was deeply interested in economic questions and wrote several books dealing with the economic exploitation of India by Britain.
8. Fenner Brockway (1888-1958) was a British left-wing politician who campaigned strongly for nuclear disarmament. Converted to socialism early in life, he was one of the first to be imprisoned for being a conscientious objector in World War I. He wrote many books on subjects like pacifism, nuclear prohibition, and economic exploitation.
9. Dadabhai Naoroji (1825-1917) was a great Indian national leader. He started life as a Professor of Mathematics and Natural Philosophy in Bombay in 1854, but resigned after a year to go to London to join a business firm. There he applied himself to the task of educating Englishmen inside and outside the Parliament on matters affecting India. He raised his voice against the drain of India's resources by England. He was thrice elected president of Indian National Congress. He was also elected to the British Parliament in 1892.
10. Gopal Krishna Gokhale (1866-1915) was a professor of history at Poona who resigned his job to participate fully in nationalist activities. He was a member of the Bombay Legislative Council and became president of Congress in 1905. A moderate, he was a leading proponent of self-government for India and influenced M.K. Gandhi's thinking.
11. Rajni Palme Dutt (1896-1974) born of an Indian father and a Swedish mother, was a veteran British Communist and a founder member of the British Communist Party. He was expelled from Oxford for propagating

Marxism. He was a prolific writer and wrote among other works, *India Today*, for which he is highly valued.

12. While Kipling is generally perceived as a bard singing of the glories of the British Empire, he had also his brief introspective moods. For he could also sing to 'God of our fathers...lest we should forget' where he visualizes British glory as 'one with Neneveh and Tyre'.
13. The moment any political unrest translates into an assertion of one's fundamental right to freedom, it brings in its train an insistence on certain well established (though, may be now, outworn and obsolete) symbols of religious/social identity. The last few years in India one has see the strife-torn border states of Punjab and Jammu and Kashmir face such assaults from radical/revolutionary/fundamentalist/terrorist elements. Punjab saw the insistence on the Sikh religious taboo on not cutting hair by anyone, while the women were additionally prohibited from wearing skirts or trousers. Similarly a ban on wearing of sarees (deemed as of Hindu origin) along with a compulsory covering of the female form or at least a headscarf to completely cover the hair was enforced in the Muslim-dominated Kashmir valley. Yet with a little easing of the political situation Punjabi girls are back to modern dresses while Muslim girls have dropped the ***burqa***.
14. Dinabandhu Tarkachuramani with his strong intellect, powerful rhetoric and deep dedication to his country's cause invites a comparison with Edmund Candler's ***Siri Ram, Revolutionary***. The latter novel was praised by Joseph Conrad for its 'lofty impartiality', 'sincere sympathy' and 'a distinct sense of enlightenment in the intricate matter of racial psychology' (quoted by Parry, 153). It would be a fascinating exercise to study Thompson, Candler and Conrad together as explorers of 'racial psychology'.
15. Horace Alexander was a historian by profession who took keen interest in Indian affairs and wrote about them. A moderate, he had a close relationship with Indian moderates, including M.K. Gandhi and was a spokesman of the Friend of India. Edward Thompson and Horace Alexander often exchanged views about personal as well as Indian problems.
16. V.K. Krishna Menon (1896-1974), one of the young firebrands of Congress was a prime mover of the British Centre of the India League. Thompson came in contact with him in the early 1940s when along with some pro-India Englishmen they fought a wordy war with the Conservative British through very active though small solidarity gatherings. E.P. Thompson, while talking of his father, reproduces a typical quote from Krishna Menon. 'We are not asking you to "give us freedom." We will take it when we want to. I am not here to ask you for your help but to remind you of your duty ('The Nehru Tradition', 140).

BIBLIOGRAPHY

Ackerley, J.R. *Hindoo Holiday.* London: 1932 Chatto & Windus, Revd. edn. 1952

Anand, Mulk Raj. 'Anglo-Saxon Attitudes: Twentieth Century Fiction About India' in *The Image of India in Western Creative Writing* Eds. M.K. Naik, S.K. Desai and S.T. Kallapur. Dharwar: Karnatak University, 1970.

Bhalla, Alok. 'A Plea Against Revenge Histories: Some Reflections on Orientalism and the Age of Empire' in *Indian Responses to Colonialism in the Nineteenth Century.* Eds. Alok Bhalla and Sudhir Chandra. New Delhi: Sterling Publishers Pvt. Ltd., 1993.

British Museum General Catalogue of Printed Books Vol. 238. London: Trustees of the British Museum, 1964.

Brockway, A. Fenner. *The Indian Crisis.* London: Victor Gollancz Ltd. 1930.

Candler, Edmund. *Abdication*. London: Gerald Duckworth and Co., 1955.

Carthill, Al. *The Lost Dominion.* London: William Blackwood and Sons, 1925.

Chamberlain, M.E. *Britain and India: The Interaction of Two Peoples* Newton Abbot, David and Charles/Handon, Connecticut, Archon Books, 1974.

Chirol, Valentine. *Indian Unrest.* 1910; rpt. New Delhi Light & Life Publishers, 1979.

Churchill, Winston. 'Address to West Essex Conservative Association', Feb. 23, 1931 in *Winston Churchill: His Complete Speeches* Vol. V. Ed. Robert Rhodes James. New York and London: Chelsea House Publishers, 1974.

Curzon, Lord. *Speeches* (1905) in *Lord Curzon in India.* Ed Sir T. Raleigh

Digby William *'Prosperous' British India.* London: T. Fisher Unwin, 1901.

Disrael Benjamin *Tancred* I, in *The Works of Benjamin Disraeli*, Vol. 15, 1904; rpt. New York: Ams Prek, 1976.

Diver, Maud. *The Singer Passes.* Edinburgh and London: W. Blackwood and Sons, 1934.

Dutt, R. Palme. *India Today*. 1940 Rev. Ed. Calcutta: Monisha, 1970.

Fanon, Frantz 'Algeria Unveils', *A Dying Colonialism*. 1959 in France Translakol and Punkol. New York: Monthly Review Press, 1965, pp. 63-4.

Fischer, Louis. *Empire.* London: Dennis Dobson Ltd., 1945.

Forster, E.M. *Hill of Devi.* 1953; rpt. New Delhi: Arnold-Heinemann, 1977.

Gandhi, M.K. 'Foreword', *To Awakening India* by S.E. Stokes

Godden, Jon and Rumer, Godden. *Two Under the Indian Sun.* New York: Alfred A. Knopf and the Viking Press, 1966.

Green, Martin. *Engling Novel in the Twentieth Century.* London, Malbourne and Henley: Routledge and Kegan Paul, 1984.

Griffin, Sir Lepel. 'Indian Princes at Home', *Fortnightly Review* Vol. XXXIV, Oct. 1883, quoted by Benita Parry

Howe Susanne. *Novels of Empire*. New York: Columbia University Press, 1949.

Hyndman, H.M. *The Bankruptcy of India*. London: Swan Sonnenschein, Lawrence & Co., 1886.
Iyer, Raghavan. *Utilitarianism and All That.* New York: Concord Grove Press, 1983.
Jacob, Violet. *Diaries and Letters from India.* 1895-1900. Ed. and Intro by Carol Anderson. Edinburgh: Canongate, 1990.
Kipling, Rudyard. 'The White Man's Burden' in *The Five Nations* from The Sussex Edition of *The Complete Works in Prosse and Verse of Rudyard Kipling* Vol. XXXIII. London: Macmillan & Co., 1937, pp. 241-2.
Lago, Mary. *Imperfect Encounter.* Cambridge, Massachusetts: Harvard University Press, 1972.
Lethbridge, Sir Roper. *Indian Offer of Imperial Preference* P.S. King and Sons, 1913 quoted in *The British Connection with India by* K.T. Paul cited below.
Mahood, M.M. *The Colonial Encounter.* London: Rex Collings, 1977.
Mason, Philip. *The Men Who Ruled India.* 2. vols. London: Cape, 1953-4.
Masters, John. *Bugles and a Tiger.* London: Michael Joseph Ltd., 1956.
Mayhew, Arthur. *Christianity in India* n.d. rpt. Delhi: Gian Publishing House, 1988.
Nehru, J.L, *Selected Works of Jawahar Lal Nehru.* Ed. S. Gopal Vols. VIII and X. New Delhi: Orient Longman Ltd., 1977.
Orwell, George. *Burmese Days.* London: Gollancz, 1935.
——— 'Shooting an Elephant' (1936) *Selected Essays.* Harmondsworth: Penguin, 1957.
Parry, Benita. *Delusions and Discoveries.* London: Allen Lane, 1972.
Paul, K.T. *The British Connection with Indian* London: Student Christian Movement, 1927.
Raleigh, Sir T. *Lord Curzon in India*, n.p. 1906
Ridley, Hugh. *Images of Imperial Rule.* London and Canberra: Grown Helm/ New York: St. Martins Press, 1983.
Sarkar, Sumit. 'Afterword' to *The Other Side of the Medal* by Edward Thompson. New Delhi: Sterling Publishers Pvt Ltd., 1989.
Sharpe, Jenny. *Allegories of Empire.* Minneapolis and London: The University of Minnesota Press, 1993.
Shaw, Bernard. *The Man of Destiny* (1986) in *Plays Pleasant and Unpleasant* Vol. II by Bernard Shaw. 1898 rpt. London: Constable and Co Ltd., 1959.
Spear, T.G.P. 'British Historical Writing in the Era of the National Movements', *Historians of India, Pakistan and Ceylon.* Ed. C.H. Philip. London: UP, 1961.
Stokes, S.E. *To Awakening India.* Madras: Ganesh: & Co., 1922.
Swindon, Patrick. *Paul Scott: Images of India.* New York: St. Martins Press, 1980.
Thompson, Edward. *The Other Side of the Medal.* 1925; rpt. New Delhi: Sterling Publishers Pvt. Ltd., 1989.
——— *Rabindranath Tagore: Poet and Dramatist.* Oxford: UP, 1926. rev. edn. 1940.

———The History of India. London: Ernest Benn Ltd., 1927.
———An Indian Day. London: Alfred A. Knopf, 1927.
———A Farewell to India. London: Benn, 1931.
———A Letter from India. London : Faber and Faber, 1932.
Thompson, Edward and G.T. Garatt, *Rise and Fulfilment of the British Rule in India*. London: Macmillan, 1934.
Thompson, E.P. *Alien Homage*. Delhi: UP, 1993.
Woolf, Leonard. *Autobiography.* 2 Vols. London: Hograth Press, 1960, 1961.
Manuscript Letters
From Edward Thompson to Horace Alexander. New Delhi: NMML Archives.
From Rabindranath Tagore to Edward Thompson. Shantiniketan: Vishwa Bharti Archives.

MARGIT KÖVES

The English Curator and the Buddhist Doctor: Charles Fábri's Identities in India

Charles Fábri is best known and remembered in Delhi as an art and dance critic. He was trained as an archaeologist and sought to express himself creatively in novels, plays and painting. His research as an archaeologist, an art historian and his creativity were complementary. The effort is to understand 'modern India' and link it with its archaeological, historical past and connect the creativity of the artist Fábri with the activities of the scholar. His novel *Indian Flamingo*, published in 1947, was a narrative of Indian society in the 1930s.

The problem of 'racial', cultural, linguistic and religious identities is repeatedly raised in *Indian Flamingo.* Personal history acquires importance in the light of Fábri's own life and the growing communal tension in Punjab before the Partition. The romance of the Englishman, John Fawcett and Padma Mitra, the young artist, grows into the quest for Indian identity against the background of a multilingual and multicultural intelligentsia and Punjabi society.

Fábri's novel, located in the world of modern painting, is not part of the canon of the Indian English novel. In the process of raising problems of identity and authenticity *Indian Flamingo* fictionalizes and builds a myth of Amrita Shergil. The postcolonial myth of the same figure is created by Salman Rushdie's *The Moor's Last Sigh*.

India as the scene of erotic desire and disappointment is the major theme of colonial romance—written in the last quarter of nineteenth century—based on the convention of interracial love (heterosexual or homoerotic) coupled with colonial horror and cultural disgust. *Indian Flamingo* is a late variant of romance, describing the growth of culture into nationhood.[1]

Padma's pictures interpreted by Fawcett as revelations of modern Indian art and her self-realization against all odds suggest the birth of

India as a nation through its culture and art.[2] In the era of transfer of power Fábri constructed his English narrator, John Fawcett, to involve and confront his English audience with the possibility of change, the transformation of culture into a politically independent nation. Fábri took up the theme of cross-cultural friendship and love from Forster's *A Passage to India* in a new imperial context.[3] The time of writing—1945: the period between the Second World War and the Partition-lends significance to the narrator's identity and to the issues of 'race' and culture which acquired new relevance after the Holocaust. A number of solutions in the novel betray Fábri's multiple identities as a polyglott, assimilated Jewish Hungarian, a liberal Englishman and a Buddhist convert.

I

The majority of characters in the *Indian Flamingo* were based on personalities peopleing in Fábri's world. John Fawcett, the narrator and curator of Lahore Museum, occupies a post in the novel which Fábri held after the War. Most of the pictures painted by Padma, are based on Amrita Shergil's paintings exhibited in 1937 in Lahore and reviewed in newspapers by Fábri.[4] Padma's person was modelled after Ratna Mathur, whom Fábri married in 1947.[5] The narrative conveys the sense of participation, mobility and a sharing of values, and cultural models with his Indian surroundings. Fábri searched for cultural provisions to transcend everyday existence and also to discover a more meaningful life. This interest, shared by a number of Central-European orientalists in the twentieth century was part of a cultural critique of conditions at home; it led them to the problematic taken up in their research and it also found expression in their artistic and creative activity.

Forster's *A Passage to India* (first published in 1924) concludes with the impossibility of friendship between Fielding and Aziz, the liberal Enlgishman and the Indian doctor, till India becomes independent, and a nation.[6] *Indian Flamingo* asserts the possibility of friendship or even synthesis. This was a development emerging from the new modes of contact established in the 1930s, including the intimacy of evenings spent in each others' homes by those who are sufficiently mobile and Indianized, like Fawcett, or anglicized by their education, like most intellectuals in Fawcett's surroundings.

Indian Flamingo opens with the description of an evening in the house of Elizabeth and Kishan Mitra. The Mitras are part of Fawcett's special circle of friends after the eleven years he spent in India. This is also the evening when John first meets Padma, Mitra's sister, who had just returned from college. Padma and John meet often and after John discovers that Padma is an artist they get engaged without the knowledge of the family. Saidullah commits suicide and Padma runs away to Kashmir after George's confessions of love provoke Padma's mother to lock her up. After discovering Padma's whereabouts Mitra and John together take a trip to Kashmir just to meet her. There is the promise of marriage and harmony between Fawcett and Padma.

II

When Charles Louis Fábri was born in 1899 in Budapest, Hungary was part of the multinational, multilingual Austro-Hungarian Monarchy. In the last quarter of the nineteenth century and in Fábri's childhood, in the first decade of the twentieth century, Hungary underwent rapid industrialization and modernization and this contributed to the tension between the powerful Hungarian minority, and the others: Croat, Serb, Slovak and Ukrainian nationalities who considered themselves repressed in economic and cultural terms.

Fábri came from an assimilated Jewish background, like many outstanding Hungarian orientalists before him (Ignaz Goldziher, Armin Váméry or Aurel Stein). Assimilation in Hungary was part of the liberal project of emancipation and it included complex efforts like change of language and names, purchase of aristocratic titles, greater participation in public life, entry into new professional avenues, the struggle for a new uniform civil code, and the possibility of intermarriage between Christians and Jews.[7] Mixed marriages and conversion were considered the most extreme steps taken by Jews to become Hungarians. Similar solutions like intermarriage and free choice of a religion (by the English living in India), figure in Fábri's novel ***Indian Flamingo.*** A special characteristic of the Hungarian development was that such an assimilation did not go with the closing up of distance between Jews and other groups. Many features of the Jewish past, mainly surviving among Jews coming from Galicia and Lithuania, were looked at negatively and condemned by assimilated Jews, accepting the point of view of the majority community.

Fábri's background motivated him to consider linguistic nationalism as a prerequisite of the birth of the nation and to privilege Hungarian linguistic nationalism as compared to the linguistic nationalism of the other minorities. The movement for the renewal of Hungarian language in the Austro-Hungarian Monarchy, concentrated for more than a hundred years, all efforts on developing the Hungarian language through purification from foreign elements and creation of the narrative of pre-history through the linguistic analysis of etymological roots. ***Indian Flamingo*** considers language as the centre of one's identity and lack of sufficient knowledge of one's mother tongue the cause of insecurity. In the novel a sense of dislocation is created by insufficient knowledge of Hindustani in the English educated Indian middle class of Lahore.

Growing up in the first decade of the twentieth century in the Austro-Hungarian Monarchy also meant an adaptation to a semiotic network of cultural behaviour and a dexterity with languages which enabled Fábri to move with ease in Europe. In his documents submitted for naturalization Fábri listed several European (and two Asian) languages spoken by him.[8] Part of the semiotic network was a peculiar decorous and solicitous relationship to women, reflected in Fábri's novel in the description of Padma's and John's developing relationship and in the discussion of race, gender and art.

The limitations of Jewish emancipation and extremities of assimilation reinforced the reflection on the relationship between the individual, community and the universe. A number of orientalists focused attention on the public and the private sphere and the place of the individual in the societies of the East.[9] These problems are taken up by Fábri in *Indian Flamingo* in the context of English presence.

The outcome of the War, the collapse of the Austro-Hungarian Monarchy and the failure of the short-lived Workers Republic reversed the course of emancipation.[10] After his school leaving examination Fábri was enlisted in the army as an officer in reserve.

As a result of intellectual and Jewish participation in the Workers Republic of 1919, the antidemocratic and antisemitic potential of official and academic nationalism gained force after the First World War. The Department of Indology in Budapest, established in 1873, was closed down in 1919 as a punitive measure against participation in the revolutionary council of the university by József Schmidt.[11] The first anti-Jew laws were introduced in 1920 in Hungary, fifteen years before the Nuremberg laws in fascist Germany. The laws restricted the number of Jewish students studying in the universities and virtually made employment of Jews by the state administration impossible.

The prospect of an academic career in Hungary for a person of Jewish origin, like Fábri, was unachievable. In the course of the War the Fábri family became impoverished, and Fábri, when studying in the University of Pécs, subsisted on giving French, German and English lessons.[12] In the absence of regular formal classes Fábri chose philosophy as his main subject and studied Indology, Eastern art along with art history in the course of his "doctoral self-training". This meant an informal way of learning further through a wide reading of specialized literature, through discussions with colleagues, and visiting the oriental art collections in London and Berlin beyond what he was taught of European art history. Zoltán Felvinczi Takács, the Director of the Museum of East-Asian Art, could serve Fábri as a model.[13] Felvinczi Takács, like Fábri had a training in painting under Simon Hollósy in Munich and was equipped to contribute articles both on the history of art and archaeology. Felvinczi Takács also served as a link in Fábri's international contacts.[14]

After he was awarded his doctor's degree in 1927, Fábri joined the Kern Institute in Leyden and contributed to the series *Annual Bibliography of Indian Archaeology*, edited by J.Ph. Vogel. At the same time he also studied with Professor Sylvain Levi who was one of the first visiting foreign professors in Shantiniketan and who guided a number of Indian students in Paris.[15]

Fábri first reached India in 1931 after Aurel Stein, the archaeologist and explorer, invited him to participate in his expedition on the route of Alexander, the Great. Fábri was the only European ever to be present in a Stein expedition. Stein appreciated Fábri's eagerness to learn and his ability to work tirelessly. He joined Stein in Lahore in November 1931 who described him to his friend as 'thoroughly businesslike, an indefatigable worker and in addition very modest and genuinely attached. There is some risk of his spoiling me by his solicitude for my comfort and ease.'[16]

Fábri was first exposed to an Indian environment in Punjab, in Lahore, on the banks of the Jhelum river and in the Salt Range of Punjab. In the course of archaeological expeditions Stein located sites, measured distances, collected linguistic and anthropometrical data like body and skull measurements. The loyalty of the people to the British Raj in the Salt Range contrasted pleasantly for Stein with the nationalist upsurge elsewhere in Punjab.[17] Fábri was both stimulated and excited by the direct contact with Indians, excavations and camp life. Stein was happy to have an assistant who could take dictation in four languages and with whom, after the days work was done, one could sit around the campfire reciting poems of János Arany, the nineteenth century Hungarian poet.[18]

For all his admiration for Stein's work, Fábri's approach to his Indian surrounding was different. Unlike Stein and the earlier generation of orientalists he was giving way to the sensual involvement with the field, an experience known to anthropologist and orientalitsts but which has been accepted as part of academic observation only since 'the reflexive turn' in anthropology. (This meant the acceptance of the anthropologist as a participant observer sharing common needs in the field. This can also be a source of emancipation of the subject of observation, of being an outsider and having an insider's perspective.) In Fábri's case it meant the acceptance of the political and cultural self-understanding of Indians of his own class and intellectual milieu. While Stein saw irrationalism in nationalism, *Indian Flamingo* shows that Fábri had accepted the political participation of Indians in creating their society. The source of his understanding was the complex sensual and emotional involvement and the 'absorption in both worlds.'[19]

Following the archaeological excavations and trailing Alexander's route, Fábri returned to London in May 1932 to arrange the findings jointly with Fred H. Andrews in the British Museum.[20] In 1934 Fábri was invited to give lectures in Shantiniketan and Calcutta. Later the same year, he edited the *Annual Report of the Archaeological Survey of India,* clearing in six months time a backlog of four years. His next assignments in India in 1935 took him to Lahore as officer on special duty to supervise the excavations at Mohenjodaro and Harappa. In the novel *Indian Flamingo* John Fawcett spends five days with the Mitras and George before Saidullah's suicide at Harappa.

Fábri was later appointed to rearrange the collection at the Lahore Museum and in 1938 he was still in Punjab on a new appointment as field director of the Punjab Exploration Fund. During this period he also wrote on diverse fields like education, reviewed books and exhibitions, and gave extension lectures on the history of Indian art at the Punjab University in Lahore. His lectures were appreciated[21] and his efforts in the Museum highly valued.[22] His knowledge of Sanskrit and Hindustani, his interest in Indian history and art, placed him in the category of those Englishmen 'who seemed to love India and threw their roots deeply into its soil'.[23] Fábri occupied the space established for the English by Indians.

He was able to take on an English identity because of his mobility, his gift of talk and the ability to impress.[24] But this was only a public identity, similar to the character of the narrator in *Indian Flamingo.* Privately he cultivated most of the accidental factors of his birth. He applied for English citizenship only in 1938 when the Second World War seemed to be a distinct reality. Hungary became an ally of Germany, and Fábri as citizen of an inimical country, would have been interned in India. An additional reason was that in 1938 and 1939 the anti-Jew laws were introduced in Hungary, and emigration was a constant preoccupation with Jews in Hungary like elsewhere in Central Europe,[25] and Fábri was a Jew according to the Nuremberg definition. He became a naturalized British subject with little delay in 1939. Perhaps he unwittingly remarked in his original naturalization papers that he was uncertain where he was going to stay after naturalization, but the administration marked this section and sent this form back for revision.[26] In his conversation with Gandhi about prayer, meditation, intellectual conviction, and the right of a person to kill oneself, Fábri introduced himself as a Buddhist and a Hungarian scholar, 'a stark rationalist' whose scriptures were the *Bhagavadgita* and the *Dhammapada.*[27] He wrote *Indian Flamingo* after his army service in 1945 when he was the curator of the Lahore Museum. The novel was, to a great extent, shaped by his chosen and accidental identities as liberal Englishman, born a Hungarian Jew, and as a Buddhist.

III

Liberal notions of culture and class, belief in the universality of culture and in the importance of 'the knowledge of Greek, Latin, and Eastern antiquity' as well as a rejection of philistinism shaped, Fábri's writings to a great extent. Cultural issues like language, education, art and religion are presented and interpreted by the narrator of *Indian Flamingo*, John Fawcett along dichotomies such as bigotry and enlightenment, irrationalism and reason, authenticity and modernity. Fawcett and his Indian friends Saidullah, the Mitras, and Digvijay share similar intellectual and aesthetic values while others, like Brigadier Hollingworth, Miss Holden, Padma's mother and Chotu Lal Narayan Das are excluded from the class of education and culture and ridiculed as philistines.[28]

Fawcett is the curator of the Lahore Museum and this throws up the reference to Lockwood Kipling, father of Rudyard Kiplng, who established the Lahore Museum and was it's first curator. Kipling's novel Kim opens with the picture of the *ajaib-ghar*, the wonderhouse, which is often the background of *Indian Flamingo.* Just as Fábri follows the British tradition of providing India with a linear history, unearthing the past through excavations, defining the value and meaning of objects to be collected, classifying and displaying them in museums,[29] so too does Fawcett establish and collect data, organize and distribute information collected from his informants. He is an omniscient narrator who guides the reader into homes, museums, to archaeological sites, the Punjabi countryside. His unceasing verbal energy shows the desire to evaluate, to order, to inhabit and to cultivate. His enthusiasm often bordering on 'elation' contradicts the image of the educted Englishman, the dignity of an intellectual professional[31] and this suggests that his desire to merge, to make himself Indian[32] is burdened with anxiety and ambivalence.

The intimacy of the opening section—the December evening after dinner in the Mitra's house, the conversation about langauge, poetry, and politics—indicates that since the early decades of the Raj, the social situation of *A Passage to India* (where the collector tells Fielding that intimacy of any sort is not possible with Indians), new modes of social contact came into existence. The memory of the evening in the Mitras house is heightened with nostalgia. The distance of time and the constant use of the past tense presents the sense of idyll in the mixed company of Indian and English guests. Fawcett's relations with the Westernized educated Indian middle class enables him to see racism and nationalism through their eyes. The Indian village wedding and the countryside enhance these idyllic qualities of intercommunity peace and this is later contrasted with the news of riots and unrest carried by Fawcett's newspapers. The perspective of nostalgic memory is based on the sharp communal and political polarization of the 1940s which led to the partition of India.[33]

The story of Fatimah's adultery, followed by Saidullah's suicide, breaks the tone of nostalgia and George's death also associates the romance with tragedy. Padma's prodigious talent, her alliance with John, Elizabeth's and Kishan's future child, carry a note of optimism. These are concessions on the future of the Indian nation connected with the presence of the English while the two deaths (a Muslim's and an Englishman's) anticipate the tragic potential of Independence and Partition. The solutions in the novel reflect a feeling of participation on both sides which had become an element of English liberal tradition by the 1940s.[34]

Right at the outset in the novel, language, customs and religion are discussed in terms of authenticity and uprootedness. George Lindhurst, one of the guests at the Mitras, brings up the topic of a memorial plaque to 'Lawrence of the Punjab' to be installed in English and in Latin in the Lahore Officers Mess. The other guests feel that it would be more appropriate to write the memorial in English and Hindustani. (p.10) Cultural and political conflict which is described by Saidullah and the narrator as 'the clash of two vast civilizations' is first associated with language.[35]

The special role given to Hindustani in *Indian Flamingo* is the affirmation of its role in nation building. Language is an area elaborated in great detail in the novel and Fábri emphasizes it in a warning at the beginning of the novel (p. 6) that his system of transcription of Hindustani is a literal rendering, more authentic than Kipling's or any other previous attempt.

This insistence on linguistic evidence in a work of fiction is quite extraordinary. Fábri's training with Vogt in Leyden, his post-doctoral research with Levi in Paris, and his study of the classics in Latin and Greek in the Hungarian Gymnasium prepared him for the collection of linguistic evidence and the presentation of Hindustani. The excessive concern with language almost turns the initial sixty pages of the novel into a textbook of Hindustani, part of the nineteenth century Punjabi *Sharif* culture and etiquette.[36] These examples also demonstrate the social space and everyday use of Hindustani in an English speaking milieu as it is used by children within the family or in a work situation — as it is spoken with his subordinates in the museum.[37] Fawcett describes his own adjustment to India as the path which takes him from knowing 'macaronic' Hindustani to a proficient use of the language and the 'way of the people' (p. 58).

The degeneration of the English and their cultural arrogance is demonstrated through the decline of the first colonizers, like Henry Lawrence, to the various representatives of the day who can make themselves ridiculous. Brigadier Hollingworth and Miss Holden (a school teacher) who live and work in India but do not speak Hindustani receive satirical treatment. Lawrence who was the initiator of the 'Punjab tradition' is glorified as a linguist and dehistoricized.[38]

Examples of 'this lovable language', Hindustani presented and separated from the English text by italics and by their translation address the language issue by adopting a philological method, translation of separated roots of words: *ek bat* all one speech; *Namaste, Hazur* I worship you, Your Presence; and *Dhanyavad* Words of Gratitude. Translation of a phrase, expression, or a sentence would normally present the meaning in the context of the whole, the translations in the novel dissolve the interconnection between the roots of words, present them with that meaning and put them together again in their combination, supplemented with their original dictionary meaning. As a result, Hindustani displayed in the novel is archaic.

What is labelled in the novel by Saidullah as the clash of civilizations can also be seen as a cultural contest for a new linguistic hierarchy. Saidullah in the novel expresses his thoughts in everyday conversation most naturally in English but writes modern Urdu poetry. The tension created by English as medium of instruction for the professional middle class is further complicated by the plurality of languages: English, Hindustani, Hindi, or Urdu. The question of language and its cultural importance were issues, raised in India already in the nineteenth century and were part of the emerging national consiousness. This was reflected in the linguistic contest between English and various vernaculars which could be outright antagonistic or could be more intricate with one Indian language being elevated to official eminence over other Indian languages.[39]

Paradoxically the translation of Hindustani phrases in the novel, intended to demonstrate the right of Hindustani language spoken by the communities living in India[40] a the authentic language of the people, establishes the monopoly of English. Linguistic hybridity which is natural in a bilingual situation is not presented except in the form of satire, in an official letter to Fawcett from Chotu Lal Narayan Das (an aged Hindu Babu, p. 89). The Hindustani words and phrases in italics supplemented by their translation, isolate them even where they could be understood from the context. Idiomatic English is established as monoglossia, the language of the narrator and the Indian middle class, separate from Hindustani and 'baboo' English. The declared aim of the novel to show the 'authenticity' of Hindustani becomes ambivalent through the monopoly which the narration establishes over the interpretation of Hindustani.

Etymologyzing translation of the kind presented in *Indian Flamingo* aims at manifesting the original meaning of words part by part instead of targeting the equivalent of the phrase in the context. The Hungarian language reform, the renewal of the language in the nineteenth century, set out to replace 'alien', 'foreign' (German) words, phrases and structures by newly created or archaic, 'authentic' Hungarian words and suffixes and encouraged their use to prove their birthright.[41]

Privileging Hindustani in the novel had secular and democratic potential, justifying and legitimizing the demand for Hindustani as the language of communities living in Hindustan. This exercise is reversed by the narrator. While the novel ridicules cultural arrogance, it approaches imperial decline with a sense of regret, drawing a parallel between the dissolution of the British Empire in India and the Pax Romana in the Near East (p. 56). The colonial nostalgia for erstwhile greatness simultaneously ignores the fact that the same tradition led to economic and cultural exploitation and made racial prejudice part of everyday practice. This was further complicated by the historical fact in the background of the novel that linguistic contradictions existed within the Freedom movement.[42]

IV

While the possibility of friendship was suggested between Fielding and Doctor Aziz in *A Passage to India,* Fawcett's and Saidullah's friendship in *Indian Flamingo* reflects a shift of perspective. Saidullah was Fawcett's "most civilized friend", his *bhai* his "best friend". He and Fawcett share a common ground in the love of poetry, art and a critical relationship to imperial narrow-mindedness on the basis of hierarchy of education and belief in the universality of culture. They belong to the same class of culture and education, the dividing lines separating 'civilizations' and race are relocated along class lines in the novel.

Saidullah's wish to live in the 'equalitarian brotherhood of man' (p. 122) and his belief in universality are disappointed. He has 'no patience left' (p. 123) and his irritation is fueled by racial and religious hostility around him (p. 123). His talk of 'hatred' (p. 132), his 'desperate passion' and 'great despair' like the 'violent, mad, raging', 'fury' (p. 139) of Padma's mother are pitched against the ethical system of Pali Buddhism represented by Fawcett. The emotions of *dukkha* displayed by Saidullah and Mrs. Mitra can be countered by the norms of Buddhism, the ethics of kindness and self-command. This is what Fawcett conveys to the school-children about Buddhism on their visit to the Buddhist

Gallery of the Lahore Museum and in his decision not to expect Padma's return of his love (following the teachings of the Blessed Buddha ... I shall try to give her happiness without asking for return, p. 57). Fawcett's compassion (*karuna*) in place of passion and his commitment to service to others (*pravrtti*) are finally rewarded by Padma returning his love.

Universality inspired Indian and Western philosophers to overcome the limitations of denominational belief. In Durban, Mahatma Gandhi advocated the reconciliation of Buddhism, Islam and Christianity.[43] Buddhism and Advaita Vedanta philosophy were incorporated into a syncretic philosophical system by Radhakrishnan and Tagore.[44] Kosambi's work underlined the radical, democratic, and anti-caste character of Buddhism; Radhakrishnan and Tagore emphasized those elements which enabled Hinduism to accommodate Buddhism.[45]

Buddhism gradually occupied a place of privilege in the nineteenth century orientalist scholarship which considered Buddhism, a "new, pure religion", the chance of salvation which was allowed to pass by. In consequence excavations, collections and compilations about religion and history, and the philosophy of Nietzsche and Schopenhauer allocated a place of pride to Buddhism.[46] Philosophical speculations perceived Buddhism as 'the most radical negation of existence' similar to Christianity, but rising above Christianity in its rejection of mediocrity.[47] Theosophy at the turn of the century in Europe provided a space for Buddhism and it was also utilized by anticapitalist cultural critique, often advocating a praxis for the transformation of society.[48] Modern literature and art in Europe and Hungary by the first decade of the century was strongly shaped by Buddhism.[49]

Inspite of all his love of Buddhist art which had developed only in the later phase of Buddhism, Fawcett in *Indian Flamingo* draws a line between early and late Buddhism. Fawcett holds up the ethical system of early Buddhism as a model against the blind faith in devotion which toor over in late Buddhism, the "foolish faith that the recitaton of words would lead to a state of happiness" (p. 65). Integrity of personality and a course of actions controlled by reason is possible only if the words of the dying Buddha are followed 'Be ye lamps unto yourselves, islands of refuge unto yourselves' (p. 133). Fawcett's daily reading, the *Majjhima-nikayah,* is the earliest source of Buddha's teachings about extinguishing desire and suffering.

In July 1939 Fábri while interviewing Gandhi at Abottabad asked for Gandhi's opinion about meditation and prayer, about dogma and critical judgment, about the right to kill oneself because of physical pain or the inability to continue to struggle. Fábri argued for the critical faculty of reason and meditation to be more important than senseless muttering in prayer, while Gandhi asserted that prayer helped him to achieve many things in life. It allowed him... 'to lose himself ... in the divinity' in him due the intensity of his faith. Gandhi maintained that it is immodest to ascribe extreme power to one's reason and intellect as the analysis of one's own thought itself is limited.[50]

The Boddhisattva Manjusri in his usual form wields the sword of wisdom to fight his enemy, namely ignorance. In the novel the statue of the Goddess Manjusri,[51] a female form propagating learning and the arts[52] is identified, cleaned and adored by Fawcett. Only those who recognize the importance of intellectual horizons like Padma or Pandit Vats share the admiration of Manjusri with Fawcett. The opposition of wisdom and ignorance, measure and excess postulated in the novel and confirmed by the figure of Manjusri, overlaps the notion of reason as constructed by the Enlightenment. The qualities of European self-definition (reason posited against emotion, sense against non-sense, measure against excess) in *Indian Flamingo* are ascribed to Buddhism. The novel relates emotion and excess to Saidullah (a Muslim), Padma's mother (old Hindu woman) and George (a young Englishman).[53] Though the novel subsists on the surrender of European identity, the values of Enlightenment are inscribed in the presentation of Buddhist ethics.

V

The narrator, Fawcett as an archaeologist and a linguist links, inhabits and interprets the cultural universality that Mohenjodaro, Buddhist art, Mughal miniatures and modern art represent while other characters in the novel like Vats, (the Sanskrit scholar), Mitra, (the judge), or George, (the young Englishman), can only represent their immediate group or social class. The dedication of the novel to Amrita Shergil and "her sisters and brothers" suggests that the birth of modern art in India is the founding moment of the nation. In the multilingual surroundings of India with many religions Padma's art represents the uniting element confronting fragmentation. In the figure of Padma Mitra, a young Indian woman, the novel combines the 'celebration' of the Indian woman and the discussion of antiracism.

In his reviews of Amrita Shergil's exhibitions Fábri always emphasized her half-Hungarian parentage, the long years she spent in Hungary and in Europe as a child and her training in Paris.[54] In the novel Padma studies in Beasgarh College, in the Punjab her father and brother are judges (her other brothers are doctors), and they are part of the English edcuated professional middle class in the Punjab. Her mother is "the member of the last, old generation" (p. 142), who "could read Hindi and had read nothing but religious and mythological texts" (p. 179) and who in retaliation to Padma's marriage to Fawcett, (a white man) could go as far as have her daughter poisoned or murdered (p. 142). Her revulsion against Europeans comes from the same source as the racism of Europeans who are repulsed by "the touch of black skin". The source of Saidullah's unhappiness is also based on the Muslim custom of a traditional marriage arrangement with a cousin. The contrast between Padma and her mother is understood as the key of transformation in the novel. As her brother says "rebellion in the homes comes when the girls start it" (p. 181).

In the 1930s the first and second generation of college educated women were about to enter the social scene. This coincided with reports on the Hindu Women's Inheritance Bill, Hindu Women's Bill on Property, the Child Marriage Restraint Act, the employment of women teachers, and the entry of women into the medical profession. In 1937 the first election took place in which women voters also participated.[55] All these raised new expectations and hopes in connection with women's education and position in Indian and Punjabi society.

In *Indian Flamingo* a group of schoolgirls come to visit the Lahore Museum and inspite of their limited syllabus ask Fawcett intelligent and brave questions who guides them to the Buddhist Gallery. Padma studies in Beasgarh in the Missionary college and spends one year in Europe. Fábri wanted to show the newly found independence of Indian women yet he created a contradictory image of passivity with *flamingo* indicating Padma in the title of the book and in later references. Backwardness, prejudice, hatred, ignorance which were earlier ascribed to India in orientalist literature are relegated in *Indian Flamingo* to women who did not get educational opportunities in English and who are described as 'primitive'.

The issue of race, gender and the desire for "fresh experience" are combined in the discussion on art.[56] Aesthetic and erotic desire as a counter to racism is present in the novel in the discussion on art. Fatimah reminds Eric of the miniature paintings representing ladies at the Mughal court (p. 14); Padma looks with her heavy eyelids, enormous black eyes, and bronze-coloured arms like a princess from an old Ajanta fresco. This collapsing of aesthetic and erotic desire is even more evident in the description of the Manjusri statue. As Fawcett dusts the 'cream-coloured sandstone with sensual softness' and 'nipple, painted bright brick-red' it reminds him of the 'subconscious longings' of the monk who carved the statue. He decides not to undress a 'delicious, naked' woman in front of the chaprasis. As Fawcett shows the statue to Padma, the continuous transgression from the aesthetic to the erotic becomes even more palpable and this creates a sense of discomfort in the reading because the text is never far from prurience.[57]

The sexual invasion of art in the context of interracial contact goes back to the nineteenth century debate about race which focussed on the issue of sexuality and sexual unions between blacks and whites. "Affinities" and "repulsions" among the males and females of certain races was an issue of speculation.[58] Though Fábri reverses the racist argument, the terminology of his argument remains the same and reaffirms the distinctions between the barriers of races.

After the Second World War, when Fábri wrote *Indian Flamingo,* theories of race were completely discredited. But at the time of the novel's narrative in the 1930s newspaper articles in England often raised the issue of racist discrimination exercised against Gandhi and Nehru and their class of people who were educated in England with regret. Discrimination against other classes or Indians was not discussed.[59]

The visual and verbal imagery of *Indian Flamingo* is saturated with the vocabulary of race and this is disturbing for the reader specially because of the interplay of the aesthetic and the erotic. The use of the language of eroticism is peculiar also because it is obvious that racism is disapproved in the novel and issues of women's education and rights are raised.

The system of arguments widely used at the turn of the century during the Habsburg Monarchy suggesting that man was pure spirit while woman was pure matter wanting to be treated as an object, continued along with the emergence of new possibilities and professional avenues for women. In art and literature there was a cult of the *femme fatale*, a symbolic representation of woman's erotic and 'spiritual' power. Padma's creative force and her irresistible attraction leading two men to commit suicide, resemble the *femme fatale* of the turn of the century. The recognition of women's abilities in the culture of the Monarchy is inconsistent with a highly formal decorum, a special semiotic behaviour with women, emphasizing the gender difference. This split of values was a formative force in culture of the turn of the century and some of the most emancipated men of the first decade of the century, like Georg Lukács or Béla Bartók believed in it.[60]

VI

Padma's paintings, her prodigious talent and the resistance she displays in the face of her mother's opposition bring in a new dimension in the novel. She goes to Kashmir alone and spends her time painting till her brother and Fawcett find her and give her the news of her mother's stroke.

The fate of culture, the birth of the nation, depends on whether it is able to come to terms with modernity. The thought of how modern

India can come into its own and how it can synthesize western achievements in various areas was taken up again and again in the thirties.[61] In the novel Indian modernity is represented by the purely Indian identity of the young artist. She is Indian in her essence and this matches John's English essence. Fawcett unlike many Englishmen in India was brought up and educated in England. John and Padma are driven to a fusion, a "synthesis" similar to the process of assimilation, giving up an identity to be transformed by the other in Hungary.[62]

Padma's 'phenomenal' talent manifests itself in its self-progenitory nature. She develops her talent without a teacher, in isolation from any school of painting or academic teaching. Fawcett is the first person to see her paintings and her work is revelation ("arrived at last was the great painter this country had been waiting for" p. 148) and it could be interpreted and fully appreciated by him as an English curator.

Fábri was committed to the idea of the continuity of ancient Indian civilization with the later Muslim civilizations. He also considered that modern India could look back to an organic continuous past tradition of art and crafts.[63] Inspite of this, in the novel the only connection between Padma's art and the Indian past are the Ajanta paintings. This served to build up a myth of the founder of modern Indian art.

Fawcett's analysis of Padma's work rests on a dynamic of thought, which defines visual perfection in painting on the basis of a set of dichotomies. The technical mastery over visual material is European ("the hand and the eye of a westerner"), and the intellectual is Indian ("heart and mind—Indian"). Her treatment of line is described in terms of austerity and measure, and the handling of colour as sensuality and excess. The perception of the oriental scene and the brilliance of colour brings Padma's art close to Gauguin's.[64]

Padma brings into the plane of visibility social classes which had so far been invisible in Indian painting. Labourers are brought forth on the canvas in their "lean, hungry, tragic hopelessness", women "lost" and "forlorn" (p. 76). Fábri's first reviews of the figures in Amrita Shergil's paintings[65] as well as his later writing emphasized the "sad, thin faces with their dreamy, lost look"[66] and the tragic loneliness", the "sorrow, misery, lonely solitude" of the painter.[67] Padma sends her paintings to Fawcett when she leaves Lahore and her "tragic and marvellous" pictures fill John in turn with humble submission and joyous celebration. Her paintings are the revelation of 'the very soul of these people'and as Fawcett hangs her paintings in his rooms he gives way to his wish to be one with India with a sense of surrender (Oh, this was India, my India, my Punjab! ... 'Let me drink the cup of suffering to its last dregs. This my world. This is my Punjab, these are my people, painted by my bride.' p. 148)

VII

Indian Flamingo addresses the question what is the foundation of Indian nationalism. The historical past preserved in museums, a single language (Hindustani) and religion, permeated with Enlightenment ethics are not sufficient to guarantee the existence of the nation. Art is the basis on which the nation could be born. The novel describes the politicization of the educated middle class, their relationship to the English and to British colonial institutions.

Describing Padma's art as authentic ascribing essentiality to her figure, the novel denies art the level of politicization it went through in the decades of the Freedom Movement.[68] Fawcett interprets the villagers in Padma's pictures in their aesthetic presence, analysing them in a language verging on sentimentality similar to Fábri's early reviews about Amrita Shergil. The studies of Indian peasants in the novel ("long, haggard faces, lean and hungry" p. 148) and the four portraits of the staff of the American mission in the novel ("happy in their faith", "with the background of a prosperous, well-to-do country" p. 148) underline the difference that American welfare could do for that nation.

This suggests that all classes were to be included in the concept of the nation including labourers even if there is no clear social dimension attached to them in the novel. The nation was to be created through Padma's art in the novel, but paradoxically, however political the concept of nation was, Fábri wanted to keep art free of politics. Though colonial practice and injustice against the Indian middle class is registered, Fábri as a liberal did not accept politics mediated through art.

Central-Europeans living in India occupied a space allotted to Englishmen by Indians and often adopted an English identity.[69] This assumed English identity was often reinforced by their emigree status as exiles and further complicated by their choice of India as residence and by the Freedom Struggle. Modernity understands migration as trauma, homelessenss and the interchange of xenophobia and xenophilia must have reminded Fábri that the choice of a home, the desire to merge remains unfulfilled and it may meet with various responses, similar to Jewish projects of assimilation.

The identities of Padma and Fawcett as Indian and English serve the purpose of the myth of modern Indian art in consistence with nationalism which in general elevates authenticity as protection against the threat of infiltration.[70] Although in literary-historical terms Fábri's novel is not seen as part of the canon of the Indian English novel and its sheer merit is open to debate, it raises interesting problems of identity and authenticity and locates them in the world of modern painting which did not enter the mainstream of the Indian English novel.

Fábri introduced himself to Gandhi as a Buddhist scholar and a Hungarian, and this reflected his plural identity. His experiences of nationalism and the powerful system of European arguments about the nation predestined him for the quest for fusion and assimilation as the only East-European solution to identity. "Merging of essences" leading to universality advocated for the educated middle classes is an ambivalent project as the European experience, the persecution and annihilation of Jews, Gypsies and all alien element showed in the Second World War. In the liberal English framework it meant a special place assigned for the English and those who had links with the English. Submission and assumption of a new Indian identity is rehearsed in the course of the novel several times.

At the time of the transfer of power Fábri envisioned that the passage from a culture to nationhood in 1947 would mean privileging Hindustani language, Buddhist religion, the English educated middle class woman whose creativity is the potential prerequisite to the birth of the nation. Rejecting hybridity, Hindustani is isolated and English is established as monoglossia. The qualities of European self-definition: reason, sense and measure are confirmed as Buddhist ethics. Racism and violence is attributed to the uneducated. Labourers and villagers are an unpredictable quality either removed into the idyllic, intercommunal harmony of the past or sentimentalized in the aesthetic space of Padma's painting.

Overcoming the split between artistic and scientific mimesis the novel reflects Fábri's milieu in Lahore, his major aesthetic and social concerns. Fábri's interest in the issue of Indian modernity remains central in his critical writing as he claims cultural authenticity for modern Indian art. The agency of emancipation is ascribed to the Indian middle class. The alliance of Padma and John is the concession given to liberal English presence claiming a special place for art and its interpretation. This is the course of their transformation into the representative cultural institutions of independent India.

NOTES

1. Benita Parry, ***Delusions and Discoveries, Studies on India in the British Imagination 1880-1930,*** London, 1972; Sara Suleri, ***The Rhetoric of English India***, Chicago, 1992.
2. This is also what the dedication of the novel also refers to. "To the beloved, undying memory of Amrita and her sisters and brothers of the

new India" Charles Fábri, *Indian Flamingo,* London, 1947, p. 5. All subsequent page numbers refer to this edition.

3. Fábri apparently wanted to write a novel similar to Forster's *A Passage to India*, (a verbal information from Bisham Sahani). This refers to a meeting with Fábri which probably took place in Bombay in 1945.)
4. *The Civil and Military Gazette,* 20-1 November 1937; *The Tribune,* 21 November 1937.
5. Géze Bethlenfalvy, *Charles Louis Fábri, His Life and Work,* New Delhi, 1980.
6. Though there is a reconciliation between Aziz and Fielding, the response to Fielding's suggestion "why can't we be friends now" is "No, not yet". See in E.M. Forster, *A Passage to India,* London, 1989 pp. 315-16; Sara Suleri *The Rhetoric of English India,* Chicago, 1992, pp. 132-48.
7. Viktor Karády, Asszimiláció és társadalmi krizis [Assimilation and Crisis in Society] in the monthly: *Világosság* [Light] vol. XXXIV, March 1993, pp. 33-60, and András Kovács, *Identitás és Etnicitás, Zsidó Identitásproblémák a háború utáni Magyarországon* (Identity and Ethnicity. Problems of Jewish Identity in Hungary after the War), in: *Zsidóság, Identitás, Történelem* (Jews, Identity, History) ed. by M. Kovács, Yitzhak M. Kashti, F. Erös, Budapest, 1992, pp. 97-113.
8. The order of languages is according to Fábri: English, Hungarian, French, Italian, German, Dutch, Spanish, Hindustani, Irani. National Archives of India F/10/104/38-public.
9. Armin Vambery (1832-1913), Justified imperialism in Turkey, Iran, and Caucasus in *The Story of my Struggles,* 1908. Ignaz Goldziher (1850-1921) worked on the problem of religion as an element of private life and the organic and inorganic elements in the process of national formation. *A Spanyoloszági arabok helye az Iszlám fejlödése történetében* [The place of Arabs of Spain in the development of Islam as compared to the Eastern Arabs], *Mythos bei den Hebraen* [The Myths of Hebrews], Aurel Stein (1862-1943) saw global, classical past as the possibility to overcome national, communal, and religious differences *On Ancient Central Asian Tracks,* London, 1933.
10. From the last quarter of the nineteenth century Jewish emancipation was a controversial process as the lives of three Hungarian scholars of international standing reflect. Ignaz Goldziher (1850-1921) who wrote about Islam and Arabic history spent his life sidelined as the secretary of the Jewish parish in Budapest, Aurel Stein (1862-1943) left Hungary in search of an academic career and later joined the British administrative service. Georg Lukács (1885-1972) could never get a university position inspite of his outstanding pre-war books on modern drama, his early essays and the important place he occupied in Hungarian intellectual life and in Heidelberg as Max Weber's student.
11. Géza Bethlenfalvy, *India in Hungarian Learning and Literature,* New Delhi, 1980 pp. 28-30.
12. Fábri's letter to Rabindranath Tagore dated 13 October 1926, File No., 113 Rabindra Bhavan, Shantiniketan.

13. Pál Miklós, Elöszó [Forward] in: Zoltán Felvinczi Takács, ***Buddha útján a Távol-Keleten*** [On Buddha's Path in the Far-East] pp. V-XXIII, Budapest, 1990.

14. Fábri gave Felvinczi Takács' name and address in the East-Asiatic Museum as contact when he seeking an appointment to meet Tagore at the time of Tagore's visit to Hungary in 1926. Fábri's letter to Rabindranath Tagore dated 13 October 1926 File No.113, Rabindra Bhavan, Shantiniketan. About Tagore's visit to Hungary see: Gyula Wojtilla, ***Rabindranath Tagore in Hungary*** New Delhi, 1983.

15. It is possible that Tagore helped Fábri to establish contacts with these important centers of Indology. In a letter written to Tagore on 2 November 1926 after a personal meeting in October in Budapest Fábri requested Tagore for a letter of reference to M. Winternitz, Professor of Indology in Prague or "anybody else" of Tagore's choice to enable Fábri to continue with his interests in Sanskrit and Indian philosophy. File No. 113, Rabindra Bhavan, Shanti Niketan.

16. Annabel Walker, ***Aurel Stein, Pioneer of the Silk Road,*** London, 1995, p. 291.

17. Ibid., p. 292.

18. László Szörényi, Aurel Stein in: Aurel Stein, ***Azsia halott szivében*** [Hungarian selection of Stein's writings: In the Dead Heart of Asia], Budapest, 1985, pp. 438-55.

19. "Life, life in India, life in a Punjab town had thrown us together, six men fond of eath other, feeling and thinking in much the same way, similar in many respects, whatever our roots were, but similar in this particular matter most of all, that we both belonged to the West and East. It was—among other things that attracted us in each other—this intellecutal absorption in both worlds, this living in a period of transition and moulding, that threw us together, us, who belonged to this curious, torn, double-headed monster world, where some of us may have expected a clash, others may have hoped to avert it—at least avert a clash in ourselves, within. "***Indian Flamingo*** p. 11 See also Kirsten Hastrup, ***A passage to Anthropology, Between experience and theory,*** London, 1995.

20. Charles Fábri, Ruined Town Near Bhera in: ***The Civil and Military Gazette,*** 15 January 1938.

21. "Mr. Darling at the close of his lecture said that throughout his stay in India of over thirty years he had never spent so delightful an hour in a lecture room. He congratulated Dr. Fábri on his brilliant performance." ***Civil and Military Gazette,*** 6 February 1937. Darling was the vice chancellor of Punjab University, Lahore, and author of the classic ***The Punjab Peasant.***

22. Regular reports followed the opening of new galleries in Lahore Muzeum in May and November 1937 and in March 1938.

23. Prakash Tandon, ***Punjabi Saga 1857-1987***, Delhi, 1988 p. 29.

24. Jawaharlal Nehru, ***Selected Works,*** vol., 7. In September 1948, Nehru asked Azad to accomodate Fábri in the Archaeological Department and expressed that he was impressed by Fábri's qualifications and conversation.

25. Sándor Révész and Aczél György, the Hungarian monthly ***Mozgó Világ***, July 1996, p. 99.

26. National Achives of India, File No. 10/104/38-Public.

27. "A Dialogue with a Buddhist. The Meaning of Prayer", *Harijan*, August 1939. (Mahadev Desai who noted down the interview referred to Fábri as to "the Buddhist doctor".)

28. In the novel the word 'civilization' is used in both meanings in the sense of material culture and also overlaps the notion of 'culture language, education, religion, symbols, and practices. Matthew Arnold, The Function of Criticism at the Present Time In: *Selections from Matthew Arnold* with introduction and notes by V.S. Seturaman, Delhi, 1980, p. 58. See also Freud's reference to the question of difference between culture and civilization as reported by his English editors: 'In view of Freud's sweeping pronouncements: ("I scorn to distinguish between culture and civilization") and of a similar remark towards the end of "*Why War*", it seems unnecessary to embark on the tiresome problem of the proper translation of the German word "*Kultur*". We have usually, but not invariably chosen "civilization for the noun and "cultural" for the adjective. See in: Sigmund Freud, *Civilization, Society and Religion,* London, 1991, p. 182. See also Eric R. Wolf, *Európa és a történelem nélküli népek* [Hungarian translation of: Europe and the People without History], Budapest, 1995; Raymond Williams, *Keywords* Glasgow, 1979.

29. Bernard S. Kohn, 'The Transformation of Objects into Artifacts, Antiquities and Art in Nineteenth Century India' in: Barbara Stoler Miller, *The Powers of Art, Patronage in Indian Culture,* Delhi, 1992, pp. 301-27.

30. "A curious elated feeling seized me. A feeling of elation that seizes me sometimes when I encounter unexpected difficulties, a feeling reminiscent of the elation that one experiences when emerging on the pinnacle of a mountain difficult to climb. My back was up. I *must* show these children. I *must* show myself, that I *could* do this, that I could give a talk in this thin air, in this atmosphere of unreality, this preposterous situation of having to talk about Indian art to Indian pupils who knew nothing of the history of their own country. I was too conceited to throw up the sponge. I was going to do this almost impossible labour... ", p. 24 [italics mine].

31. "Elizabeth Mitra had the quiet, self-assured manners of an Englishwoman whose family of university professors and doctors for three generations had inherited and bred the simple dignity of "professional" class of well-to-do black-coat workers." p. 13.

32. Charles Fábri's claim about Amrita Shergil, Antoinette Shergil and about himself in: *Notes towards a Biography of Amrita Sher-gil.*

33. The political polarization of the 1940s did not exist in the 1930s but divisive forces were already at work. See Mushirul Hasan, *Nationalism and Communal Politics in India,* Delhi, 1991, pp. 282-93.

34. Identification on both sides is reflected increasingly after Forster's *A Passage to India*. See Edward Thompson, *An Indian Day*, New Delhi, 1986; Paul Scott, *The Jewel in the Crown.*

35. Fábri anticipated Huntington's thesis about "The Clash of Civilizations". Huntington describes civilization as homogeneous blocs organizing themselves on linguistic, religious and cultural frontlines in: *Foreign Affairs*, Summer 1993, pp. 22-49.

36. David Llelyveld portrays this in its interconnection with English education, see: *Aligarh's First Generation,* Delhi, 1996.
37. Only recently, linguistic research in the area of cultural space and the use of Indian language has been carried out: R. Agnihotri.
38. Henry Lawrence "gathered round him a brilliant band of young assistants and the "Punjab tradition" began, hard work through all the scorching head of summer, vigorous and if need be ruthless government and devotion to the welfare of the people, specially the peasant cultivators" and he played a very complex historical role in the takeover of the Punjab. See: Sir Penderel Moon, *The British Conquest and Dominion of India,* London, 1989.
39. Sisir Kumar Das, *A History of Indian Literature,* Vol. VIII, New Delhi, 1991; Amrit Rai, *A House Divided*, Delhi 1991; David Lelyveld, 'The Fate of Hindustani: Colonial knowledge and project of a National Language 'in: Fate *Orientalism and the Postcolonial Predicament*, Delhi, 1994, pp. 189-214; Christopher R. King, *One Language Two Scripts,* Delhi, 1994.
40. Mushir-ul-Haq, *Muslim Politics in Modern India,* Meerut, 1970. Hungarian nationalism rallied around the issue of the langauge when in 1784, the Austrian Habsburg monarch Joseph II issued a decree to make German the language of administration and the language of schools and the Church. The Hungarian Academy of Sciences was established by István Szechenyi in 1825 for the cultivation of Hungarian language and along with the economic and political struggles of the 1820s, Hungarian langauge was reformed and spread as the medium of science and the press. See: Dezsö Pais, *Nyelvünk a Reformkorban* [in Hungarian: Hungarian in the age of Language Reform], Budapest, 1955.
42. Hindi was accepted as the official language but the cultivation of both Hindi and Urdu was suggested by the Congress Party in 1945.
43. Gandhi was also interested in the Judgement of Western scholars about Buddhism as the authoritative reference and the element of *moksha* in Buddhism. Mahatma Gandhi, *Collected Works*, 26 November 1894; 1 February 1895.
44. In his lectures in Oxford, in 1930, Tagore advocated a creative life-world based on creativity, spontaneity, positive attitude and sharing the love and wisdom of *Isha*, the Super Soul of the Upanishad. This was also an area in which Fábri was already interested in 1926. In his letter to Tagore dated 2 November 1926 he asked Tagore how would he interpret part 6 of the Isa-Upanishad: "He who recognises all beings in his own Soul, and in all beings his own Soul: he has no doubts more", Rabindra Bhavan, File No. 113, Rabindranath Tagore, *The Religion of Man,* Delhi, 1994.
45. It is possible that those who were not Hindus identified the sudden popularity of Buddhism in the Independence Movement with its brahmanical and not universal and democratic dimenson. "The chowkies on the right of the dais were adorned with Buddhist priests. Many languages were spoken. English, Sanskrit, Arabic, chaste Hindi. But not a word in our precious language (Urdu)....." Begum Anis Kidwai, 'In the Shadow of Freedom' in: Mushirul Hasan, *India Partitioned*, vol. 2 pp. 170-1, New Delhi, 1995.

46. Bernard S. Cohn, 'The Transformation of Objects into Artifacts, Antiquities and Art in Nineteenth Century India', pp. 301-29 in: *The powers of Arts,* ed. by Barbara Stoler Miller, Delhi, 1992.
47. Alfred Weber, *Vallás és kultúra* (the Hungarian translation of *Religion und Kultur*), Budapest, 1983, pp. 248-69.
48. Jenö Henrik Schmitt, *Krisztus és Buddha* (in Hungarian: Christ and Buddha) Budapest, 1904; *Die Gnosis* Budapest, 1911; Georg Lukács, *Soul and Form,* London, 1974; *If jukori Müvek (1902-1918)* [in Hungarian: Works by the young Lukács], Budapest, 1977; *Curriculum Vitae*, Budapest, 1982; Béla Balázs, *Napló* [in Hungarian: Diary 1903-22], vol. I-II, ed. by Anna Fábri Budapest, 1982; *Hét mese* [in Hungarian: Seven Tales], Gyoma, 1918; *Trisztán hajóján* [in Hungarian: On the ship of Tristan], Gyoma, 1916, Oszkár Jászi, Eröszak vagy passziv rezisztancia, bolsevizmus és a gandhizmus vitája [in Hungarian: Violence or passive resistence? The debate of Bolshevism and Gandhism] in the volume: *A kommunizmus kilátástalansága és a szocializmus reformációja*, Budapest, 1989, pp. 117-25.
49. The reference is to the writings of Yeats', Rilke, A Dialogue with a Buddhist. The meaning of Prayer it. Harijan, T.S. Eliot, Mór Jókai, Béla Balázs, Sándor Weöres and Lörincz Szabó.
50. A Dialogue with a Buddhist. The meaning of Prayer, *Harijan*, op. cit.
51. Alice Getty, *The Gods of Northern Buddhism,* Delhi, 1978, pp. 110-13; B. Sangharakshita, Buddhism in the Modern World in: *2500 years of Buddhism,* ed. by P.V. Bapat, Delhi, 1956, pp. 447-82.
52. "holding a sacred book in one hand, a book full of wisdom; and raising another hand in a gesture of reassurance, saying, "Have no fear"; and a third hand turned towards the worshipper, bestowing the gift of kindness, in the "Gesture of the Boon"; and there, in that fourth hand, was the symbol of beauty: a beautiful lotus flower; a day-lotus...."p. 66.
53. "Oh, how I wanted to be one of this country" p. 80; "I felt I belonged to these people .... "p. 112.
54. 24 November 1937 *The Civil and Military Gazette; The March of India,* Vol. IV n.1, 1951, reprinted in *Charles Fábri* op.cit., pp. 93-7; Charles Fábri, *Notes towards a Biography of Amrita Sher-gil,* Lalit Kala Akademi.
55. Reports in the *The Civil and Military Gazette* on: 24 January 1937; 7 April 1937 and 1 April 1938.
56. "Primitive" is the person who is not "naturally attracted by fresh experience", while the "civilized man" in Fawcett's definition "looks for further knowledge"; and ... "fascination for the white skin springs from the same source as for the brown one; an urge, a penchant, to taste new fruit, explore new worlds, find fresh knowledge, expand our limited existence into a wider world of humanity." p. 106.
57. Elizabeth's and Mitra's glance at each other in the sitting room sets off phantasies about the way "they searched for each other's breast and arms" in bed, p. 14.
58. Robert Knox in *Races of Men* (first published in 1850) devoted a chapter to the question of 'hybridity' along with other works by Gobineau, Nott and Paul Broca, which discussed the issue of race in terms of sexuality and pairing. See: Robert J.C. Young, *Colonial Desire : Hybridity in Theory, Culture and Race*, London, 1995.

59. M.J. Durai *'Civil and Military Gazette'*, 9 April 1938.
60. Otto Weininger, *Geschlecht und Character. Eine prinzipielle Untersuchung*, Vienna, 1908.
61. An example of such speculation about "modern creative urge in India" is Tandra Devi's article entitled "The Indo-European Orchestra" in *The Civil and Military Gazette*, 2 September 1938, which suggested that westerners should abandon fixed ideas about harmony and Indians corresponding should forget about *ragas*.
62. In all his critical writing about Amrita Shergil, Fábri emphasized the fact of her mixed parentage. The focus is there on Shergil's half-Indian and half-Hungarian identity, her choice of a Hungarian husband, and her place to paint India which reinforced her double heritage as an Indian and as a Hungarian and her symbolic identity as a bridge between India and Europe.
63. As documented in his Punjab University Extention Lectures, reported by the *The Civil and Military Gazette*.
64. "The simplicity of Gauguin ...his suppression of unnecessary, unwanted detail." *Indian Flamingo* op.cit., p. 76. In his analysis of Amrita Shergil's work, Charles Fábri elaborates the differences of "ties". Gauguin was excited by the "sensual" world, "the paradise of *others*" while India was Shergil's natural milieu. Shergil went further in the reduction of shadows in her late paintings completely dismissing the source of light. Stronger stylization of plants and vegetation and the use of white patches are characteristic of Shergil's later paintings. Charles Fábri, *Notes towards a Biography of Amrita Sher-gil*, Lalit Kala Akademi.
65. 24 November 1937, *The Civil and Military Gazette*.
66. *The March of India*, Vol. IV No. 1, 1951, reprinted in *Charles Fábri*, op. cit., pp. 93-7.
67. Charles Fábri, *Notes towards a Biography of Amrita Shergil*, Lalit Kala Akademi.
68. Partha Mittar *Art and Nationalism in Colonial India 1850-1922*, Cambridge, 1994.
69. Joseph Weingast, an Austrian who became a naturalized English citizen in 1938 asked for the change of his name to Mr. Joseph Rex Wyning. The fact that he was a musician only confirms the hypothesis that there was an expectation that he should take on an English identity. See National Archives of India. F. No. 10/113/37.
70. Theodor Adorno, *The Jargon of Authenticity*, London, 1986, p. 31.

RADHA SHARMA

India Mirrored in Contemporary French Writings

Over the centuries, India has served as fodder for the West's very fertile imagining of the Orient. The various images of this Indian alterity that have been regurgitated in Western literature vary from the utterly poetic, overly romantic, rose-tinted to the banefully prosaic, completely mundane and murky. From exotic myth to sordid tale, from the sublime to the squalid, from paradise to festering canker, the range of avatars that India seems capable of assuming is seemingly elastic enough, seemingly ambivalent enough to accommodate an entire range of contradictory representations.

The sheer abundance of texts and writing produced over the years testifies to the extent of the West's interest in the Orient in general and India in particular. The subject of innumerable studies, books and even films, India has attracted scholar and adventurer alike, inspired philosophers and writers, enticed travellers and nirvana seekers, enthused missionaries and hippies, been the muse of photographers and film makers. "No country can evoke passionate feelings to the degree that India can. Her landscapes, people, noises, smells have excited Western imagination for centuries, filling with wonder some, appalling others."[1] Moreover as Jean Biès remarked, though he was speaking specifically of French writers, rare were those that India left completely indifferent. "To my very great surprise, I observed that a significant number of writers had been, from the least to the highest degree, and in every possible way, disconcerted, seduced, bewitched or terrified by India, and that there was not even a single one who had not mentioned India at least once in his work."[2] The large volume of documentation produced, the scale of "knowledge" of the Indian Other requiring that these writings be examined instead of being rejected off-hand on the claim that they lack substance or are born of suspect motives. The main focus of this brief critique is not the discourse - orientalist or otherwise - of Indologists but rather that of contemporary French writing whose readers are drawn from the lay public and which is essentially of a more enduring nature, namely books and not press articles. The texts examined include literary as well as popular writing and cover fiction, mainly novels, as well as non-fiction, such as travel accounts and essays. However, before dwelling on contemporary depictions of India it is necessary to locate them historically so as to examine the evolution if any, in the presuppositions that underpin such constructs and images of India that are recreated and propagated at the end of the 20th century.

CONTEXTUALISING THE ICONS OF DISCOURSE

Western imagination has created an imaginary India. India, the "country of monsters" and India, "the cradle of wisdom", are two frequently recurring themes that have fashioned the archetypal image of India since Antiquity and that are to be found even today though in different forms.[3] India in the Western perception could be likened to a two-headed creature incarnating at the same time the civilised and the barbaric, wisdom anu crass ignorance, the beautiful and the monstrous. Which of India's faces was highlighted varied from one epoch to the next. In one of the earliest known pieces of foreign writing on India, the c.400 BC account by Ktesias, India emerges as a land of untold wealth, exotic landscapes, unknown spices, rich brocades, brilliant jewels, inhabited by the wierdest fauna and the most curious looking people. Ktesias's version, reinforced a century later by the account of Greek envoy Megasthenes, ***Indika***, recreated India as a mythical land of marvels, the fabulous and the monstrous. The birth of India as a country of wisdom in Western perception dates back to Alexander's campaign and encounter with Indian gymnosophist as well as by philosophers accompanying him. Both these representations of India were to endure. At varying times, like in the Age of Enlightenment, the emphasis was on the glory and antiquity of India's past - India was perceived as one of the cradles of ancient civilisation but was at the same time viewed through the prism of the "marvellous", at others, as in the 19th century, aided by the romanticism inspired vision of writers, India became a space, for which even hyperbolic terms such as utopia or terrestrial paradise ("a paradise on earth, if there ever was one" - Judith Gautier), seemed highly inadequate. However, this space was perceived at the same time as a breeding ground of brutal crime, barbaric acts, despotic regimes, idolatrous practices and superstitious beliefs. It was essentially "true" eye-witness accounts by envoys, travellers (Al Biruni, Marco Polo, Bernier, Tavernier etc.), Jesuit missionaries and adventurers that were to make

India known in Europe over the ages. India's entry into French fiction occurred largely in the 18th century (Voltaire, Bernadin de Saint-Pierre) and coincided with the discovery of Sanskrit texts in translation followed by a nascent Western interest in Indian philosophy and philology but it was with the establishment of the French colonial enterprise in India that India's claim as a subject of novels and literature in France was really ensured. The 19th century saw the proliferation of texts on India by a host of authors who for the most part never made it to India. Writing about the last century, Catherine Champion says,

> Through the accounts of travellers and the translations of sacred texts that the public now had at its disposal, India acquired one of the most alluring reputations as far as a novelist was concerned. Out of all the countries of the Orient, India appeared the most extreme in horror as well as in beauty. India was such a different land, such an incomprehensible land that it was perceived as the most terrible of places ever frequented by the most intrepid traveller. It offered the most varied landscape. It corresponded, more than any other country, to the romantic vision that is founded on the myth of the eternal Orient, by associating the contemporary Orient with the antique one.[4]

"ETERNAL INDIA"

This Western representation of an ancient, eternal, immutable India has remained tenacious and continues to form the framework of the contemporary French discourse[5] on India. Raymond Schwab observed in 1950 that India has a "past that was not dead but remained 'an antiquity of today' and always"[6] or as Malraux put it "remote from ourselves in dream and time, India belongs to the Ancient Orient of our soul"[7]. Half a century of independent and sovereign existence, yet what continues to exercise fascination for the French reader today - or so the kind of books produced would seem to indicate - is the India of the colonial era, French India, Mughal India, the India of palaces and maharajahs, India as a place of unparalleled seduction, a country of unheard of riches, a land of fabulous decors, famous for the powers of her fabled fakirs, known for the intrigues of her Brahmins.

In terms of numbers, contemporary French literary works on India appear marginal, around 100 during the last 25 years - but as compared to similar works set in or pertaining to non-European or non-Western cultures, these figures are not all that insignificant. These works include all the genres - short stories, novels, theatre, poetry, travel accounts etc. but the pride of place is occupied by the novel as well as travel accounts which are a genre that India somehow seems to engender particularly.

Since we are dealing in some measure, though neither primordially nor exclusively with fictional texts, as travel accounts and essays form a large part of our corpus, a remark on the liberty of fictional representation needs to be made at the outset. The problematics within which this analysis is located is predominantly one of the mimetic relation between the texts and a given pre-constituted reality i.e. India and as with all exercises of this kind, could suffer from the inadequacy of subordinating the text to this pre-constituted reality, of measuring the fictional against the real. We have tried to minimise this as far as possible by limiting ourselves to texts in which the representational practice of writing dominates the formalist practice of writing, a practice in which creative expression and the way of writing prevails over the textual-real. It is for this reason, for example, that works such as Marguerite Duras's *Le vice-consul* and *India Song*, which are set in a famine stricken, leper inhabited India, have been left out of the analysis as in them India counts for strictly nothing. The setting is India, it could easily have been another location without subtracting an iota from these literary creations. We have put the focus on texts whose *raison d'être* seems to be India, that pre-constituted reality.

The India that numerous novelists prefer to recreate is the India of yore - *Le Roman de la Begum Sombre*[8] (The Novel of Begum Sambru), *Le Temps d'un royaume, Jeanne Dupleix 1706-1756*[9] (The Time of a Kingdom, Jeanne Dupleix), *Le Nabab*[10] (The Nawab), *La femme sacrée. La Maharani de Jhansi*[11] (The Anointed Woman, The Maharani of Jhansi), *Jahanara ou les mémoires d'une princesse moghole* (Jahanara or The Memoirs of a Moghol Princess)[12], *Le gardien du Gange*[13] (The Guardian of the Ganges) and *Pour l'amour de l'Inde*[14] (For the love of India), the story of the relationship between Lady Mountbatten and Pandit Nehru which describes India on the eve of independence, to give a few examples. All these evocations, not only of another space from the French point of view, but also of another time, serve the purpose of the anachronic discourse generally resorted to when reporting knowledge about the Other.[15]

These attempts to go back in history, this temporal distancing of the Other, are part of the exotic vein as a source of literary inspiration, exoticism being one of the traditional ways of accessing the Orient. Exoticism and immutability, these two key elements of the fictional reconstructions of history are to be linked to the atemporal character attributed to India by Orientalism. Freezing India, through writing, at distant moments of her past, allows India to be presented in her "natural" invariability, thus ignoring totally the march of time, progress, development and modernity.

Even with a shift in construct, when the textual setting is the geopolitical space of independent India, the over-emphasis on stagnation, underdevelopment and tradition, the constant labelling of India as a country of the Third World, on the one hand, and the perception of India as the epitome of spirituality and other-worldliness, as a modern day escape route from the plagues of the world, a place of instant nirvana, on the other, only serve to reinforce the myth of India's unchanging face, the cliché of her timeless existence. Contemporary French writing on India mirrors this attraction/repulsion, this enchantment with Indian otherness whose other face is dread of this very alterity.

THE ULTIMATE PILGRIMAGE

The literary trend that represented India as an elsewhere that is an invitation to real as well as imaginary peregrinations, as a Mecca of spirituality, the ultimate pilgrimage to basics, to the source of being, began in the 19th century and was reinforced in the 20th. Various French writers like Chateaubriand, Lamartine, Hugo, Nerval, Gautier, Vigny, Leconte de Lisle, Gide, Pierre Loti, René Guénon, Michaux, Alexandra David-Neel, René Daumal, Lanza del Vasto, shared this depth of feeling for India. But the most passionate response was undoubtedly Michelet's, for whom Asia was like "a medicine for the soul" and India "the womb of the world". Michelet wrote in la *Bible de l'humanité* (The Bible of Humanity), "One must breathe, regain one's breath, remake oneself at the living waters that retain eternal freshness. Where to find this, if not in the cradle of our race, on the sacred summits from where descend, here, the Indus and the Ganges, there, the torrents of Persia, the rivers of paradise. [. . .] Here I have found what I was seeking, the Bible of goodness".[16] To the quest for exoticism and material riches was added the quest for spiritual riches, for inner peace and tranquillity. The perception of India as an immense material treasure house was replaced by the perception of India as a spiritual haven or as Jean Biès remarks with a play on words in French, "à la route de la soie succède la route du Soi" ("the road to silk is followed by the road to the self'),'[17] the disenchantment with the European lifestyle was an incentive to create a new self, to become the Other or to quote Heinrich Heine "the West, disgusted with its weak and cold spirituality, seeks the warmth of the Orient's breast".[18]

In short, the pilgrimage to Asia answers our need to know that the sacred exists somewhere, just as there is a pope in Rome and there are pyramids in Cairo. The Orient is both a foreign land and a familiar landscape towards which we return as though to our lost origins. We look at these nations with an eternal vision that does not take into account their own history. The little shiver at the novelty of it all is always followed by a feeling of recognition. This allows one to attribute to the religious success of these continents a normative character, an absolute value, that we are pleased to assume as being immutable.

This Orient as a cultural model is therefore the result of a fiction rather than a correctly apprehended reality.[19]

India is constructed as a land steeped in ancient wisdom, the spiritual/ mystical counterfoil to Western rationalism, its negative mirror image as it were, reinforcing the cliched metaphor in circulation in Indological texts that Indian thought is neither rational nor scientific stemming as it does from imagination rather than reason[20].

This trend of perceiving and representing India as a spiritual haven gathered momentum with the advent of the beatnik generation and the hippie phenomenon which saw the influx into Asia, and notably India, of waves upon waves of young Westerners driven by the Occident's "moral bankruptcy" to seek salvation and comfort in the arms of the Orient. In a reversal of situations the former colonised becomes the spiritual master - from the country where Jesuits came in search of lost souls to convert to Christianity, India comes to a full circle with Jesuits who come to India with this intention of offering salvation, staying on and not only losing their own faith but undergoing an Indian metamorphosis.[21] In post 1968 France when the passage to India was very much in vogue, this led to the publication of books such as René Barjavel's *Les chemins de Katmandou*[22] (The Paths to Katmandu), an account of the voyage to Asia by this generation of young people, a voyage away from dissatisfaction towards inner harmony and Muriel Cerfs *L'antivoyage*[23] (The antivoyage), the latter tinting the quest for harmony with the hues of a hedonistic mission. In Laurence Cossé's *Le premier pas d'amante*[24] (The first step of a girl in love), India is a new beginning, a new assurance for the Westerner with unanswered questions. However, though Cossé's heroine finds the truth she is looking for, Cerf's quest for absolute freedom ends in disappointment. The oriental bubble bursts. The promised land turns out to be a mirage. Far from furnishing all the answers, India seems beset by monumental problems. "Reality" is the depiction of the full range of clichés about India, from the sublime to the sordid.

"THROUGH A LOOKING GLASS DARKLY"

However, a new trend has been added to the existing slants of the traditional discourse on India, a trend that revels in the sordid. This trend emerged in part out of historical transformations, namely decolonisation and the independence of India, for soon after becoming independent, India began to be defined as a country of the Third World with all its attendant characteristics. Third World being a term applicable mainly to countries that had been created after the process of decolonisation and that had largely adhered neither to the capitalist nor to the socialist camps. Generally poor, with a low level of development the countries of the Third World are characterised by high birth and death rates, a low level of industrialisation, low spending in the food, education and public health sectors in comparison with the countries of the North which are rich, industrialised, underpopulated, literate. In other words, the Third World means in general a mass of humanity, an illiterate therefore uncivilised mass of humanity that is subject to hunger, poverty, lack, disease and death. And these are precisely the recurrent motifs that a section of contemporary French writing on India resorts to, for India is perceived through the prism of the Third World.

In part, as also pointed out by Gisela Bonn,[25] this perception of India as a land of abject misery and poverty is the indirect outcome of the metaphysical quest of the hundreds of young people who came to India in the 60s and 70s, for, in the process of self-reinvention and spiritual regeneration they became junkies or the victims of gurus and godmen of dubious character and intent. While reporting on this phenomenon of the disappearance into India and Nepal of scores of young people, their travails and the agony of their kin, the international press put the spotlight firmly on the poverty and unhygienic conditions in which they lived. In the Western world's perception India became synonymous with misery and degradation and the fact that these are realities of drug addicts, lives the world over was completely overlooked.

However, these motifs of poverty, disease and death are not new, having made their debut in French writing a long time ago. An example is Loti who speaks of those "poor little skeletons with huge astonished eyes at so much suffering, who chant the song of famine or who yell it at the entry to villages, at road crossings, while holding their frightfully hollow stomach in both hands" or those "mummies, [those] emaciated mass of bones, whose eyes remain in the hollow of their orbits and voice in the depths of the throat, who walk around asking for alms."[26] A reading of Loti shows that at the beginning of the 20th century these were familiar images but these vivid images with negative connotations are offset by others that are equally real but much more positive. Loti depicts India through a tone that is critical but far more objective at the same time.

In sharp contrast to earlier writers like Loti, Alexandra David-Neel and others, an important trend of contemporary French writing on India focuses exclusively testimonials of the inferior status of India, signs of the stagnation of India as compared to the concepts of progress in the West. Does this subjective perception of India by France and the West wherein only one, the most ugly of India's facets is revealed, stem from a conscious or unconscious urge to affirm the superiority of the West or is it simply the expression of a desire to freeze India in its past, to recreate the myth of "eternal" India by stressing economic stagnation and lack of progress? One justification that is often advanced is that from the perspective of the North, a perspective of abundance and development what strikes is the lack and underdevelopment. "The period when one came here [to India] to exclaim about the extravagance of the rajahs, of the Mughals, is well and truly dead. Today, one goes to India to become indignant. The country of tigers, pearls and caparisoned elephants has become the abscess of the planet, the largest museum of infamy."[27] A clear shift of focus from prince to pauper. An explanation proposed by Christian Petr - an explanation that may hold when applied to the 1960s and early 1970s - is that instead of vexing Western sensibility this poverty takes on positive social connotations for the materially disillusioned Westerner in search of ways to sublimate the self: "Through modern novels India is offered to us as a solution to the moral, philosophical and religious crisis of the West.... *its last temptation*."[28] In both cases, irrespective of whether the prime motivating factor is righteous indignation (with its concomitant of moral superiority) or the elevation of the self, this portrayal of India as a country of abject misery and little else makes the interest of the Other wholly subservient to that of the self and bears out the truth of Said's observation that "European culture gained in strength and identity by setting itself off against the Orient as a sort of surrogate and even underground self."[29]

"THE CALCUTTA SYNDROME"

Explanations and justifications not withstanding, at the end of the 20th century, India is thus firmly identified as a Third World country in fictional prose. Far from offering French readers a promise of an earthly paradise, the French writer who tries to recreate independent India in his work, finds nothing more enticing to attract the reader than titles such as *Parias*[30] (Pariahs), *Le mendiant des étoiles*[31] (The beggar of stars), *Le bain du Paria*[32] (The pariah's bath), *Dans la peau d'un intouchable*[33] (In the Skin of an Untouchable), *Les Parias de Ceylon*[34] (The Pariahs of Ceylon). Incidentally, a similar phenomenon is apparent if one looks at the list of Indian works translated into French and published in France: *Parole de femme intouchable*[35], *Oupra: L'Inde des intouchables et des maudits*[36], *Ma vie d'intouchable*[37], *Le journal d'un intouchable 1969-1977*[38], are a few examples.

In general, right from the opening lines[39], the reader who lets himself get enticed by these "realistic" titles, or by other more evocative, nostalgic, promising or neutral ones such as *La tentatlon des Indes*[40] (The temptation of the Indies), *L'Inde des grands chemins* (The India of great paths)[41], *Indes*[42] (Indies), *La cité de la joie*[43] (The City of Joy) or *Un voyage vers l'Asle*[44] (A voyage towards Asia) - of course, a few inevitable exceptions exist - is plunged into a whirlpool of images that evoke the "daily horrors" of life in a country of the Third World such as India. He is submerged by waves of staggering misery, swept away by a flood of adjectives of remarkable virulence and purulence.

What do you expect? This is India. This explanation is supplied by Lucien Bodard in the preface of the book *L 'Inde des grands chemins* by Jack Thieuloy,

Immense swarming, immense canker. India, for him [that is to say Thieuloy], is the pits. Everything happens as if over there, there is nothing but dregs. This makes Thieuloy happy. [...] Thieuloy depicts this loathsome India with obvious relish. He shows carrion everywhere. [...] This book is a hallucination - but a hallucination that is the literary expression of reality. [...] Is this book likely to shock? I do not think so as it corresponds to a truth about India.[45]

This is a "truth" about India... Other truths that French fiction has taken on the task of unveiling are overpopulation and misery or poverty, the two being inextricably linked. For the Westerner, India is overpopulated to such an extent that it is apparently impossible not to speak of it in literature. How not to evoke the mass of people, the immense swarming, the torrent of peoples? It follows logically that since this incredible swarming mass of humanity, this milling India is at its most dense best (or worst, if you prefer) in the large cities, the Indian itinerary chosen for the reader must therefore necessarily go to those places where these two critical components of the fictional representation of India are to he found. That means an obligatory halt at Bombay, Calcutta or sometimes Delhi.

Sometimes Delhi but not necessarily. For according to some authors such as Guillebaud,

Delhi is not India: its avenues are more in flower, its pavements less filthy and beggars more rare. It's a privileged area where the true noises and smells of the subcontinent only surface in homeopathic doses"[46] Whereas for others, such as Boulet, Delhi is very much India. "[...] the sun shines on Delhi and the army of pavement dwellers have not yet begun squatting on the street. But I am very much in India. Swarms of flies follow me and the air stinks of bogs.[47]

Bombay merits descriptions such as "In the white morning light, the plane plunges down over the world's largest shantytown: a vast expanse, as far as eye can see, of shacks made of rusty metal sheets, slashed by sharp angled passages. Bombay is the economic capital of

India."[48] or "At the beginning of the 1980s, Bombay was one of the craziest cities of Asia: eight million inhabitants, nine million rats, [. . .]"[49]

But what city better than Calcutta to describe this "milling hideousness" (Guillebaud) for it offers both "mass and filth" (Bodard), two essential elements of India according to a particular Western perception?

In Calcutta, "the bodies are there, everywhere, haunting, standing up, crouched, but more often than not lying down across, straight, at angles."[50] "Stretched out forms at the base of pillars, corpses almost that could be mistaken for small piles of dust, lepers brandishing their stumps at taxi windows; old British splendour of colonial palaces that resemble ruins engulfed by fetidness; reddish façades of the ancient Empire of the Indies, gnawed today by decrepitude, assailed by mini-shantytowns that proliferate like cankers right upto the roofs."[51] Calcutta, where "the night [is] inhabited by hundreds of Indian gazes that lightly brush over you, repulsive like insect wings."[52] "Calcutta, it has been said often enough, is a "thing" that breathes and listens to itself as a matter of priority. [...] Louis Malle can sleep undisturbed, the film he shot here in 1969 is not outdated."[53] Calcutta, where the abiding principle is the principle of ruin:

> In overpopulated Calcutta, in the city that the poor have besieged and occupy, the dream of founding cities to enshrine the name of man in his humanity and universality is inverted by the rule of universal inhumanity, and the modern idea of progress is replaced by that of a cycle, in which the principle of ruin dominates. Ruin in this case is an active principle and not a result: an action, not a state of being. The inordinately poor man, the man who is beyond misery, the man who is hungry and eats nothing, the sapped man doesn't live in cities: he congregates in a mass and forms a block with other bodies, he sinks into airless niches, under stinking covers, he sleeps everywhere, in the sun as in the shade, in cars, between your legs, in the slimy dust and the grease of cars and in the smoke of exhaust pipes; he lights fires on the pavement and scratches to eat the refuse that he snatches away from dogs, crows, young goats and cows.
>
> Here it is not reason that triumphs nor is it insanity, but the regression towards absolutely unsatisfied naked need. The city has become nature once again.[54]

Calcutta is summed up by pavement after pavement of "deathly looking", "skeleton-like" bodies, of the walking dead, lepers, beggars. It is the story of hordes and hunger, disease and death.

As for death, fiction on India abounds in descriptions of cremation sites, funeral rites, pyres that are lit along the Ganges, Benares being the favourite place to speak of death. From the "humblest of [solitary] funerals" given to a young man by two dogs who tear his corpse apart on the banks of the Yamuna just behind the Taj Mahal[55] to the "dead, wrapped up on their bamboo biers placed on the narrow stairs along the terrace [who] await their turn."[56] We also have references to "stacks and stacks of logs of wood" which according to Thieuloy "tell us a great deal about the constant movement of the dead."[57] In fact, so frequent are the allusions to corpses floating in rivers, littering the pavement or mounting up on *ghats* that Jean Herbert, an indologist who was responsible for liberating French Indian studies from the narrow confines of academia, felt obliged to declare of the Ganga, "I never glimpsed even the slightest corpse in it, not even that of a dog or rat, as one gets to see so often in the Seine."[58]

After having seen corpses in various degrees of cremation, and after having roamed around ghats and cremation sites, the reader is inevitably asked to bear witness to life in a slum or shantytown. He is asked to experience firsthand the "zero degree of the picturesque, to sniff the "fetid mud", the "blocked drains"; the sewers that overflow, to smell "the sharp odour of slums, consisting of burning cowdung, rot and excrement."

In fact, several writers evoke what Michel Tournier calls the "outrageous lavatorial presence."[59] "I am not exaggerating", says Marc Boulet. "All around the station, men piss standing up or crouching, wherever they feel like, without hiding and generally close to a wall. Some use the occasion to let out a lot of shit. Simply, without a fuss. Their task over, they pull up their trousers and bye bye! The shit remains and enriches the scent of urine. In the heat, all this ferments."[60] To be Indian according to the perception of this author, is not to hold back when one feels like urinating or defecating. Explaining the logic that underlies this "very Indian habit" the writer declares with religious overtones about the Indian, "When he goes out, if he feels like urinating or defecating, he does not hold back. Why retain impure matter within one's self, it would be crazy, and hup, he [that is the Indian] pulls his pants down by the side of the road."[61] Boulet, who wishes to transform himself into an Indian in order to experience the life of an "untouchable", therefore has to rid himself of all notions of public hygiene. He must, in addition, learn to blow his nose with his fingers (the explanation supplied - "the Indian does not want to be saddled with his snot by wrapping it in his hanky"[62]), he must learn to belch, spit, dig his nose in full view and fiddle with his testicles in public without any embarrassment. As he says "In the person of Ram Munda, I must not hold back, it will give me a very local touch. [...] Indian men of all castes scratch their balls, reposition them in their pants throughout the day. In the street, in shops, and even in front of women. Of course, there is the heat, the sweat that sticks to the genital organs, but this lack of reticence in public also reveals the desire and pleasure of asserting in this phallocentric society that one is a male and that one is equipped with one."[63]

This is not an isolated case. Frédéric Coste, the narrator of *Pariahs*, an autobiographical account under the thin veneer of a novel, expresses his anxiety at seeing Dominique who "had become like a native", a phenomenon which meant that he "felt no shame at relieving himself in the open, anywhere he fancied, in gutters, drains, groves, openly and publicly, cleaning himself in the oriental way, without paper, with the fingers of the right [sic] hand dipped in a little water. He [...] picked his nose shamelessly all the time, in front of everyone, played with his testicles, pulled them up, rolled them in his palms as though he feared they would fall to the ground. Worse, he had learnt to expectorate in the manner of natives by clearing the bottom of the throat and coagulating the mucus at the tip of the tongue so that it remains whole and forms a pretty bubble when it reaches the ground." However, without expounding further, Coste confesses that he "had become Indian in the most superficial sense of the term."[64]

Glossing over or ignoring the multiple threads that are interwoven to form the fragile fabric of "Indianness", to be Indian for the majority of these writers is to be Hindu. Indian is very often synonymous with Hindu. The almost exclusive focus on Hinduism, its beliefs, practices, gods, rites, notwithstanding the presence of 110 million Muslims, not counting the Buddhists, Jains, Christians etc., enables French fiction to dwell on an aspect that holds a great deal of fascination for the French, namely the caste system,[65] and to speak of the lot of the lowest castes, to show the social exclusion that exists. This overwhelming interest does not stem as one might imagine from a desire to right social wrongs, set the record straight or give a voice to the subaltern but is a severe hegemonic indictment of India's record of development and social progress which only serves to reinforce Western stereotypes about Indian society and strengthen Western claims to a superior status as dispensers of economic and humanitarian aid "The Indian loves his poor and rejoices at discovering his inferiors. [...] The destitute comfort him in the belief of his own superiority, he revels in their ignominy, likes to squelch around in their servility"[66], Victor Habersham, an American agronomist who "impresses with his erudition" tells us in *Pariahs*. The same could well be said of the sections of the French reading public that devour works of this kind.[67]

The attitude of the Western protagonist of these writings on India *varies from* the intrinsically Christian one of *the poor shall inherit the kingdom of God* to the overtly racist position of viewing them as *the scum of the earth*. The Western protagonist is far from apathetic when confronted with this inhuman condition. He very often takes on the mission of liberating all these destitute poor, these "pariahs", these "slaves" (term employed by Parturier), these "untouchables" from their miserable fate. The path adopted to reach this goal *varies from* Christian charity (*Le mendiant des étoiles, The City of Joy*) to extreme violence. This is the case of Victor Habersham of *Pariahs* who exterminates the poverty-stricken from the face of India.

Such is my illness: I can no longer tolerate this incurable disease called Asia. This complacency towards misery, this loving cohabitation with garbage, this respect of the poor man who is honoured like a god and deprived of the means to escape from his condition: this is what I have taken a violent dislike to. [...] I must exterminate all those who practise the intensive culture of the small alms bowl, wipe off the face of the earth this mafia of carrion crows.[68]

Though couched in noble motives the dominant connotation of this discourse of liberation remains racist. The exterminating mission is undertaken in order to improve the country, this "laboratory of human degradation" for to leave without doing anything to appease hell after having seen it, is not a solution for someone who "loves India more than Indians."[69] However, therein lies the crux, for love that is transformed into violent aversion, is what finally constitutes "a link that is far stronger than love."[70] In a few of these works, after a bout of illumination, this aversion is indeed inexplicably transformed into a curious feeling of oneness with India, even, as in the case of Frédéric of *Pariahs*, an abandonment of identity by the self in an attempt to become the Other.

In conclusion, what these contemporary writers offer us is less a representation of India than a series of fragmentary, fractured and superficial visions and perceptions of India and Indians. Some are even conscious of this fact. In the words of Guillebaud, "This country would really like it if the outside world could perceive that slowly, she is becoming something else."[71] Though Guillebaud recognises that "India [is] a large modernised nation that trains her own pilots, manufactures automobiles, develops agriculture and has a say in the affairs of the world"[72] for others nothing is modern "not even the atomic reactors patched up with bits of string, comparable to mildewed ears of corn."[73] or as Pier Pablo Pasolini declares with authority, "In the end, it [India] is a small country, with only four or five large cities of which only one Bombay is worthy of the name, without industry or almost."[74]

Whereas the historical novel, with India as a setting, recreated the India of yore, while some writers like Germain Thomas (a rare category) still perceive India as a paradise on earth, and others look to India for what is no longer available in Europe ("the essence of being"), still others only perceive India as mirroring the Third World with an overabundance of wretchedness, filth, abject misery. For them "India is a long poem that begins in the sky and finishes in the sewer."[75] This sentiment of repulsion is only the movement of the pendulum that is in the natural order of things according to Francois Chenet for the exaltation of the myth is followed inevitably by its savage demolition, it is illusion in fact that always fosters disillusionment: "The price of idealisation and the tribute that has for too long been paid to the sublime in fiction [...] was the inevitable feeling of disenchantment that would lead to the inverting of images of India."[76] French discourse on India has plummeted from exaltation to revulsion.

However, what gives a semblance of cohesion to these varied perceptions of a far-off elsewhere, to these fragments of French contemporary discourse on India, is the insistence on immutability that is perceived and presented as stagnation. For responding to the double sales imperative of exoticism and realism, French writers recreate India in a time warp - either the India of sages and sagacity, the India of princes and palaces or the India of millions and misery. The end result remains the same: eternal India or poor India, the effective connotation is the antipode of modernity. This incapacity of French writers today to apprehend and depict India in her indisputable modernity and modernisation cannot fail to startle the discerning reader. France's attempt to construct relations with the Indian Other is founded in the perception of difference as distance not so much in space as in time. The cliched assumptions about India are indicative of a political praxis whereby mystical, traditional and impoverished India serves as a counterpoint to the rational, modern and developed West. Which of the two emerges stronger after this exercise is self-evident.

NOTES

* All translations except where otherwise stated are mine.

1. K. Marius-Gnanou, *L'Inde,* Paris, Editions Karthala, 1997, p. 7.
2. Jean Biés, *Littérature française et pensée hindoue,* Paris, Librairie C. Klincksieck, 1992, p. 9. First edition 1974.
3. See Catherine Weinberger-Thomas, "Introduction, Les yeux fertiles de la mémoire. Exotisme indien et représentations occidentals" in C. Weinberger-Thomas (ed.), *L'Inde et l'imaginaire,* Paris, Ed. de l'Ecole des Hautes Etudes en Sciences Sociales (coll. "Purusartha", 11), 1988, pp. 9-32.
4. Catherine Champion, "La fiction populaire française" in D. Lombard, *Rêver l'Asie,* Paris, Ed. de l'Ecole des Hautes Etudes en Sciences Sociales, 1993, p. 50.

5. Though we are referring here very specifically to literary discourse it is worth noting that even the discourse of scholars on India can reflect a longing for an immutable India. Speaking of *devadasis,* their "excellent education, absence of vulgarity, high standards of behaviour" and "the high regard that this profession continues to be held in", Jacques Dupuis takes the position that "One should be allowed to deplore the fact that, in the name of religious reform, India did not know how to preserve one of the most authentic testimonies of her culture." Jacques Dupuis, *L'Inde, une introduction à la connaissance du monde indien,* Paris, [Pondichéry], Kailash, 1994, p. 60-62. Quoted by K. Marins-Granan, *op.cit.,* p. 191.
6. Raymond Schwab, *La renaissance orientale,* Paris, Payot, 1950; English translation, Gene Patterson-Black and Victor Reinking, *The Oriental Renaissance,* New York, Columbia University Press, p. 6.
7. André Malraux, *Antimémoires,* Paris, Gallimard, 1972, p. 17.
8. Michel Larneuil, *Le roman de la Begum Sombre,* Paris, Albin Michel, 1981.
9. Rose Vincent, *Le Temps d'un royaume, Jeanne Dupleix, 1706-1756,* Paris, Ed. du Seuil, 1982.
10. Irène Frain, *Le Nabab,* Paris, Jean-Claude Lattès, 1982.
11. Michel de Grèce, *La femme sacrée. La Maharani de Jhansi,* Paris, Olivier Orban, 1984.
12. Lyane Guillaume, *Jahanara,* Paris, Stock, 1989.
13. Guy Deleury, *Le gardien du Gange,* Paris, Robert Laffont, 1994.
14. Catherine Clément, *Pour l'amour de l'Inde,* Paris, Flammarion, 1993.
15. See Johannes Fabiann's insightful work *Time and the Other,* New York, Columbia University Press, 1983, particularly Chapter Three/Time and Writing About the Other.
16. Michelet, *Bible de l'humanité,* Paris, F. Chamerot, 1864, pp. 2-3.
17. J. Biès, *op.cit.,* p. 557.
18. Quoted by Pascal Bruckner, *Le sanglot de l'homme blanc,* Paris, Ed. du Seuil, 1983, p. 155.
19. Bruckner, *Ibid.,* p. 159.
20. See Ronald Inden, *Imagining India,* Oxford, 1990.
21. See for example Laurence Cossé, *Le premier pas d'amante,* Paris, Gallimard, p. 52.
22. René Barjavel, *Les chemins de Katmandou,* Paris, Presses de la Cité, 1969.
23. Muriel Cerf, *L'antivoyage,* Paris, Mercure de France, 1974.
24. Cossé, *op. cit.*
25. Gisela Bonn.
26. Pierre Loti, *L'Inde (sans les Anglais)*, Paris, Calmann-Lévy, 1903, pp. 270 and 277.
27. Pascal Bruckner, *Parias,* Paris, Le Seuil, p. 70.
28. Christian Petr, *L'Inde des romans,* Paris, [Pondicherry], Editions Kailash, 1995, p.12.
29. Edward Said, *Orientalism,* London, Penguin Books, 1985, p. 3.
30. Bruckner, Paris, *op. cit.*
31. Michel Tournier, "Le mendiant des étoiles", *Le Médianoche amoureux,* Paris, Gallimard, 1989.

32. Louis Frédéric, "Le bain du paria" in *Corps Ecrit - Rêver l'Inde,* No. 34, Presses Universitaires de France, Juin 1990.
33. Marc Boulet, *Dans la peau d'un intouchable,* Paris, Le Seuil, 1994.
34. Gérard de Villiers, *Les Paries do Ceylon,* Paris, Plon, 1917.
35. Baby and Shantibai Kamble, *Parole de femme intouchable,* Paris, Côté-femmes, 1991.
36. Laxman Mané, *Oupra : L'Inde des intouchables et des maudits,* Paris, Maren Sell, 1987.
37. Daya Pawar, *Ma vie d'intouchable,* Paris, Editions la Découverte, 1990.
38. Madhau Kondilker, *Le journal d'un intouchable 1969-1977,* Paris, L'Harmattan, 1985.
39. Bruckber, *Parias, op. cit.,* first page :

    "We had just turned into an alley pervaded with the smell of paper. [...] when a young girl, thin to the extreme, a baby in her arms, accosted us with hand outstretched.

    —Baksish, Baba, baksish.

    She filled the street with a plaintive litany, mouth twisted, full of repressed sobs. Scaly white spots disfigured her hands. [...] The little face [of the baby], swaddled in dubious rags, was almost blue. The minuscule head nodded gently on a neck that was too thin to support it. A fetid odour emanated from him.

    —Caress that child, ordered the American in a toneless voice.

    I was going to intervene. But Menviel, so prompt to obey, had already lightly touched the baby's cheeks.

    —He's stone cold.

    —And do you know why he's stone cold? exclaimed the American. He's stone cold because he's been dead for the last two or three days and this young bitch is making money with his corpse. We gave a start. [...]

    —You knew? You knew? faltered out the archaeologist on the verge of feeling sick, Why did you ask me to touch it then?

    —To get you to put your finger on Indian reality. There's no better initiation than this."
40. Olivier Germain Thomas, *La tentation des Indes,* Paris, Albin Michel, 1981.
41. Jack Thieuloy, *L'Inde des grands chemins,* Paris, Gallimard, 1971.
42. Jean Clausel, *Indes,* Paris, Editions Payot et Rivages, 1994.
43. Dominique Lapierre, *La cité de la joie,* Paris, Robert Laffont, 1985.
44. Jean-Claude Guillebaud, *Un voyage vers l'Asie,* Paris, Le Seuil, 1979.
45. Thieuloy, *op. cit.,* pp. 11-12.
46. Guillebaud, *op. cit.,* p. 72.
47. Boulet, *op. cit.,* p. 24.
48. Clausel, *op. cit.,* p. 13.
49. Bruckner, *Parias, op. cit.* p. 133.
50. Tournier, *op. cit.,* p. 170.
51. Guillebaud, *op. cit.,* p. 118.
52. Cerf, *op. cit.,* p. 203.
53. Guillebaud, *op. cit.,* p. 118-119.

54. Danielle Sallenave, *Le principle de ruine,* Paris, Gallimard, 1994, inside cover page.

55. Françoise Parturier, *Les chiens du Taj Mahal,* Paris, Albin Michel, 1987, pp. 9-10.

"Silence. The curved immobility of vultures settled on dead trees sandpapered by the seasons. They are waiting. The corpse is there, the corpse that the dogs have dragged onto the bank of the Yamuna right upto the foot of the ramparts that hold up the terrace of the Taj Mahal. The corpse of a very young man, thin, narrow, triangular, extremely triangular, legs and arms apart - like a fork and cross at the same time - , a discreet body, already inorganic, a sandy grey like the sludge on which it lies. Two large dogs, the kind of stray dogs that are common in Asia, one white, the other yellow, two alive clear commas, are eating it.

They do not devour it. They're not dogs from Athalia's dream.

They work as a team - without haste or frenzy, calm, methodical and efficient.

What is most strange is their absence of fear, not even a trace of the edginess that animals always have, none of those pauses, those furtive glances of an animal with a prey.

Nothing distracts them.

Busy, skilled, they have the rhythm of technicians and are good anatomists. Specialists. Very quickly the skeleton appears. The white dog turns it over, moves up to the skull, holds it so that his companion can tear away the double membrane that still protects the nape of the neck. The rustling of two bits of taffeta being torn.

The vultures, dark shadows, medieval cutouts against the backdrop of a golden red sky, straighten up. They too are good anatomists.

A sharp short cracking sound rang out, not unlike the clap that is used during shootings to announce the shot. The birds quivered. Then came the sound of castanets and the horrible demolishing, the hideous laughter of the Mexican carnival, the skull shaken, teeth exposed, bloodcurdling jerks. The jaws rattle, laugh, the skull jiggles about.

This grotesque, obnoxious scene, this unexpected disorder only ceases when the white dog manage to plunge his mouth into the throat and eat the tongue."

56. *Ibid.,* p. 44.
57. Thieuloy, *op. cit.*
58. Quoted in Biès, *op. cit. p.*
59. Tournier, *op. cit.*
60. Boulet, *op. cit.*
61. Boulet, *op. cit.*
62. Boulet, *op. cit.*

Explanations are proffered on almost everything under the sun. An example: "Do you known why Indian restaurants are so dimly lit? In a country where three quarters of the population is starving, meals in public are almost a clandestine act. The partaker must hide from public view; here one feasts in the shadows." P. Bruckner, *op. cit.,* p. 27.

63. *Ibid.*
64. Bruckner, *op. cit.*, "references p. 137.
65. This is a point made by Ronald Inden, *op. cit.* ...
66. Bruckner, *Parias, op. cit.*
67. To give an example, *Dans la peau d'un intouchable* by Marc Boulet crossed slaes of 50,000 copies in six months. This "non-fiction" book is an account by the author who, having already written *Dans la peau d'un chinois* (In the skin of a Chinese), convinced one of France's leading publishers, Seuil, to pay him an advance that would enable him to disguise himself as an Indian "untouchable" - skin suitably darkened, hair dyed - live as a beggar in Benares for several weeks and record his experience as an "insider". By his own admission, he learnt Hindi for six months in Paris through a Teach Yourself method which was followed up by three months in India before he began his experiment. Though the books - promoted on its back cover as "An unparalleled testimony but also an uncompromising portrait of modern India that remains largely governed by the caste system that has however been abolished by the Constitution" - strains the credulity of Indian readers its veracity is unquestioned by the French for, it is fast becoming recommended reading for Frenchmen desirous of knowing more about India. It was in the number 2 spot of such a list of 5 books proposed by the French news magazine *Le Point* in its 19 April 1997 special issue òn India, "*Un* géant du XXIe siècle" (A Giant of the 21st Century), an issue which attempts to tell it like it really is.
68. Bruckner, *Parias, op. cit.*, p. 73.
69. *Ibid.*, p. 67 and p. 65.
70. *Ibid.*, p. 173.
71. Guillebaud, *op. cit.*, p. 72.
72. *Ibid.*, p. 72.
73. Bruckner, *Parias, op. cit.*, p. 71.
74. Pier Pablo Pasolini, *L'odeur de l'Inde,* Denoël, Paris, 1984, pp. 77-78.
75. Bruckner, *Parias, op. cit.*, p. 71.
76. F. Chenet, "L'Inde au miroir de la littérature contemporaine", ("India in the mirror of French Literature") in *Crops Ecrit - Rêver l'Inde,* 34, PUF, June 1990.

CHITRA HARSHVARDHAN

Bridging Differences? Translation Anthologies: Constructing the "Other"

In this age of globalization anthologies of translation mark another milestone on the path to achieving the reality of the global village.[1] This is borne out by the fact, that despite having been in existence for centuries, there is today a renewed interest in them. There is a growing awareness that translations are increasingly becoming the site for the clash of cultures, revealing the configurations of the power relations at play. The act of translation as also that of compiling an anthology is an act of rewriting. Both represent the original but are not in fact identical with it; yet both are creative activities often producing indelible impressions. The intervention of the translator as well as that of an anthologist is decisive in the reading of the text. Any translation is merely reading of a text at a given moment in time. The presentation of a piece also influences its reception—here the foreword or afterward, the blurb, the title, the subtitle, the cover illustration, the other pieces constituting the whole, play a crucial role in the reading of the piece. As such anthologies of translation would be doubly potent, combining both activities in the attempt to ostensibly bridge differences and promote intercultural understanding and harmony.

An anthology may be compiled for various reasons:

> in an effort to present what anthologists consider to be the best or most characteristic texts (or other printed matter) in a given field or what they judge to be most useful for a given group of readers; in an attempt to stabilize—or, for that matter, to revolutionize—received ways of behaviour or conventional perspectives; in the hope of producing a commodity that sells well; etc.[2]

There is an underlying principle governing the compilation of an anthology: an anthology may be introductive/prospective[3] i.e. introducing authors for the first time of it may be retrospective[4], offering a selection of the writings of already established writers. It can be generic, if it focuses on a single genre, seeking to reveal its development and hence to highlight its characteristic features. If an anthology seeks to present a certain epoch, the emphasis would be on the literary trends and movements of that period. A chronologically ordered anthology would seek to expose its readers to both authors and their styles and to the significant developments in the literary field, attempting to provide a historical balance. If an anthology is thematic[5] as opposed to literary, the stress is on the extra-literary features such as the socio-political aspects reflected in the collection. The underlying assumption here is that literature represents reality. The fact that literature constitutes an escape into the realm of fiction and is thus itself a construct is pushed into the background.

A translation anthology however, usually has its primary focus on the transfer of the cultural and literary values[6] of the source language culture. Thus it serves as an ethnographic rewriting[7], providing easy access to another culture, striving to explain it or at least to render it more comprehensible to the reader. Hence, it projects a certain image of this culture, defining its contours by determining what should be translated and what precluded.

Moreover in the case of translation anthologies, very often, even authors who are established writers in the source culture are unknown in the target culture. The anthology in translation cannot therefore, be considered as retrospective in the target culture except for the initiated. Then again there is the problem of a time-lag between the first publication of a work in the source culture and that in the target culture.[8] This is especially true in the case of thematically compiled anthologies in translation. The thematic criteria far outweighs the other criteria as far as translation anthologies of distant cultures are concerned.

Translation anthologies, presenting the literature of a country, whether from a generic period or thematic perspective, tend to foreground the shared nationality of the authors, suggesting commonality of experience, hinting at a national identity and promising an insight into the ethos of the concerned culture. Implicit is the fact that the best or most characteristic of that culture is on offer and display, providing an insider's view of its 'essence'. Such collections then frequently play down the tensions of multiculturality in the interest of unity; concommitantly the glimpse provided is coloured by the intention of the anthologist.[9]

Anthologies by their very nature, are a medium of dissemination. As Walter Höllerer puts it, they reveal the interplay of literary-history, poetics and sociology."[10] Characteristic of anthologies however is the criterion of selectivity[11]. In fact,

> anthologies can do for texts what museums do for artefacts and other objects considered of cultural importance: preserve and exhibit them and, by selecting and arranging the exhibits, project an interpretation of a given field, make relations and values visible, maybe educate taste. In short, anthologies attempt to give structure to (a branch of) culture. . . .[12]

This apparently comprehensive introduction to a culture makes anthologies popular in this age of information explosion and retrieval. They appear to facilitate the reader's task of rapidly acquainting himself/herself with the literature and culture of other nations. Anthologies are indeed a very powerful medium either in the breaking of prejudices or in reinforcing them, since they contribute to the establishment of the canon. The emerging canon can be accepted, enlarged in subsequent anthologies or even subverted,[13] through the deletion of authors included earlier or the inclusion of others, who represent an opposing worldview.

Anthologies reflect both, public taste as well as serve to mould it[14]: a case in point are the anthologies of women writers. The sudden spurt in anthologies of short stories by women writers in India as elsewhere. The Deutscher Taschenbuch Verlag (DTV) has for instance brought out a whole series of anthologies of short stories by women writers; each volume being devoted to one particular country, including one on India, which will be examined in detail in this paper mirrors the apparent desire to alter existing canons to include women writers and their perspectives on society and the gender issue.[15] Perspectives vary and that what is projected in the anthologies reveals the anthologist's position on the question: Is it one of consciousness-raising and empowerment or one of merely a 'sharing-in' of the privileges hitherto enjoyed by a certain section of people by virtue of their class, race, gender, nationality, etc. ?

Another significant reason for the sudden upsurge of interest in women's writing is the profit motivation of the publishers. Women and women's issues currently have a ready market. Publishers prefer to avoid taking risks, here anthologies on women's writing appear to guarantee success as regards turnover. Sales figures also reflect public taste. Thus the shifts and changes in the constitution of translation anthologies from the same culture over a period of time reflect change in public tastes. Moreover, since the readership for translation anthologies from the so-called developing world is relatively small, publishers attempt to attract the largest possible number of potential readers. In the capitalist world this leads to competition amongst the publishers[16] as well as to promoting an image which sells. It very often results in endorsing existing prejudices, although in real terms this is detrimental to the avowed goal of bridging differences and initiating a dialogue of cultures.

Since no culture is today perceived as being homogeneous or a monolith, the question is, whether this fact notwithstanding, an attempt is to be made to project and represent the culture as being homogenous and thus privilege the dominant mainstream? If, on the other hand, pluralism, heterogenity or multiculturality are accepted, then in that case, which are the voices to be represented, and which are to be suppressed through conscious omission? Which are the images of social life to be projected? Is the translator or anthologist resorting to so called universal experience to deny particularity? One has to critically examine the question of what image and why such an image is being projected at all and moreover if it is at variance with the declared aims and goals of the translator or anthologist as enunciated by him/her in the preface. These questions assume significance as they reveal the manner of the construction of the "Other"; at the same time they betray the "positionality"[17] of the translator/anthologist. In the light of this, manipulation and distortion are very real possibilities.

II

This paper seeks to highlight these concerns analysing and comparing two anthologies of short stories by Indian women writers, which have been translated into German, with a view to examining the image projected of Indian women. The anthologies are: *Frauen in Indien. Erzählungen*, and *Die Zeiten haben sich geändert. Frauen in Indien.*[18] The first of these has been compiled by a German, Anna Winterberg who spent seven years in India. She is the anthologist and also the translator of most but not all the stories. This volume is a translation of Indian English short stories by various Indian women writers, taken largely from collections of stories by the respective authors. The anthology itself is thus originally in German and published in 1988. The second anthology, the original title of which is *In Other Words. New Writing by Indian Women,*[19] has also been published in German by the same publishers, namely the Deutscher Taschenbuch Verlag in 1995 but interestingly, the anthology existed in Indian English originally brought out by the publishing house Kali for Women in 1992. It was subsequently translated into German, after the rights had been acquired by the dtv. Thus in the case of the first anthology, it was compiled for a specific German readership, whereas the second had been compiled in the original for primarily an Indian readership. This has been translated as it is, without any changes and without any translator's note. The translator is Susanne Aeckerle. The blurb of this anthology in translation is an edited version of the original. The only new information included is on the editors of the volume, that they are at the same time the publishers also of the only women's publishing house in India, viz., Kali for Women in New Delhi. Interestingly, the catalogue of New and Forthcoming Books for 1995-6 of Kali for Women, proclaims it as being merely 'India's first women's publishing house. . . .?

The nationality of the consumer-readers appears to have influenced the selection of the short stories, resulting in the emergence of two diverse images of the "modern Indian woman". Thus giving credence to the assumption that the question of identity of the "Indian woman," as sought to be conveyed by these anthologies is predetermined by the vision and understanding of this phenomenon "Indian woman" and all that it constitutes by the respective anthologists. The very concept of the prototype of an "Indian woman" modern or otherwise is in itself open to question. That both anthologies seek to focus on writing by women is evident from the respective titles. Women writers are being viewed as narrators of "their" universe and experiences, and at the same time as being representative of that of women. They are supposed to be the authentic, authoritative voice, portraying reality. This is clear from the blurbs provided in both books. The blurb on the inside of the Anna Winterberg anthology states.

> The western image of woman in India is shaped by such diverse images such as the powerful Indira Gandhi on the one hand and female foeticide and bride burning, with a view to collecting more dowry, on the other. The stories in this volume focus not so much on such horror stories, as they do on the daily life of women within their marriage and family, the demands made on women by a patriarchal and traditional society and on the attempt by women to fight for the right to be the arbiters of their own lives.

The blurb in German on the other anthology reads,

> With new-found self confidence and poise, they describe their own, modern world, as well as the old world, as seen through the eyes of their mothers and grandmothers. It is with humour, intellect and accuracy that they variously exemplify that times have indeed changed in India.

In fact the German translation of the title reads, *Times have changed. Women in India.* There is thus a translational shift in the meaning, for whereas the original title *In Other Words. New Writing by Indian Women* emphasizes woman as "Other" as well as the contemporaneity of the writing, the German title lays stress on modernity versus tradition. The fact of modernity in the German version is further underscored by the cover illustration which brings a supposededly traditional Indian woman face to face with a modern one, as is self-evident from the attire and hair style of the women depicted. The cover illustration is by Rotraut Susanne Berner and is obviously the reproduction of the popular imagination of the "Indian woman", providing an exotic touch. In contrast the cover illustration of the original is by Arpana Caur and titled "Threat". It shows a woman ablaze, and another seated with books falling around her. Clearly the two illustrations transmit very different signals, generating very different moods and expectations. Anthologies, more particularly translation anthologies, may therefore be said to present a selective vision of "reality".

Stefan H Kaszyński, in his article *Übersetzungsanthologien als Medientrager im internationalen Kulturtransfer* claims that anthologies should ideally be objective and unbiased, but this is not always the case. He further states that for an anthology to be exceptional it must have a distinct identity, a special quality which goes beyond the norms of compiling an anthology.[20] In this context, Susie Tharu and K. Lalitha's *Women Writing in India. 600 B.C. to the Present* merits consideration on the grounds that it seeks to

> create a context in which women's writings can be read, not as new ***monuments*** to existing institutions or cultures (classics are, by definition, monuments) but as ***documents*** that display what is at stake in the embattled practices of self and agency, and in the making of a habitable world, at the margins of patriarchies reconstituted by the emerging bourgeoisies of empire and nation. Our stress is on what forms the grain of these women's struggles. . . . . Most important, and this has been the major principle for our selections: what modes of resistance did they fashion? How did they avoid, question, play-off, rewrite, transform or even undermine the projects set out for them?
>
> In other words, we are interested in how the efforts of these women shaped the worlds we inherited, and what therefore, is the history, not of authority, but of contest and engagement we can claim today.[21]

In their attempt to achieve this goal, the editors have read against the grain of literary histories, paying particular attention to those who have been marginalized or around whom controversies have raged. They have sought to understand 'what it meant for a writer to live in times and in situations where she was doubly "Other" as woman and as colonized person'.[22] Moreover in their chronological presentation they strive for an understanding of a shift in themes or the transformation of certain recurring figures, such as the Hindu widow. All this makes their quest remarkable.

In contrast the blurb on the inside of the Anna Winterberg anthology makes an allusion of correcting the prevalent false or distorted consciousness with regard to Indian women, in West German society. This however is belied by the choice of stories and themes as well as by the statements made by Anna Winterberg herself in her afterword as also by the blurb on the back jacket, which seeks to lure the reader with the question. *How does a woman feel, seeing her groom for the very first time, at the marriage ceremony?* Or again the blurb on the inside of the book proclaims, *"Hardly anything worse, than not having children, especially sons, can befall an Indian wife.... for a woman's worth is seen in terms of the sons she produces. Therefore Radha, the wife of a policeman in the story, "The Childless", has to accept her husband's marriage to another."* Anna Winterberg, writes in the afterword, that her first encounter with India in 1968 was marked by "revulsion and fascination."[23] This is a rather cliched reaction of Germans to India since the time of Goethe himself. She further explains that literature as a means of understanding the milieu was inaccessible to her since Bengali was a particularly difficult language to learn. She claims that Indo-Anglian literature provided a limited access to a world she had hitherto been acquainted with, only through the books of Kipling and E.M. Forster. In India, her own initiation into this world is through the short stories of Ruth Prawer Jhabvala, who was born in Germany, of Polish parents, educated in England and married to an Indian architect. Currently she lives mostly in New York. Interestingly this author, two of whose stories are included in this volume, has always considered herself as a European and is on record as saying. "When one writes about India, as a European and in English (as I do), inevitably one writes not for Indians but for Western readers."[24] Winterberg's justification for bringing out a German volume of Indian short stories in English is that English is spoken by perhaps 2 percent of the population, which is "afterall 14 million people."[25] Moreover it is the link language for the various regions of India; added to this it is the language of the sciences, the administration, the highest court. Further according to her the most important newspapers are all published in English and finally, if all this were not reason enough, she believes English facilitates close contact with the West in various fields. Winterberg states that English is spoken by the upper middle class and the upper classes. What is however dubious is her claim that

> woman have from the very beginning played a more significant role in Indian English literature than they could in other Indian literatures, since it is only women from these classes who have access to the necessary education and later have a well-paying job or—and this is more often than not the case - a husband

with a lucrative job to provide for them, so that they have enough leisure to write.[26]

As regards the selection of stories in this volume, Anna Winterberg first makes a general statement on the broad themes of Indian-English prose writing, which according to her are: social critique, the national movement, with the horrors of partition and its aftermath and finally the issue of cultural confrontation between East and West and the search for identity. She admits that these issues have been tackled by authors of both sexes and are not gender specific. What makes her selection peculiarly women-oriented is, according to her, the focus on women's themes, such as the problem of being a spinster or a childless woman, the emancipation of a woman within the family or vis-a-vis the husband, the search for identity in a job etc. Further the anthology is intended to provide an insight into the traditional and future prospects as well as into the way of thinking and behaviour of women within their social milieu.[27]

Anna Winterberg's afterword alone demonstrates explicitly that she has reduced the so-called "Indian woman" to an epitome of a middle class woman. Marriage and her status within it seem to form the essence of womanhood; her very existence is to be defined by this institution, the rigidity of which the anthologist prefers to favour in order to accentuate the difference, in this otherwise universal institution, as exotic. The anthologist's own attitude towards Indian women writers as a class is visibly disparaging—as non-serious writers, leading affluent, complacent lives, being provided for by indulgent husbands. Such writers can hardly be expected to critically interrogate the socio-economic and political context which constitute the multilayered cultural construct of woman's identity. Consequently there is no trace of critiquing a system, or striving for an understanding of the underlying causes of oppression and domination, rather it is an attempt at achieving equality within the existing social framework.[28] It is thus a projection of the liberal feminists' agenda, exciting neither disquiet nor agitation. There is no concern for women of other classes, no attempt to transform society, no attempt to provoke introspection. Winterberg's easy dismissal of the reach, impact and importance of regional writers is fallacious as there is sufficient evidence to the contrary.

Winterberg's cultural construction of the so-called "Indian woman" as manifested in the afterword is reinforced by her choice of authors and stories. Of the 15 authors, only one is born after independence; of the 12, whose dates of birth have been mentioned, 10 were born either before or by the year 1940. Again of the 15 authors, 6 have for the past several years been living abroad[29] and not all writers perceive themselves as women writers focusing on women's issues, although it remains the reader's prerogative to read the text from that perspective. Bharati Mukherjee has, for example, time and again emphasized that she neither thinks of herself as a woman writer nor in fact as an Indian writer. In his article on Bharati Mukherjee, M. Sivaramkrishna quotes her as dismissing Indian-English writing as "very, very provincial" and its' future as being "pretty dim". Mukerjee held the interesting opinion that Indo-English literature is non-existent as a category but very much extant as a 'voice'. Denying categorically that she is an Indo-Anglian writer, she observed to me, 'there are no Indian themes, American themes or English themes. What I'm trying to produce is a voice perhaps. The word "voice" has a special place in my aesthetics.'[30] R.K. Dhawan writes of her, "she is clear about where her loyalties lie today and is at pains to emphasize that "she is an American writer".' She has stated that the aim of her writing is 'to expose Americans to the energetic voices of new settlers in this country.'[31]

Anita Desai is another writer, who has never really identified herself as first and foremost a woman writer. Her novels tend to explore alienation, the collapse of a value system, rootlessness, though undoubtedly she creates strong women characters. To quote Jasbir Jain, "Anita Desai while disassociating herself from specific feminine concerns, has gone on to portray women whose femaleness leads them to suicide, murder or withdrawal from the outside world."[32] Shashi Deshpande as a writer fits in rather well with Winterberg's own goals, for her "fictional world is a world of joint families, of male domination, of a horde of uncles and aunts, of multi-faced loyalties, where women struggle for basic rights: right to education, to take up a job, to have or not to have a child, to think in terms of self-fulfillment.[33] The short story, *The First Lady,* published in this volume is a deviation from this normal pattern. While the crisis in the marriage is the point of departure for the woman's introspection, it ultimately leads her to contemplate on the lack of morals today as compared to the idealistic days of the freedom struggle and thus as an extension of the betrayal of those ideals and the corruption of the value system.

Although the stories selected by Winterberg span a period of 33 years, having been published in the original between 1953 and 1986, yet they provide neither a glimpse into multiplicity of the Indian experience nor do they explore the woman's subjectivity, hinting at the emergence of a new sensibility. As already stated explicitly in the afterword, the majority of the stories deal with issues relating to marriage and family. These can be broadly classified under the following subcategories: childlessness, finding a partner and problems within marriage. The problem of childlessness is central to four of the stories, the oldest of which was published in 1953 and the latest in 1980.[34] Common to all the stories is the social stigma attached to being childless and the desire of all the women for a child, reinforcing gender stereotypes of the maternal role, in which alone 'the woman' finds fulfillment and attains womanhood. Similarly, the problems within marriage touch upon the rather formal relations between husband and wife. Thus, the protagonists of the short stories, *The Fastidious Housewife* by Dina Mehta and *One Never Knows* by Sujatha Bala Subramanian, are willing to overlook the infidelity of the husband. Indrayani Sowkar's story *The White Dove* portrays the dehumanization of the woman. This story as well as that of Rita Singh Mathur on dowry death, *The New Home,* also raise the question of the woman's body being used to assuage male desire - is the Indian arranged marriage then legalised prostitution, especially when the issue of dowry is raised or is it legalised rape? While not denying the validity of such an interpretation of the Indian arranged marriage in some cases, would not an uncritical presentation of these issues alone, again serve to reinforce existing prejudices and popular images of the downtrodden and oppressed "Indian woman" rather than shatter and fragmentize pre-existing biases by introducing a differentiated understanding of the problem?[35] And in that case, is it not in contradiction to the goal of the anthology? Jhabvala's story *Aliens* in fact emphatically underlines the difference between whites and blacks by perpetuating the myth of the civilized white in comparison with the primitive, uncouth and over-sexed black. The finding of a partner is also shown rather conventionally, even in those stories[36] where a love-match is achieved or where the woman is portrayed as defiant. This is so, because in no case is the woman emancipated enough to openly take a stand. The relationship is either clandestine and gains legitimacy through intrigue or the momentary crumbles in the face of male liberalness, the woman again conforming to the patriarchal assumptions of the feminine.

In this collection of 19 stories, it is only three which critique social values (those of Anita Desai, Shashi Deshpande and Vishwapriya Iyengar). Gender stereotyping has been upheld, the women coming across as emotional, incapable of shaping their own lives, submissive, practising self-denial, indulging in escapism; there is also a clear division of labour on the basis of sex: the woman's domain being the home, the man's the outside world; if women are working, then they are depicted as perusing typically feminine jobs. Another striking feature is the role played by superstition, fatalism and spirituality in these stories, endorsing existing notions of Indianness and Indian women, rather than correcting the widespread false consciousness or understanding, attached to the same in the Federal Republic of Germany, as is claimed in the blurb.

The anthology *In Other Words, New Writing by Indian Women,* although also a collection reflecting a middle class, urban milieu, is not confined solely to forging an identity within the bonds of marriage and family. According to the blurb in the original "*In Other Words brings you 14 of the most innovative and adventurous of contemporary Indian women writers. . . . All the authors except two, belong to the post independence generation.*" These lines have been reproduced in the German version of the blurb as well. The blurb further claims that the "*Preoccupations (of the writers) range from an observation of the past through the lives of their ancestresses to that of the present, through their own*". Although some of the stories in this collection also reflect tradition and superstition, yet on the whole they seek to transcend the narrow confines of the home, either through an attempt to link with it the reality outside, or the home is peripheral to the larger issues being raised. Thus Vishwapriya Iyengar's story *No Letter from Mother* highlights the alienation of the post-colonial school girl from her mother tongue and thus by extension from her roots and culture. Three other stories critique the Establishment and the accepted norms of success.[37]

Shalini Saran's *Mallika Farida* is a sketch of a woman's attempt at living a clean and honest life, independently. Her influence on the women of the slum arouses insecurity amongst the latter's menfolk, leading to the defilement of Farida's body by the neighbourhood pimp and the delivery of a sharp warning from the Mirza Sahib, her landlord, who reminds her, the shrine where she dwells, is a sacred place to which she retorts, "There is no shrine as sacred as one's body".[38] Or Manorama Mathai's *Sara*, which questions the values of "respectability and adaptability" upheld by partriarchy or the fact that female desire continues to remain taboo. Then again Urmila Banerjee's *The Tamarind Tree Murder*, demonstrates how a relationship of domination and bondage, albeit between a mother and her children, more especially a son, lead to fear, violence and the crippling of a personality. It questions hierarchy, the oppression of expectations and status. Achla Bansal's *Thanks Anyway* touches upon the very topical problem of the parents of the Indian diaspora. In Githa Hariharan's *The Remains of the Feast,* Rukmani, the great grandmother, a few weeks prior to her death goes against all that she has held holy throughout her life, as though to truly liberate herself from the chains of caste and social taboos. Deep Bedi's story *The Manuscript* explores the upholding of values even when surrounded by decadence. Shama Futehally's *The Portrait of a Childhood* depicts the intrusion of the masses into the world of the privileged, resulting in feelings of guilt in the face of the deprivation of others.

This collective evinces, at least, on the surface a greater global or macro awareness, which hints at a change in perception and values, that is to be encouraged and critiqued. The catalogue of New and Forthcoming Books for 1995-6 of Kali for Women claims that the objective of this publishing house "is to increase the body of knowledge on women in the Third World, to give voice to such knowledge as already exists, and to provide a forum for women writers, creative and academic." This, perhaps, explains the choice of the stories, since clearly there is no common theme underlying this collection as opposed to the first. Consequently the concept of modernity and its' concerns is given expression from a different perspective, keeping also in mind, that the anthology was initially intended only for an Indian middle class urban readership. This anthology too is limited to Indian English writers and does not include translations of work by women writers in regional languages, thereby privileging the national identity over the regional and the urban over the rural.

The obvious shortcoming of this collection also, is that the woman inhabits a world restricted by the concerns and aspirations of the middle class.[39] While not denying that literacy is a prerequisite for writing, and that in a largely illiterate country such as India, this ability is thus the privilege of the upper classes, yet it is not a natural corollary that authors (although by and large belonging to a certain class of society) limit their vision to this class only, especially since India is more than just its elites. Several Indian authors have indeed sought to throw light on the immense political and economic problems confronting the country and their impact on its' social fabric. Writers in the regional languages are more prominent in picking up this challenge, although the consciousness of all writers as well as others in India has been shaped by multiple influences, both regional and national. It is unfortunate that in recent times the vision of Indian English writing has been myopic, restricted to middle class urban concerns. None of the stories in either volume touches upon inter-caste or inter-communal realationships. Similarly the exploitation of peasant women at the hands of the feudal landlords finds no mention. There is no story demonstrating women's role in ecologial movements; nor do any of the stories reflect women's fight against alcoholism and other social evils. Political themes are totally ignored; the trauma of the riots of 1984 or the militancy widely prevalent in certain parts of India find no expression. Much of the social and political upheavals in the country have gone largely unheeded as raw material for literature in Indian-English. In contrast literature in the regional languages is rich in such themes, which also effect the lives of women, since they are not isolated incidents but rather symptomatic of the deeper malaise affecting society and thus contributing to the condition of women in this country.

III

Women writers in regional languages have taken up issues throwing light on the political and economic problems confronting women. In Bengali Mahasweta Devi's short story *Draupadi* for instance focuses on the plight of tribals as well as on the government crack-down on the Naxalite movement in the early seventies. Malini Bhattacharya's street play *Meye Dile Sajiye* (*To Give a Daughter Away*) is a effective campaign against domestic violence and dowry murders. In Hindi Nasira Sharma's *Ibne Mariam* deals with the aftermath of the Bhopal gas tragedy, especially the collapse of families with young brides being turned out of their homes for fear they might beget abnormal children. It also highlights mankind's voyeuristic commercial interest in the suffering of others. Geetanjalishree *Bel Patr* explores the problems of a Hindu-Muslim marriage, the social pressures it is subjected to, resulting in tension within the marriage. Mannu Bhandari's *Saza* (*The Sentence*) is a case of justice delayed, justice denied with its concommittant destruction of home and personality. Krishna Sobti and Mridula Garg are known for their feminist stances. Rajee Seth's *Andhe Mode Se Aage* shows the protagonists' developing consciousness of herself as an exploited human being.

In Urdu Ismat Chugtai's writing questions accepted social mores. Her famous short story *Lihaf* (*The Quilt*) is centred on a lesbian relationship. Saliha Abid Husain's *Ek Savaal* (*A Question*) questions the sincerity and commitment of social activists, hinting that most pursue this line of work with the goal of achieving personal recognition. The story also provides an insight into the debasement, toil and despair of the lower classes and in the face of rampant inequality and oppression, the significance of freedom in independent India is questioned. In Wajida Tabassum's *Utran* (*Castoffs*), the protagonist, the daughter of the wet nurse, resents having to constantly wear the clothes cast off by the rich daughter of the house. Her sense of self-respect is outraged by the fawning attitude of her mother. Finally she turns the tables on her young mistress by seducing the groom of the latter on the eve of the marriage.

In Oriya Binapani Mohanty's short stories *Lata* and *Asru Anala* (*Tears of Fire*), the protagonists are extremely poor—Lata, the daughter of a landless peasant and Ketaki, the vegetable vending lower caste widow both rebel against the unjust society. Lata, who has been abused by her in-laws flees to the shelter of her father's home, only to be raped by 'respectable' villagers during his absence. She confronts society with its hypocrisy and double standards, revealing the names, shaming the congregated mass of villagers, seeking to render her homeless again,

Ketaki, whose meagre earnings barely stretch to providing a meal for the family, initially cows down to extortionists demanding protection money; but on discovering that these hoodlums have murdered a young girl activist, who took up cudgels on her behalf, she avenges the death by taking the law into her own hands and ritualistically executing the killers. The story critiques the complicity of the law enforcement agencies in the oppression of the poor and defenseless.

Women's writing in Malayalam appears to have a long tradition of a feminist consciousness. Jancy James writes:

> Resistance assumed different faces in women's writings in Malayalam. Some took up cudgels and declared themselves fighters of sexual oppression (K. Saraswathi Amma). ...The second category of resisting women writers indulged themselves in an irrepressible vein of melancholy....(Rajalekshmy)...(Sugathakumari). Resistance crystallized as interiority syndrome in the youngest generation of women writers. ...
>
> Yes, morbidity, bitterness, avenging sensuality, and a sardonic dalliance with death have become the hallmarks of writing by the present generation of women in Malayalam. ...Manasi, Sara Joseph, Vatsala, Gracy, Ashita, Sobha Warrier—the list is not very long but their literature is on a par with some of the fiercest discourses in feminism.[40]

K. Saraswathi Amma's *The Soil That Grows Diamonds* is a critique of a society where young girls are sold off to men old enough to be their grandfathers in order to save the family from penury. Ashita's *Incomplete Stops* is again a powerful critique of a society, where a young woman, on being deserted by her husband, finds herself in a mental hospital. Ten years later she is summarily discharged for want of beds. In the meantime she has become conditioned to carrying out orders. As a result, at the time of her discharge, she is not equipped to cope with the reality of the society outside and is taken advantage of by a policeman. K.M. George, in his foreword to the anthology of Malayalam women writers notes, 'Not only are all the protagonists female, but by and large, their search for meaning in their lives, or for liberation does not take the shape of imitating the male idea of freedom and power.'[41] Short stories in Kannada also focus on the interdependence between society and the individual. According to B.C. Ramachandra Sharma, 'An aspect of the present day short story in Kannada is the phenomenally expanding universe of experience that characterizes it. Dalits, women and Muslims have come into the field of fiction, having resolved to be heard and this has resulted in enriching the genre.[42]

Jahnavi is both a Dalit and a woman writer and writes from that perspective. Anupma Niranjana's *Ondu Ghatane Mattu Anantara* (*The Incident - and After*) is a powerful indictment of the complicity of a hypocrisy-ridden society in the humiliation and debasement of women, where a man out of cowardice abandons his wife to rapists and then wants to shun her. The wife holds him in contempt and walks out of the marriage. In Veena Santeshwar's *Avaala Svatantrya* (*Her Independence*) the accomodating working wife realises that despite India having won independence in 1947, women continue to remain chained and oppressed. Vaidehi's short story *The Confession* focuses on the violence perpetrated on women through marriage, which aims at the dissolution of womanly bonds.[43]

Marathi also has a rich tradition of Dalit literature. Although the Dalit voice is predominantly male, yet there are Dalit women writers in Marathi also: Shantabai Kamble, Kumud Pavde, Baby Kamble, Mukta Sarvagod. Dalit women writers are better known for their autobiographies.

> Their autobiographies trace the contours of untouchability at the personal, familial and societal levels. What makes them valuable is the record of the unbelievable courage with which these women as girl children from the Dalit community and therefore twice devastated—first by the canker of caste and second by being female—transcended their limitations to realise the dreams of a new, seemingly impossible selfhood.[44]

Several of the authors discussed above are also available in English translation, although it is always better to translate directly from the language in which the text has been written originally. Moreover women's writing in regional languages has been included in translation anthologies in English. Kali for Women have also brought out anthologies of women's writing in translation. The anthologists/publishers themselves could also have individually compiled an anthology including short stories from the regional languages. Such a selection would perhaps do more justice to the aim of introducing "women in India", for, as must be evident from the examples cited above, regional literatures are indeed a rich reservoir for exploring the multiple identities of Indians. Regional and social fragmentation give shape to these identities. Literature cannot be viewed in isolation. It is the outcome of the socio-historical and cultural dynamics of the concerned region. The task of representing India or Indian women for that matter, thus necessitates contextualizing the various regional literatures, since each literature reflects a differently evolved and constituted consciousness rooted in the socio-economic and historical variables involved in its development. In this connection, it might be worthwhile for translation anthologies, especially thematic ones with clearly ethnographic overtones, not to be compiled on the principle of gender; some male authors have also written sensitively about the condition of women.

NOTES

* All translations are mine.

1. Evidence of this is hitherto unprecedented research being undertaken in this area; an excellent example of this is the special project on anthologies being carried out by the Göttinger research centre 'Die Literarische Übersetzung.' The project is entitled *Anthologies of Literature in Translation—Part 1. Establishing World Literatuer: A Paradigm of German Translation Culture.*
2. Helga Essmann and Arnim Paul Frank, 'Translation Anthologies: An Invitation to the Curious and a Case Study', in *Target, International Journal of Translation Studies* 3.1, 1991, pp. 65-90, p. 66.
3. Arnim Paul Frank and Helga Essmann, 'Translation Anthologies: A Paradigmatic Medium of International Literary Transfer', in *American Studies (Amst.)*, *Vol. 35* No. 1, 1990, pp. 21-34, p. 24.
4. Ibid., p. 25.
5. See Essmann and Frank, 1991, op. cit., p. 72. See also Gabriele Pisarz-Ramírez, 'Internationale Kurzprosa in Anthologien der Deutschen Demokratischen Republik: Die Reihe "Erkundungen" ', in Harald Kittel, ed., *International Anthologies of Literature in Translation,* Berlin, 1995, pp. 199-238, p. 204.
6. Thus according to Frank and Essmann translation anthologies also reflect the desire of the anthologist to either promote interest in the source literature or to contribute to the renewal of the target literature by furnishing qualities deemed to be lacking in the latter. Frank and Essmann, 1990, op. cit., p. 30.
7. Gabriele Pisarz-Ramírez explicitly states that the anthology serie *Erkundungen* in the former G.D.R. was in the nature of an expedition, exploring the unknown, opening up new vistas of reality and broadening the literary horizan. In fact its slogan was ' "Erkundungen" is the prose ticket to the world.' Gabriele Pisarz-Ramírez, op. cit., pp. 208-9. Anil Bhatti also draws attention to the "ethnological attitude" underlying much of the literature in translation from distant cultures. He points out that a "reverse ethnology" is normally not possible in the case of German texts being translated for an Indian readership because most educated Indians would already be conversant with many German authors through English translation. This demonstrates the inequality prevalent in intercultural relations. This demonstrates the inequality prevalent in intercultural relations. Anil Bhatti, 'Anmerkungen zur Vermittelung indischer Literatur in deustschen Anthologien', in Harald Kittel, ed., op. cit., pp. 107-16.
8. For further details see Frank and Essmann, 1990, op. cit., pp. 28-9.
9. According to Kittel, anthologies reveal not only the role and intention of editors, but also the social make up of authors and readers, their participation in the forming of literary tastes as well as the changing attitudes towards the literary achievements of the past. Kittel, Ibid., p. XI.
10. Quoted in German in Frank and Essmann, 1990, op. cit., p. 22.

11. Several anthologists after having listed the criteria for selecting the texts for the anthology, admit in the introduction/foreword, that in the ultimate analysis the selection does indeed reflect the personal preferences of the anthologist - amongst others Bhisham Sahni, Sara Rai, Ranga Rao and M.U. Memon. The anthologies are: Bhisham Sahni, ed., *Anthology of Hindi Short Stories. (tr. Jai Ratan),* New Delhi, 1993. Sara Rai, ed., *The Golden Waist Chain. Modern Hindi Short Stories.* New Delhi 1990. Ranga Rao, ed., *Classic Telugu Short Stories.* New Delhi 1995. M.U. Memon, ed., *The Colour of Nothingness. Modern Urdu Short Stories.* New Delhi : 1991.
12. Essmann and Frank, 1991, op. cit., p. 66.
13. Andre Lefevere, 'Anthologizing Africa', in Andre Lefevere, *Translation, Rewriting, & the Manipulation of Literary Fame,* London : 1992, pp. 124-37, p. 127 ff.
14. Frank and Essmann, 1990, op. cit., pp. 21ff. See also Kittel, op. cit., p. XII.
15. That women perceive reality differently and that this is reflected in their creative writing, is a widely held view and anthhologists often mention this as one reason for the compilation of an anthology, having gender as its basis. See for instance Lakshmi Holmstrom, ed., *The Inner Courtyard. Stories by Indian Women.* Delhi, 1991. K.M. George also mentions this in his foreword to K.M. George, Jancy James et al., eds., *Inner Spaces: New Writing by Women from Kerala.* New Delhi, 1994 and this is echoed in Syeda S. Hameed and Sugra Mehdi, eds., *Parvaaz: Urdu Short Stories by Women.* New Delhi, 1996. According to Tharu, much of the feminist criticism of the early seventies in America also reflects this belief. Susie Tharu and K. Lalita, eds., *Women Writing in India: 600 B.C. to the Present. Vol. 1.* Delhi, 1993. p. 14.
16. Lefevere, op. cit., p. 125. In comparison Pisarz-Ramírez mentions that under socialism, since the profit motive was not the determining factor, literatures of little known cultures were also published. Moreover there was no duplication or overlap with regard to the area of publication. Thus the publishing house *Volk und Welt* was responsible for publishing translations of the literature of the twentieth century, whereas another publishing house was responsible for publishing the classics of world literature, etc., pp. 209ff.
17. See Luise von Flotow, 'Translating Women of the Eighties: Eroticism, Anger, Ethnicity', in Sherry Simon, ed., *Culture in Transit. Translating the Literature of Quebec,* Montreal 1995, pp. 31-46, p. 32. Positionality refers to the subjective aspects of translation.
18a. Anna Winterberg (ed.), *Frauen in Indien. Erzählungen,* München: 1988.
18b. Urvashi Butalia and Ritu Menon (eds.), *Die Zeiten haben sich geändert. Frauen in Indien,* (tr. Susanne Aeckerle), München: 1995.
19. Urvashi Butalia and Ritu Menon, eds., *In Other Words. New Writing by Indian Women,* New Delhi, 1992.
20. Stefan H. Kaszyński, 'Übersetzungsanthologien als Medienträger im internationalen Kulturtransfer', in Arnim Paul Frank, Kurt Jurgen Mass and Fritz Paul, eds., *Überserzen verstehen Brücken bauen:*

geiteswissenschaftliches Übersetzen im internationalen Kulturaustausch, Bd. 8, Teil 2, Berlin: 1993, pp. 578-86, pp. 580-5.

21. Susie Tharu and K. Lalita, eds., *Women Writing in India 600 B.C. to the Present, Vol. 1: 600 B.C. to the early Twentieth Century,* Delhi, 1993, p. 36.
22. Ibid., Preface, p. xix.
23. Winterberg, op. cit., p. 245.
24. Vasant A. Shahane, 'Ruth Prawer Jhabvala: Talent and Technique', in Krishna Nandan Sinha, ed., *Indian Writing in English,* New Delhi: 1979, pp. 156-68.
25. Winterberg, op. cit., p. 245.
26. Ibid., p. 246.
27. Ibid., p. 248.
28. Interestingly the selection of so-called typically women's themes endorse the view that women are remaining within the boundaries chalked out by men as being of especial interest to them for "as the Bengali writer Nabaneeta Dev Sen also points out, should a women writer venture beyond the family and the lyrical expression of her feelings into territories regarded as male, there is an immediate outcry." Quoted in Susie Tharu and K. Lalita, eds., *Women Writing in India: 600 B.C. to the Present. Vol. 11.* Delhi: 1995. p. 206.
29. These are : Ruth Prawer Jhabvala, Kamala Markandaya, Rita Singh Mathur, Bharati Mukherjee, Santha Rama Rao and Indrayani Sowkar.
30. M. Sivaramkrishna, 'Bharati Mukherjee', in Madhusadan Prasad, ed., *Indian English Novelists: An Anthology of Critical Essays,* New Delhi: 1982, pp. 71-86, p. 72.
31. R.K. Dhawan, ed., *Indian Women Novelists. Set 1, Vol. 1.,* New Delhi: 1991. Introduction, p. 23.
32. Jasbir Jain, 'The Feminist Perspective. The Indian Situation and its' Literary Manifestations', in Niaz Zaman, Shawkat Hussain et.al., eds., *'Other Englishes'. Essays on Commonwealth Writing',* Dhaka: 1991, pp. 66-75, p. 71.
33. Ibid., p. 72.
34. Attia Hosian's *A Woman and Child* 1953; Jai Nimbkar's *The Childless* 1971; Raji Narasimhan's *A Village Story* 1978; Sunita Jain's *A Dead Wife* 1980.
35. In her book *Real and Imagined Women. Gender, Culture and Postcolonialism.* London: 1993, Rajeshwari Sunder Rajan points out that the western media tend to sensationalise events such as 'sati', deliberately suppressing information on protest action taken by women's groups, etc. (p. 15). Depending on how stories are presented, they too can evoke a similar reaction. Hence a story, where the protagonist actively resists or where protest actions are incorporated in the story, would be more appropriate to the aim of the anthology. Malini Bhattacharya's *Meye Dile Sajiye (To Give a Daughter Away),* which is mentioned in the paper later is an example. The other possibility open to the anthologist, is the inclusion of an informative discourse on the issue in the foreword/afterword.
36. These are Dina Mehta's *Marriages are made in Heaven* and Rita Singh Mathur's *Love Marriage or Arranged?*

37. These are Subhadra Sen Gupta's *Dooz, Charu and the Establishment,* Ruchira Mukherjee's *Dying like Flies,* and Manjula Padmanabha's *A Government of India's Undertaking.*
38. Shalini Saran, 'Mallika Farida', in Butalia and Menon, eds., op. cit., pp. 146-55, p. 155.
39. A possible reason for DTV in choosing to publish anthologies projecting the urban middle class identity of the Indian woman, is the relative ease with which a German readership can access such an identity, since it would probably have more in common with the West than an immage defined by its regional identity, which might prove to be alien and alienating for the readership. This in turn would imply that otherness is perceived in known categories.
40. Jancy James, 'From Veneration to Virulence: A Case for a Women's Literary History in Malayalam' in *Social Scientist, Vol 23, Nos. 10-12, 1995, pp. 98-111, pp. 108-9.*
41. K.M. George, Jancy James et al., eds, *Inner Spaces, New Writing by Women from Kerala.* New Delhi: 1994. p. XVII.
42. B.C. Ramachandra Sharma, 'Kannada Short Story Today', in *Indian Literature, Vol 168, No. 4, 1995,* pp. 9-11.
43. These stories have been culled from the magazine *Hans* and various other anthologies. These are: K.M. George, Jancy James et al., op. cit.; Tharu and Lalita, Vol II, op. cit.; Syeda S. Hameed and Sughra Mehdi, op.cit.; Githa Hariharan, ed, *A Southern Harvest,* New Delhi: 1993; Gayatri Chakravoty Spivak, *In Other Worlds, Essays in Cultural Politics,* New York and London 1987; and *The Slate of Life. An anthology of stories by Indian Women,* Kali for Women, New Delhi: 1994.
44. Meera Manvi, 'Girl Children Reaching for the Sky and More. Marathi Dalit Women's Autobiography', in Vinay Kirpal, ed., *The Girl Child in Twentieth Century Indian Literature,* New Delhi: 1992. pp. 105-111, p. 106.

RANJANI MAZUMDAR

Orientalism Redifined: Studies of *Salaam Bombay* and *Mississippi Masala*

Oreintalism is premised upon exteriority, i.e. on the fact that the Orientalist poet or scholar, makes the Orient speak, describes the Orient, renders its mysteries plain for and to the West. He is never concerned with the Orient except as the first cause of what he says and writes, by virtue of the fact that it is said or written, is meant to indicate that the Orientalist is outside the Orient, both as an existential and moral fact.

—Edward Said

It is now more than a decade since the grand debut made by Mira Nair with her first fiction film, *Salaam Bombay* in the Western world. In Derek Malcolm's words;

"Mira Nair's triumph at the Cannes with *Salaam Bombay*, which won the prestigious Camera D' or award for the best first feature and the prize given by the paying customers as the most striking and enjoyable film they had seen, was a much needed shot in the arm for the Indian cinema."[1]

Salaam Bombay was the story of street children in the city of Bombay. Highly acclaimed for her 'humanist' and 'realist' portrayal of the plight of slum kids, Nair was described by the Western press as *the* woman filmmaker who shows deep concern for the context of her country. With the accolades received for the reception of her film at International Festivals and circles, her next venture, *Mississippi Masaala*, a film about the contempt Indians hold for Africans/African Americans, also attracted a lot of attention.

This essay critically examines issues raised in Mira Nair's films—those of inequality, migration, race and sexuality in the context of production of cultural commodities in Third World societies, for the Western filmgoer. Such as process, even by film-makers of Third World 'origin', not infrequently, deploys notions of identity and difference geared towards the gratification of fears about otherness. I believe that films like *Mississippi Masala* and *Salaam Bombay* contain a politics of power, which is often obscured by mainstream commentators who cite them as a welcome change from the 1960's type 'political film-making'. An examination of *Salaam Bombay* and *Mississippi Masala* will help to bring out the tensions arising from the imagining of otherness and self taking place across the West and the 'Third World'. Both these films are peculiarly transnational—though from somewhat different vantage points.

THE FILMS EXAMINED

Shot in the urban slums of Bombay, *Salaam Bombay* is the story of Krishna, a ten year old boy who is thrown out by his mother because he has ruined a bicycle. Krishna starts working for a travelling circus, but is abondoned when the employers move away abruptly. He then heads for Bombay, and gets a job working as a tea boy and is called Chaipau—one who gets tea and bread. The film centres around the brothels of Bombay. Chaipau's daily deliveries to the brothel introduces him and the audience to various characters—Baba, the leader of the red light district and drug business, Chillum, a 25 year old drug seller who sells Baba's drugs, Baba's 8 year old daughter, Manju, and her mother, Rekha, a prostitute. Chaipau's story runs parallel with the story of all these characters. He becomes friends with Chillum and Manju. His trips to the brothel also introduces him to Solassal (sweet sixteen) a Nepali girl, who has been kidnapped to bring the brothel a lot of money in return for her virginity.

A guiding thread in Nair's narrative is her insistence on the essential 'goodness' of her characters even in the face of drudgery and a dehumanizing day to day existence. Chaipau for example is thrown out of his house, is working for a miserly tea shop owner, under the most inhuman conditions. Yet he remains a 'good' human being. Not only does he make a lot of friends, but also tries to help them at every stage. When Chillum is ill, it is Chaipau who gets money from Rekha for his medicines, it is Chaipau who tries to help 'sweet sixteen' escape from the brothel, it is Chaipau who gets picked up by the police while helping Manju and again, it is Chaipau who kills Baba to help Rekha escape. So in the worst conditions, Chaipau does not have any self-interest, he is busy helping the others in his life. The cruelty of poverty seems to leave no scar on his unblemished character. He appears undaunted in the pursuit of the 'good'.

The character of Rekha underlines both Nair's strengths and weaknesses. Her strengths are obvious. Rekha, spared from the brutality of the brothel gains relative freedom living with Baba, while at the same time being exploited and used by him as a source of income. Her relationship with Baba is frustrating yet erotic at times, shadowed by the fact that Rekha continues this relationship for the sake of her daughter Manju. Nair's great weakness is to again present Rekha as essentially 'good' unaffected to a large extent by the brutality of her day to day existence. Even in the portrayal of Baba, the main villain—in her effort to extract virtue out of him–Nair goes to absured lengths to establish a supposed complexity in the former's character.

Salaam Bombay, also takes great lengths to insist on the capacity of those marginalized for joy, indeed the film underlines that this is one of their sources of strength in confronting the drudgery of everday life. Take the short sequence in Rekha's room, as an example; Chaipau, has just come into the room wet; Rekha takes off his shirt, wipes him with a towel and then both, Chaipau and Manju, start dancing happily, to a popular Hindi film song. My argument here, is not that the poor can never have their moments of happiness or fun, but the duration of this sequence, the extensive use of close-ups of the children's faces, directly facing the spectator, reminds us of what John Berger had to say about Hal's painting of the Laughing Fisherboy.

These people belong to the poor. The poor can be seen in the street, outside or in the countryside, pictures of the poor inside the house however are reassuring. Here the painted poor smile as they offer what they have for sale. They smile at the better off to ingratiate themselves, but also at the prospect of a sale or a job. Such pictures assert two things: that the poor are happy, and that the better off are a source of hope for the world.[2]

This dance sequence seems to almost make an appeal to the spectator to come and help the 'helpless'. The 'how cute' image of these children is also very successfully shown in the cinema hall sequence, where the kids are seen imitating a dancer on screen and also the horse carriage ride at night, where the children are slightly drunk. The reason for such imagery becomes clear in one of Nair's interviews:

After seeing the film I don't think anybody will say that this film is a film showing the depression and misery in India. On the other hand, they will conclude that it is a film that celebrates the survival of the human being in the face of odds.[3]

Nair's appeal to an abstract 'humanism' conceals the ideological basis of her project—the packaging of Third World misery through the device of a refurbished orientalism. 'Humanism' towards the poor of the Third World, shorn of its socio-economic and class moorings as is the case with *Salaam Bombay*, becomes an empty phrase which conceals more than it reveals. Nair would like to celebrate the survival of the human being against odds, but she would do well to remember that for every one who survives there are twenty who perish under the most gruelling and dehumanizing circumstances. Thus Robert Stam and Louise Spence have shown the essential emptiness of bourgeois humanist categories, used by cinema in its image of the 'Third World':

> And just as the camera might therefore be said to inscribe certain features of bourgeois humanism, so the cinematic and televisual apparatus, taken in their most inclusive sense might be said to inscribe certain features of European colonialism. The magic carpet provided by these apparatuses flies us around the globe and makes us, by virtue of our position, its audio visual masters. It produces us as subjects, transforming us into armchair conquistadors, affirming our sense of power while making the inhabitants of the Third objects of spectacle for the First Worlds voyeuristic gaze.[4]

This is precisely what seems to have happened with *Salaam Bombay*. Apart from the dance sequence with the children, there are various other sections where the film operates as a 'Third World spectacle' for a 'First World audience'. There is a sequence where a man visits Baba (Nana Patekar) along with a foreign woman journalist. All of them are sitting on the terrace with Manju, the daughter in the background. As they are talking, Baba shouts for Chillum and asks him to get some tea. When the tea arrives, Baba decides to have some fun to impress the journalist. He starts hitting out at Chillum with a belt, a grotesque smile on his face. The journalist gets up in disgust and walks away. The white woman journalist's disgust, and subsequent departure from this scene of 'bizarre violence' constructs the 'brutalized' *other* who inhabits the underside of the city of Bombay.

Nair's organizing principles in *Salaam Bombay* come to their fruition in her conclusion which would gladden any Orientalists heart. As both Rekha and Chaipau stagger out of the house after Baba's murder, they are confronted with a Hindu religious procession (the Ganesh Chaturathi). The camera focuses on the grotesque pagan deity of Ganesh, the frenzied mob, oblivious to all social events surrounding it. As Chaipau and Rekha are separated from each other in the course of the procession which is entirely oblivious to their situation, we are left with a picture of the East—both barbaric and cruel, exotic, eternal and primitive, incapable of sensitivity towards the major social sores of its time. This is a familiar motif—if the East is incapable of settling its own problems, then a 'modernizing' force from without is both necessary and welcome. Edward

Said's merciless criticism of such tendencies would certainly hold true for *Salaam Bombay's* conclusion.

Many critics and reviewers have compared Nair's venture to Hector Babenco's *Pixote,* De Sica's *Shoeshine* and Truffaut's *Four Hundred Blows*. Few have, however, compared it to Luis Bunuel's classic *Los Olvidados*. A comparison with *Olvidados* would perhaps help in illuminating what seems to be the real problem with *Salaam Bombay* i.e. Nair's inability to articulate a critical theory of reality. *Salaam Bombay* phenomenally, deals with the situation of the marginalized, in an urban capitalist milieu, without making any effort to situate the latter within the framework of accumulation and inequality on a world scale. There is much that we see in *Salaam Bombay* that is present in New York just as there is much resembling downtown Manhattan in the Metropolis of Bombay. The poor in *Salaam Bombay* seem to represent the generic voice of the Occident's 'civilizational other', of societies that are not torn by struggles, glaring inequalities and contradictions but by a 'levelling poverty'.

In Bunuel's masterpiece, the opening sequence shows as shots of the port of New York, the Island of Manhattan and its sky scrapers, the Eiffel Tower, Big Ben and then downtown Mexico city. The voice over says that these structures conceal:

> pits of misery, hiding unwanted hungry, dirty, and uneducated children ... a fertile breeding ground for future delinquents. Although modern society attempts to correct these evils, the success of its efforts are still very limited. ... Mexico, a great and modern city is no exception to this universal truth ... and this film based on real life is not optimistic ... but leaves the solution of this problem to the progressive forces of our times.

Bunuel's vision is informed by a healthy holism, for whom poverty and the poor are depicted and shown in the unrefined reality of urban misery. *Salaam Bombay* on the other hand seems to be a film where Nair has to demonstrate to a Western middle-class audience, that Third World poverty need not necessarily be only a picture of suffering and struggles but also one of joy and happiness. It is interesting that Bunuel does not try to evoke an identification with his characters, but on the contrary revulsion and pain. If the marginalized were shown to be capable of joy as we know it, Bunuel would then argue that the struggle for a better world would be rendered superfluous. For example, the mother in *Los Olvidados*, unlike Rekha in *Salaam Bombay*, is shown to be cruel, insensitive, even towards her own son. Rekha, on the other hand displays a strong sense of familial love towards her daughter and even with Chaipau.

Bunuel's project was clear, a demystification of poverty, camera work that went against the usual techniques of social films. Nair, on the other hand, posits a redefined aesthetics of poverty. The drabness and grey of *Los Olvidados* stands in sharp contrast to *Salaam Bombay's* almost teasingly sensual use of colour. In the final analysis, while *Los Olvidados* mocks the audience, savagely denying any space for middle class sentiments, *Salaam Bombay* tries to seduce the viewer into accepting and gaining pleasure from viewing the life of the marginalised. Nair's reduction of the Indian experience of poverty, to an essence that animates joy and the capacity to endure suffering, feeds well into older Eurocentric narratives of the 'timelessness' of the East. It is a commentary on a 'national' experience but transnational in focus, largely for the Western spectator.

A glimpse at some of the reviews that followed the grand opening of *Salaam Bombay* will help to substantiate the dominant perception of the film that I have tried to critique.

> Yet the overwhelming impression of the film is its affirmation of the spirit and defiant flamboyance of these charming wicked innocents whom fate has given nothing except life.[5]
>
> To watch Nair's film is to enter a completely Indian world of street dwellers, chaiwallahs, pimps and drug addicts, a world with its own language, texture, signs and signifiers.[6]
>
> The movie's liveliness also comes because the film vibrates with the mad electric colours of India itself, from the painted wood with a faded patina to the gold and silver and prints of Manju's gaudy dress up clothes.[7]
>
> The poverty in the film is excruciating at first, but one adapts to it as much as Chaipau does, a hearty resourcefulness takes over. The film-makers are torn by their own perceptions which say that things are hopeless for these children yet also connect with something indomitable in the street people's lives. We can respond to the film-maker's struggle to order the events before us and make some kind of sense out of them—to pull some hope from it all.[8]

Mira Nair's *Salaam Bombay* seems to present the Indian experiene as representing the West's civilizational 'other'. To be sure, Nair does not espouse the unrefined Orientalism of the nineteenth century variety. In fact, her concern for the marginalized of India seems entirely genuine as some powerful sections of the film testify. The problem lies in her projection of Indian marginalism as something intrinsically different from similar experiences elsewhere; rather than underline (implicitly at least) that marginalism has a global character.

In *Mississippi Masala* the themes of race, sexuality and 'otherness' are examined through the prism of transnational memory and the inversion of identity in the process of migration. An unstated theme in the film is the occupation and contestation of subalternity by two non-white groups. It is important to examine whether questions of power between these two groups are explored by Nair, and whether both groups occupy the same socio-political space merely by virtue of not being white.

Bell Hooks, in her highly insightful book *Yearning*: *Race Gender and Cultural Politics,* critiques the ways in which post-colonial discourses as they have developed in the West implicate only the West and thus 'obscures the colonizing relationship of the East in relation to Africa and other parts of the Western world'. Her basic point is that people often seem to forget how Third World nationals are guilty of 'contempt and disrespect for blackness'[9] in exactly the same way as Western imperialism is. *Mississippi Masala* attempts to critique precisely this form of racist contempt that Indians have towards African Americans.

Mississippi Masala opens with scences from Uganda. Jai (Roshan Seth) and his Ugandan friend Okelo have been stopped by the police. Jai is arrested but is released after his friend bribes a policeman by risking his own life. The background to all this is the decision to banish Asians from Uganda following Idi Amin's rise to power. The trauma of leaving Uganda hangs over Jai's family. The night before their departure, we witness a conversation/argument between Jai and Okelo. Okelo tells Jai explicitly 'Uganda is for Africans, for black Africans only.'

At the bus station in Kampala, Okelo comes to see off the family. Kinu (Sharmila Tagore) and Meena (Sarita Chowdhary) bid him a warm farewell, but Jai gives him a cold shoulder. On the way to the airport, the bus is stopped by the military and Kinu is asked to step out. Opening her suitcase, she is asked to play the cassette player she is carrying. A popular old song from a Raj Kapoor film is heard. The words are:

> My shoes are from Japan,
> My trousers from England,
> My red cap is Russian, yet
> My heart remains Indian.....

The song seems to set the tone for the tension that follows in the film, yet, I would say retains a sort of ambiguity that prevents the audience from deconstructing the real significance of the words. I shall come back to this point later. The film now changes both space and time through the use of camera movement across a world map. We are now in Mississippi, in the Southern United States, and to be precise in a grocery store. Meena is introduced in this sequence, now grown-up, looking frustrated and irritated, shopping with her aunt.

The film then develops the various themes that organize it—the emerging relationship between Demetrius (Denzel Washington) and Meena (which is set off by a road accident caused by Meena involving Demetrius)—the world of the Indian community, in this case Gujarati small businessmen. Through various incidents, Nair develops what she sees as the insularity of both communities (Indian and African-American) and the tensions developing when Meena and Demetrius' affair is exposed. Portraits of socialization within each community are provided: in the case of the Indian motel business, the nostaligic and often quixotic gatherings of Gujaratis; in the case of African-Americans, Nair tries to examine the dynamics of the black family in the Deep South. Whites remain in the background in the film, functioning only as particular power-brokers — they are the police, lawyers or bankers. For Jai and his family, Africa remains the site of Utopian yearnings and a vantage point to shape present actions. Nair uses dream sequences and flashbacks of the African segments to provide a commentary on the social issues in the film, particularly that of race. As we shall see, this raises not inconsiderable problems in her approach to *power* in the film.

Nair ends the film with a resolution of the Utopian yearning expressed in the film—that of Jai to return to Uganda to get his property back, and of Meena and Demetrius to be together. The latter is done quite simply by Meena leaving Mississippi with Demetrius, thus breaking the boundaries of community. In the case of Jai, his return to Uganda produces the opposite effect of his earlier hopes, he is now convinced that his future lies in Mississippi, for 'home is where the heart is'.

I maintain that it is imperative to examine the politics of *power* in the film. This is so far the following reasons. Given that Nair's is a 'social' film, it is impossible to exclude power considerations from an analysis of the film, even within the guidelines laid down by the film-maker herself. Further, there *is* a subtle narrative of *power* in the film, deployed through the themes of migration and ethincity across the two continents.

Nair's apparent insensitivity to realities of power are most obvious in the Ugandan segments. The Indian community is largely portrayed as a hard working group of former slaves[10] under attack by a chauvinist military dictator. The class character of the Indian community is never examined fully. Indian characters occupy the space of white characters without any problems. The sentimental goodbyes of the Indian community to their African servants recalls the nostaligia of white colonial elites when departing from Africa and Asia. Nair's commitment to the Indian community in Uganda is so complete that she does not hesitate to use stereotypical images in the film.

Consider for example the sequence in which Kinu is forced off the bus by Ugandan soliders. The soliders are shown as threatening Kinu's regulated sexuality — by tearing off her *mangal sutra*, they display utter contempt for her domestic order. It is interesting however that the brutality and threatening sexuality of the soldiers is contrasted to the shifty eyed wimpiness of the Indians. The chauvinism and intolerance of the solidiers is contrasted to the internationlism of the Indians as the song makes clear. Even the final sequence of the film displays Nair's blindness to power relations in Africa. Jai's emotional journey back recalls the pulpy Raj nostalgia of the 1980s British Television shows occupying the space of the former colonial ruler. Jai returns to memories of former golden days and significantly to his old mansion now gone to seed under the Africans. The parallels with nostalgic journeys of former colonizers is so obvious that it is surprising that a film-maker of Nair's status has chosen to portray it so unreflexively.

GENDER AND IDENTITY

If the feminist movement in the West attempts to focus on female experience in order to change their lives, African women are pushed into a dilemma. Black women are disadvantaged in several ways: as blacks they are victims with their men of white patriarchal culture; as women they have to face the sexism and victimization of black men; and as black women they face exploitation on racial, sexual and class grounds by white men. In such a situation even the homeplace which was considered subversive at one point is getting undermined. Says Bell Hooks,

> Throughout our history, African/Americans have recognized the subversive value of homeplace, of having access to private space where we do not directly encounter white racist aggression. Whatever the shape and direction of black liberation struggle, domestic space has been a crucial site of resistance ..... That liberatory struggle has been seriously undermined by contemporary efforts to change that subversive homeplace into a site of partriarchal domination of black women by black men, where we abuse one another for not conforming to sexist norms.[11]

Hooks' position here seems to present a critique of essentialist positions of cultural nationalism which do not question the position of women within black culture. In *Mississippi Masala*, Nair constructs the black family and its domestic space in such a way that leads to questionable results.

The audience is introduced to Demetrius' family through a family lunch gathering organized for the father's birthday. Meena is invited to this party and so we encounter the domestic space of this black family through an invited guest, Meena. The only two black women we see in the film are Demetrius' aunt and his ex-girlfriend, Alicia. The aunt is the powerful one in the domestic space, yet she is desexualized and neutralized by virtue of being single. Since the woman in the family, i.e. the mother, is a missing member, one is able to overlook the patriarchal structures and relationship within the family.

Meena however is constructed as the sexually desirable character in the film and is contrasted to Alicia (Demetrius' ex-girlfriend). In fact Alicia puts off the audience so much by her 'overdetermined' sexuality that one cannot help but constantly compare her to Meena. Meena is the desiring subject who can freely assert sexual agency in this case by having a sexual relationship with a black man. As Bell Hooks says, these forms of representation are

> a continuation of the notion that ending racist domination is really about issues of interracial sexual access; a myth that must be critiqued so that this society can confront the actual material, economic and moral consequences of perpetuating white supremacy and its traumatic genocidal impact on black people.[12]

What then does the film have to say about the relationship between racial oppression, the aspiration of their black male protagonists and the social and sexual dynamics of the black family? The construction of emblematic black figures needs to be seen in relation to a series of prior constructions of southern Black social relations where women have been represented as either powerless or repressive (focussing on the imperilled masculinity of black men). The virility of Demetrius is a constant in the entire film, beginning with the expression of his unregulated sexuality in the early dance sequence in the bar—this is contrasted with the inability of Meena's Indian date to perform similarly. Indian men are shown as sexually incapable in the film—witness Meena's cousin Anil's pathetic attempts to enaged in sex with his bride. That this opposition between virile African/Americans and sexually limited Indians goes on to reinforce images of the alleged threatening sexuality of black men is obvious, it also however continues the recurring theme of 'feminizing' Asian men in Western cinema.

The romantic interludes between Demetrius and Meena are all performed in private space without any intrusion of the public. For example after the lunch, Demetrius and Meena walk on a beach that is totally barren. To that extent Nair is right, showing how any form of sensual relationship between these two can occur *only* outside the framework of the racial structures of American society, yet this choice allows her to avoid the complexity of the relationship where the question of both race and tradition would necessarily be affecting the perceptions of both Meena and Demetrius. Even when the two of them spend a day together, there is no effort made to contextualize this relationship through any discussion between them. We only see them on a giant wheel looking happy and then in bed. At this point, Nair tries to half-heartedly come to terms with Meena's sexual confrontation through a dream sequence from Africa, but unfortunately leaves it at that. The implications of this are not explored in further sequences.

TRADITION, MODERNITY AND COMMUNITY

In an essay titled "Post-Coloniality and the Artifice of history: Who speaks for "Indian" pasts", Dipesh Chakravarty talks about the self division of the colonial subject. In his own words:

> A historical construction of temporality (medieval/modern, separated by historical limits) in other words is precisely the axis along which the colonial subject splits itself. Or to put it differently this split is what is history; writing history is performing this split over and over again.[13]

Particularly when it comes to the construction of 'Indian womanhood' this tension between tradition and modernity becomes explicitly clear. Like other anti colonial struggles, gender and sexuality were areas of confrontation between nationalism and colonialism. The woman's body became the site of nationalist discourse. The sexual economy of 19th century English imperialism was well articulated within the cultural sphere of Indian nationalism through a combination of the themes of nationalist modernization and upper-caste cultural fears of female sexual energy and subaltern stirrings. Nationalist mythology portrayed Indian 'womanhood' as but the expression of an eternal and spiritualized past — the Indian woman, in contrast to her Western counterpart, was the repository of sexual submissiveness and an inner spirituality.[14] As Sangari and Vaid suggest,

> Both tradition and modernity have been in India carriers of patriarchal ideologies. As such neither is available to us in a value free or unproblematic self, nor is either, as they are usually conceptualized, necessarily the solution... Both tradition and modernity are eminently colonial constructs. We think it is time to dismantle the opposition altogether and to look at cultural processes in their actual complexity.[15]

This is precisely what Nair avoids in her film. There seems to be an effort to pose tradition and modernity as binary opposites. By doing this Nair falls into a linear and teleological trap of perceiving tradition as a static formation in conflict with a dynamic and constantly changing modernity. The imaging of women in *Mississippi Masala* offers a series of examples where Nair refuses to see tradition as being re-invented within the context of modernity.

Within many groups of women in India, individuality and morality has evolved through joint rather than individual action. Thus the concern with "tradition" articulates itself through much of their lives. Excluded from the hope of any inclusion in the public space in society, middle and upper class Indian women were placed outside the locations of power and authority. Hence, they pursued moral activity and a group identity in terms of family and religion, creating 'tradition' as a form of individuality, recognizing their own agency as based on interdependence.

The representation of Indian women in *Mississippi Masala* leads to notions that do not question the very tightrope on which most of these women tread. Out of the seven women we see in the film, fiver are Indians. Kinu, the mother is the typical 'spiritual' Indian woman, a carrier of tradition who reproaches her husband for not realizing that Meena is a girl who has come of age. Kinu wants her daughter to go our with Harry Patel (they meet at the marriage party and go to a bar from there) and settle down to a married life. A point to be noted here is that the father is shown to express his concern about Meena's education in the form of a pathetic sentimental conversation between him and Meena at a restaurant where the father says 'you are too intelligent to be cleaning bathrooms' and her reply to that is 'Pa there's nothing wrong in cleaning bathrooms'. The concerns of the mother are very 'typical'—to ensure that her daughter remains within the community and household, not straying too far in the public sphere. In the sequence near the swimming pool at night, Kinu affectionately caresses her daughter's hair and asks her how her date with Harry Patel went. Nair's use of sentimental music as well as the soft-lighting adds to the significance of the scene. In a later sequence, after Meena is brought home from the lockup, it is again Kinu who feels its important for her to know the family of the person Meena loves.

The other two women in the film are the "gossip" women at the marriage reception, then the aunt who irritates Meena at a grocery store and in the car that leads to the accident. By using images like this in the film, Nair not only reinforces notions of 'Indian' womanhood but projects them as a representative slice of India—an India that is 'static' 'timeless' and 'eternal'. Since most of the women appear in the film as 'individuals' responsible for their own actions and therefore to be blamed, the morality of *Mississippi Masala* constructs the autonomous individual who is supposed to be free of socio-historical constraints with no restrictions of group or hierarchy. The flip side of this argument is Meena's action, who as another autonomous individual is able to act 'progressively' according to the dictates of her conscience.

In dealing with the marginalization of Indian women, it is crucial to reiterate that all marginality is not the same—gender, caste and class create different experiences of marginality shaping different regimes of moral and political agency. Women's marginality is not a 'universal'. The history of Indian women shows that moral identity and action can be explained only through an understanding of historical experience, revealing its complexity in relation to many variables. Only by re-examining the historical context of women's location within different groups, can we hope, see and understand the social and moral values that these women created.

Mississippi Masala in that sense has the quality of a colonized/ voyeuristic gaze to use Stam and Spence's formulation that denies women living in a different society, their own realities, their own experiences in the construction of gender and sexuality. While on no account am I proposing cultural relativism as an answer since that transforms the world into unlike and distinct spaces/areas of investigation, nevertheless the views expressed in the film should have been articulated as 'situated' opinions and not as universal truths spoken from the vantage point of a more 'advanced', 'modern' and 'developed' society.

Nair's positioning and her construction of binary oppositions (tradition/modernity—archaic/modern) leads, in view of the hegemonic position of the context of her production (U.S), to a hierarchical, patronizing and distant attitude towards women in the Third World. Her basic point ultimately seems to be to show how far behind 'they' (Indians) are in their attitudes from the 'modern' values of the West. While this critique may seem a bit harsh, it is consistent with the approach she has taken in almost all her films.

For example, Meena is constructed as the exception since her only connection with India is through her parents. Her radical shift and departure from the context of other Indian women is ascribed to the fact that she grew up in the West. In the confrontation with her parents after she is discovered with Demetrius, it is Meena who says 'This is America Ma, no one cares'.[16] Apart from the fact that this statement is itself misplaced, Meena's change is seen to be the result of 'Western' and 'modern' ideas that one obviously encounters in 'advanced' societies of the Western world. What Nair fails to recognize here is that Meena as an Indian woman is tormented by the burden of knowing that she is deprived of her rights by sexist attitudes in the domestic domain and by western patriarchy and racism in the public sphere.

In *Mississippi Masla*, Nair's playing with the issues of identity, desire and choice, leads her to a kind of essentialism that turns the project of the film to an a-historical understanding of race, sexuality and in the Indian case, caste. I do believe Utopian visions need to be taken seriously if we are to transcend the boundaries of contemporary society. But this

Utopia cannot be situated outside history (as in both of Nair's endings - one in Africa with Jai happily embracing an African child, the other a sequence showing Meena and Demetrius dancing in the cotton-fields of the South) since it is only through history that the issues of race and sexuality have any meaning. Harsh though it may sound, *Mississippi Masala* in the final analysis ends up being a sentimental, harmless piece of international libertarianism.

In recent years cultural establishments in the West have eargerly promoted films like *Salaam Bombay* and *Mississippi Masala* as genuine alternatives to critical Third World Cinema. While nineteenth century Orientalism was informed by what Said calls a necessary distance from the area in question- the Orient, the late twentieth century phenomenon however is not always mediated by semi-literate colonial ideologues, but by Westernized Third World elites. The advantage of such a discourse is obvious. It is presented as a legitimate voice of the Occident's 'civilizational other', unaccompanied by a critical analysis of social change and struggle.

NOTES

1. Derek Malcolm. 'Lessons of the Street', *Cinema in India* July-Sept. 1988:39
2. *Ways of Seeing* BBC and Penguin; London: 1977: 104
3. Interview with Mira Nair in *Cinema India International,* Vol. V no. 3:1988.
4. 'Colonialism Racism and Representation: an Introduction' in Bill Nichols (ed.), *Movies and Methods,* UC Press; Berkley, Los Angeles and London : 636.
5. David Robinson, *The Times London.*
6. Brad Kessler, *Interview* Magazine at the Cannes festival, Sept. 1988.
7. Sheila Benson *Los Angeles Times* 19 Oct. 1988.
8. Peter Rainer, *Los Angeles Herald Examiner*, Oct. 1988.
9. South End Press: Boston: 1990: 93.
10. The allusion to Indians being former slaves is empirically wrong. Indians were brought into Uganda by the British to play the part of petty-bourgeois, to provide small shops and services to Africans. Only in South Africa were Indians brought to work on the railroads.
11. Op. cit., *Yearning*: 47.
12. Ibid.
13. See his 'Post-Coloniality and the Artifice of History : Who Speaks for "Indian Pasts", in *Representation* no. 37, Winter 1992.
14. 'The Nationalist Resolution of the Women's Question by Partha Chatterjee, in Kumkum Sangari and Sudesh Vaid (eds.) *Recasting Women, Kali* : New Delhi 1989.
15. Ibid : Introduction.
16. This is of course silly. To claim that people in the US are relatively unaffected by inter-racial relationships is an understatement, to say the least.

GERHARD KOCH

Franz Osten: From Munich Cinema to Bombay Talkies

Translated from German by Jyoti Sabharwal

If one were to consult books on German cinema, references to Franz Osten would be very rare. Yet this Munich born director's contribution to early Indian cinema was invaluable. Born on 23 December 1876, Franz Osten who wanted to become a theatre actor, started his training as a photographer. His father considered this to be useful, in case his son's career as an actor failed. In 1907 Osten founded the Original Physograph Company with his younger brother and produced a number of short films that established his reputation as a cinematographer. Between 1909 and 1911 he was active as an actor and director. He acted in *Die Wahrheit* (The Truth) and also directed his first full length feature film, *Erna Valeska*. The First World War disrupted his career temporarily. He resumed it again when he became the director of Emelka Company in Munich. It was his success as the director of Indo-German films, that was the high point of his career in the world of cinema.

His Indian career from 1935 to 1939 saw him directing sixteen films for the Bombay Talkies. The major works during the silent era in Bombay films were the *Light of Asia* (1925), *Shiraz* (1928) and *Throw of Dice* (1928-29). But it was *Achut Kanya* produced by the Bombay Talkies in 1936 that is considered a masterpiece on account of its storyline, histrionics and cinematography. Thus Osten played a pioneering role in the development of German cinema in the silent era and in India in the early years of the sound era. It was during the filming of *Kangan* that his career as director in Indian cinema was abruptly cut short when the British interned him at the outbreak of the Second World War. He returned to Germany but after a brief stint with the Bavaria Film Company, retired to Bad Aibling near Munich to manage a spa till his death in 1956.

Along with works on film history and the source mentioned in the text (magazines like *Film India*, *Filmfare, Cinema Vision, Lichtspielbuehn* and the *Report of the Indian Cinematograph Committee*, 1927-8), the author referred to the biodata of Franz Osten (Berlin Document Centre) and other private documents (of Ellen Osten, Bad Aibling and Mukul Roy, Calcutta) as well as interviews he conducted in 1982-3 with Amulya Bannerjee, Nimai Ghosh, Sasadhar Mukherjee, Devika Rani and Ashok Kumar in India.

Translator

German film makers made major contributions to the Indian film industry when it was still in its incipient stage in the thirties. Yet this aspect of Indo-German cultural relations has been completely overshadowed by the focus on Indology in Germany. During the era of the silent films and the early years of the Talkies, Indian film makers visited Germany to acquire the necessary know-how in German Studios since they were cheaper than the studios in the USA. They included directors such as V. Shantaram, Mohun Bhavanani and the producer N.D. Gandhi. On the other hand, the reverse path was struck by people like Paul Zils, who exercised a great influence on the Indian documentary film of the forties and fifties, the cameraman Emil Schünemann and the author Willy Haas who took to scriptwriting while in exile in India during the Second World War. Yet, the most important contribution to the development of the Indian film industry, was made by the director, Franz Osten-Ostermayr (1876-1956) whose involvement as a cameraman and director, is closely associated with the early years of Munich's film history.

Franz Osten along with his brothers, Peter and Ottmar Ostermayr, were pioneers in the field of cinema in southern Germany. In 1907 itself, the French companies Gaumont, Pathe and Eclair bought Osten's 'landscape films'. A year later, he filmed events in Munich and Bavaria for the *Pathe Journal* and the *Gaumont Week*. However, Osten worked as a director for a feature film (Erna Valewska) for the first time in 1911.

An important landmark in Munich's film history was the establishment of the Munich Society for Cinematography (Emelka) in 1919 on the initiative of Peter Ostermayr. Soon after, the foundation of the Film City, Geiselgasteig, was laid. The Emelka, rapidly developed as a counterpart to the Berlin based Ufa.[1] From 1924 onwards, the German film industry went into an economic crisis. The Emelka, however, did not suffer. During this period, an advocate, Himanshu Ray (1892-1940) came to Munich from England to tap the Emelka directorate for diverse film related activities. He planned a series of films on the lives of the founders of great religions. The Passion plays of Oberammergau, provided a model for the film made on Jesus. The Emelka, decided in favour of the film proposed on the life of Gautam Buddha. They felt it would be appropriate for a period which was marked by a fascination for qualities of leadership and healing therapies. After the end of the First World War, in Germany, Indian themes acquired great appeal both, on the screen and in literature. Joe May, made a film based on Thea von Harbous' novel, The Indian Grave in 1921; Hermann Hesse's *Siddhartha* was published in 1922, Paul Wegener, in 1924; directed the occult film, *Living Buddhas*. Ernst Lubitsch who had already filmed in 1920, an Oriental theme in *Sumurun*, was toying with the idea of making a film on Gautam Buddha, in 1927.

Emelka's decision was also influenced by the fact that Himanshu Ray had thoroughly planned his films. Financial and technical aid from Germany, was to put the fledgling film industry on its feet. Thanks to Himanshu Ray, India entered the international film arena. He was also instrumental in providing the Munich producers, the necessary know-how to create an authentic film on India, which, till now, had never been seen in German cinema halls. According to the contract, Ray had to select a team of Indian actors and arrange the requisite permission to shoot at Indian locales.

The Buddha film, *The Light of Asia* (*Prem Sanyas,* 1925) was to become, the first international co-production in the history of Indian cinema. Franz Osten, who in the meantime, had been promoted to the rank of chief director of the Emelka, directed this film. On his shooting trip to India in 1925, he was accompanied by the cameraman, Willi Kiermeier, Josef Wirsching and the folk actor Bertl Schultes from Tegernsee, who also had to act as assistant director and interpreter. While in India, Franz Osten wrote many articles for German film magazines. The accounts of his directional ventures in Jaipur, contain a rather bizarre description of a crowd scene. The extras would flee repeatedly to a shady place, to protect themselves from the scorching sun, and Osten had to seek the help of baton-wielding policemen to drive the crowd of thousands, to the front of the camera for the sake of directorial perfection.

The *Light of Asia*, shows primarily, Buddhas's childhood and youth at the palace of his father, where he grew up protected from all the inequities and injustices of life, to then one day, renounce the world when confronted with illness, poverty, old age and death. Buddha renounces his carefree life to become a wandering mendicant in his quest for truth. His spiritual biography is traced in the film with sequences which are very similar to Ufa-Cultural films of the twenties. For instance, the festive processions with caparisoned elephants, competitive games or the depiction of the rituals at Buddha's marriage to Gopa. The German film critics, highly acclaimed the authenticity of these scences. Blinded by the visual magnificence, very few realized that the film had conveniently circumvented historical facts. The most optically attractive elements were sifted out of India's thousand year old cultural tradition and pasted together. Hence, Buddha, who lived five hundred years before Christ, is shown in the film to spend his childhood and youth, in the court of a

Mughal king of the seventeenth century. This anachronistic architecture is incongrugent with the costumes worn during Buddha's marriage, which correspond to traditional Bengali marriage attire. Similar incongruities are noticeable in the outdoor sets. Disparate regions of India are shown as contiguous. Though marred by historical inconsistencies and flaws, the viewers accepted the film as an authentic depiction of historical India. The panoramic scenes depicting Indian tradition as well as the histrionic accomplishments of the Indians—especially that of Himanshu Ray, who played the role of Buddha—made the film a great success in Germany and other European countries. The director, Franz Osten was celebrated by the press as the "flag bearer" of German industry and achievement and the harbinger of German cinematic art to the international arena (Lichtbildbuehne Nr. 216/1925 p. 2).

However, Himanshu Ray's high expectations of this first Indo-German co-production remained unfulfilled. The failure of the film in India, cannot be attributed just, to its style which the Indian critics considered frivolous. It appears to be related to the sociological realities of the Indian cinema of the twenties. The elite audience, whom Himanshu Ray wanted to reach with this film to procure funds for future projects, was tuned to American and English films. Films with Indian themes and Indian actors used to run only in shabby, cheap cinema halls frequented by the lower classes shunned by the upper classes for reasons of hygiene. The poorer viewers perceived the film as too difficult and lengthy. This was attributed to the paucity of fast action sequences and the use of poetic language, influenced by Edwin Arnold's poem, *The Light of Asia* (1879). This provided the model for the script writer, Niranjan Pal. In India the film could not even break even.

By the time the film was premiered in October 1925 in Munich, Franz Osten and Himanshu, Ray planned to make another film using the same recipe: an Indian story enacted by Indian actors, filmed in India with German techinicians under the direction of Franz Osten. However, financial uncertainties led to a break up with the Emelka and the production contract was ultimately signed with the Ufa. In July 1928 the Ufa directorate started enquiry into the making of the film entitled, *Monument to a Great Love* (to be produced under the title *Shiraz*). At this time Franz Osten wrote to his friends. "The direction is very happy, the film is first class and all people have my congratulation..... I am very happy, this is the second India film, was go in all kontri from the world." [sic]

At the centre of the film's story, is a triangular relationship where the death of the woman loved by two men leads to the construction of a grave which went down in history as the Taj Mahal. The cinematic quality of the film is such that no other Indian film of the twenties had reached such standards. This can largely be attributed to the cameraman Emil Schuenemann, whom Leni Riefenstahl had wooed in vain for the filming of her NS propaganda film, *The Triumph of the Will* in 1934.

The acting career of Charu Roy, who had earlier worked as costume designer for the Buddha film, began with the film *Shiraz* (*Monument to a Great Love*) where he plays the role of Shah Jahan. After learning the ropes from Osten he started directing films himself. Satyajit Ray considered Charu Roy as one of the few serious directors of the early Bengali cinema. The Indian film historians attribute Charu Ray's first feature film, *The Loves of a Mughal Prince* as testimony to the close relationship between Charu Roy and Franz Osten, it was filmed in 1928 in the old historical quarters of Lahore. Charu Roy's impressive presentation of Shahjahan is also noteworthy. But the public had problems accepting him as a Mughal king because of his dark skin colour. When the film was screened in Patna, the public picketed the screen because they were unable to accept dark a complexioned Shah Jahan. On the other hand, this public reaction shows that despite all their fairy tale qualities, Osten tried to be realistic in his silent films; for instance, sparse use of make—up depicted the Indians in their natural skin complexion. This technique, not used in Indian cinema till the 1950s. The Madras based Indian director, Nimai Ghosh, one of the pioneers of the realistic films in India, still draws inspiration from Osten's silent films.

Towards the end of the twenties, Himanshu Ray and Franz Osten planned two more feature films. The first, *A Throw of Dice* (*Parapanachapash*) was shown in the movie halls in August 1929. The second project, *Vasantasena*—based on the Sanskrit drama of Sudraka, a drama which had had several German adaptations including that of Lion Feuchtwanger's—flopped because German studious had switched over to the talkies. These Indo-German silent film productions were assessed differently in India and Germany. A detailed account of this given in a document of the situation of the Indian film and cinematography of the twenties. This account was published in the series, commissioned in 1927 by the English colonial government. In this astounding report covering the early history of Indian cinema, a special place is accorded to the films: *The Light of Asia* and *Shiraz*. Both these films were treated as models to analyse the pros and cons of international co-productions by the Indian film industry. Himanshu Ray gave the committee a detailed account of his experiences with the Emelka and the Ufa. He strongly recommended that Indian technicians be trained in German studious, but he failed to convince the majority of the committee members, largely due to inopportune timing. *Shiraz* was still under production and from the Buddha film, the foreigners had kept a chunk of the profit for themselves. A few months later *Shiraz* was shown for weeks in the cinema halls of Bombay and Calcutta. The movie, *A Throw of Dice*, met with similar success a year later.

Franz Osten and Himanshu Ray parted ways after the *Vasantasena* project failed to take off. The former devoted his energies to make a series of 'Heimat films'[2] in Germany, while the latter wholeheartedly applied himself to improve the quality of Indian films by entering into international co-productions. In collaboration with the German cameraman Emil Schunemann and the English director J.L.F. Hunt, he produced India's first English language talkie, *Karma,* along with its Hindi version. The commerical success of this film in England enabled Himanshu Ray to fullfil his long standing dream of setting up his own studio in India. In 1934 he established the Bombay Talkies Studios and collaborated with German technicians to ensure the techincal quality of his films.

His success as a film maker lured back Franz Osten to India. This time he was accompanied by the cameraman Josef Wirsching, a laboratory technician, Wilhelm Zelle and set designer, Karl Graf von Spreti. In 1970 von Spreti's name appeared in the media in a totally different context. After the War, he embarked on a political career and when serving as German ambassador to Guatemala he was kidnapped and murdered by terrorists.

From 1935 to 1938-9 the triumvirate of Osten, von Spreti and Wirsching was synonymous with the Bombay Talkies, influencing its cinematic and commercial development.

A villa in Bombay's Malad area housed one of the most modern film studios in India, training more than 400 members according to a time and work schedule far too rigorous for Indian conditions. In turn, the members of the studio reaped the benefits of an all encompassing, systematic training in all aspects of film making. Many well known denizens of the Hindi film industry, were products of this studio: the actors Ashok Kumar, Leela Chitnis, Raj Kapoor, Najmul Hussain, Dilip Kumar; the script writer-cum-director K.A. Abbas; the influential producer, Sasadhar Mukherjee who started his film career under Franz Osten as a sound technician. Dwelling on Osten's relationship with the Bombay film industry, Mukherjee said, 'He was our guru, all of us learnt from him! Unfortunately Himanshu Ray's experiment did not elicit the expected response. The press in particular was vitriolic against the German 'guest workers'. The magazine, *Film India* was to express it in—the following manner at the beginning of 1936:

A year ago a big production was launched amidst great fanfare, employing a bevy of German experts, with their wives and children at salaries high enough to sustain fifty times the number of Indians. At that time we were evasively informed, that the foreign experts had been employed to train Indian personnel. Since then a year has elapsed yet no one has been trained so far! What is actually going on? Are we so bereft of indigenous talent that we have to import it into the country? .... *Foreigners out! should be the slogan of all producers who still have some vestiges of moral strength and self respect left in them.* (Film India, Bombay, September 1938, p.2)

This early skepticism, however, was to change into recognition and admiration once the first few films of the Bombay Talkies were completed. Within a short span of time, the Bombay Talkies studio, developed into a premier institution of the Indian cinema of the thirties. Its only serious rivals were, the Prabhat Film Company of Pune and New Theatres of Calcutta. But the production styles of these three varied distinctly from one another. The Prabhat Film Company made a name for itself through the production of popular mythological films, whereas, the New Theatre films were marked by intellectual experimentation. The productions of both these studios, had their share of hindrances and problems to contend with, while the Bombay Talkies films were slated from the beginning to be successful. A technically up to date infrastructure and professionally trained personnel formed the basis for a production system, which was regarded by contemporaries as 'American'. The validity of this impression can be corroborated by facts: within four Years, sixteen films were produced. All had the same director, (Franz Osten), the same cameraman (Josef Wirsching) and the same music composer (Saraswati Devi). Twelve films were produced with the same heroine (Devika Rani), ten had the same set designer (Karl von Spreti) and eight films had the same script writer (Niranjan Pal). This team was difficult to beat for its prolificacy and efficiency.

The commercial success of the Bombay Talkies films can be attributed to many factors. They had a marked edge over their competitiors' productions because of superior technical quality. Moreover, they set new standards of photography, editing and sound quality. This proved the point, that Western quality could be maintained despite the rigours of Indian conditions. Franz Osten, who directed about forty films, devoted himself to depict the plot sequences more realistically than in other Indian productions. However, the main attraction of these films was the actress, Devika Rani, whose success hinged not just on the photographic skill of Joseph Wirsching but to the meticulous marketing strategy of her husband Himanshu Ray.

In her appearance as well as in her lineage, Devika Rani, was vastly different from the contemporary Indian heroines. Most of the actresses of that period, were recruited largely from houses of pleasure, since the roles offered in films did not correspond to the traditional image of the Indian woman. Devika Rani, came from a well known upper caste Brahmin family of Calcutta. Her father was an army doctor and her uncle, Rabindranath Tagore, a Nobel prize laureate for literature in 1913. She also worked as costume designer for *A Throw of Dice*. After its completion in the Ufa studio, Neubabelsberg, she took acting classes in 1929-30 from G.W. Pabst. With her virginal charm, Devika Rani, who in her appearance had nothing in common with the recruits from the pleasure homes, managed to seduce the audiences completely. For the daughters of India's upper classes she became the role model. In the thirties, they flocked to the cinema halls to see her films.

What kind of films did Franz Osten make for the Bombay Talkies? *Film Indian,* the critical chronical of the Bombay Talkies, sums up the popular Hindi film of the late thirties as follows:

40 per cent song and dance sequences.
10 per cent technical stunts.

The films of the Bombay Talkies were also made according to this formula, yet Himanshu Ray always strove to use the popular film as a medium to portray socially relevant themes. Inspired by the Indian reformers of the thirties, he came to regard cinema as a vehicle for social change in India. Along with Mahatma Gandhi's philosophy and his mass movements, Jawaharlal Nehru's socialist views had a great impact not only on Himanshu Ray but on other film producers as well. The Indian film of the thirties, responded more readily and purposefully to the prevalent political trends than the other art forms, still fettered by centuries' old traditions. Thus, the incorporation of socio-critical elements led to the creation of 'Hindi socials'.

In this category fall Osten's sixteen, sound films, for they are in consonance with Himanshu Ray's didactic aims of spreading the message of the reformers. While Osten's silent films excelled as technical high quality entertainers, striving to capture the international market, his sound films were specially created for the Indian audience situated in a very specific historical constellation.

These films, take up socially relevant problems related to the caste system and its impact on traditional Hindu society. The favourite scene of action of these films was the Indian village and the main theme centred around the conflict between the 'modern' love marriage and the 'traditional' arranged marriage. Since the love marriage defied all the taboos and social norms of a caste ridden society, it represented a challenge that had to be curbed on all accounts. On the other hand the arranged marriage was shown to establish and perpetuate the ***status quo*** where the caste system is meticulously followed and social injustice prevents equitable distribution of material wealth. The proponents and beneficiaries of this decadent tradition (priests, moneylenders and charlatans) collaborate with the social pillars of corruption (administrators, police and the judiciary) to prevent the village from becoming an idyll. These representatives of the old order are met with resistance from the new forces of changes embodied by the youth, striving to do away with the falsehood of tradition. The message of the films is clear those who want to contribute to the development of a new nation should go to rural India as doctors or teachers. The Bombay Talkies' heroes are conspicuous by their academic qualifications.

No other theme, could compare with that of love and marriage to propagate the ideology of the reformers effectively. Yet, the criticism of social reality was mellowed down, so as not to offend the financiers, who were members of Bombay's influential commercial world and certainly not eager to change the status quo. The other restraining factor was the fear of censorship by the colonial state which equated social criticism in cinema with anti-colonial tendencies. To some extent, their fears were not unfounded, since the aims of the reformers were entwined with those of the national freedom movement. Through social reform, an effort was made to prove to the world that the Indians were ready for their independence. To circumvent censorship, the films made for their independence. To circumvent censorship, the films made subtle references to the freedom movement which would escape the censors but strike the right note with the viewers. The spinning wheels appeared in the films as part of the rural locale, since most films were set in the villages. The spinning wheel had become synonymous with Gandhi's demand for self governance. His homespun hit out at the British textile industry and the spinning wheel was also the symbol of Nehru's Congress party. It was able to conjure the right associations in the public mind. An ingenious way of evading censorship, is found in the opening scene of the film *Janmabhoomi*, where the last glance of a dying man is fixed on the portraits of Vivekananda, Ramakrishna and Tagore. The film *Navjeevan* made in 1939 shared its title with Gandhi's weekly newspaper. It is a comedy, where a chronic hypochondriac is cured by a magic drug and turns a new leaf. The most famous of Osten's Bombay Talkies films is *Achhut Kanya* (1936). It was adjudged as film of the year in 1937 and served as a model for the early 'Hindi social'. Jawaharlal Nehru praised it and controversial recognition was accorded by Germany. While on a holiday to Germany in 1937 Osten screened the film in Goebbels's propaganda ministry. Hitler, subsequently, cabled his best wishes to the Bombay Talkies although he was an admirer of British rule in India.

In *Achhut Kanya*, the flashback is used to narrate the story of a melodramatic love between the untouchable Kasturi, daughter of a railway gangsman and her childhood sweetheart Pratap, the son of a Brahmin merchant. A mob torches the house of the Brahmin when rumours of his friendship with Kasturi's father are confirmed. Bowing to family pressures, Kasturi and Pratap marry according to parental wishes. The caste hierarchies are thus maintained, but their love for one another cannot be suppressed. In the final climax, Kasturi throws herself before a train, to prevent her jealous husband and lover who are locked in a fight on the train from killing each other.

With the skilful handling of the suicide of the young woman under the wheels of the locomotive, Osten created the desired shock effect on the audience. The message of the film is further toned down by removing the 'happy end' sequence from the plot. Devika Rani, plays the part of the beautiful untouchable, with all the glamour at her disposal. The fact that neither skin colour nor make up nor dress evoke a resemblance with an untouchable made it possible for orthodox caste Hindus to identify with her.

The protagonist of *Achhut Kanya* is portrayed as a victim of an unjust caste system, while Protima, the heroine of *Janmabhoomi* emerges victorious in her fight against inhuman traditional values and religious bigotry. The opprressed small farmers and agricultural workers rally behind Ajay, a doctor who fights for their rights. In the last scene, the lens is placed at a tilted angle to show the masses march towards a better future, singing, 'Victory to the land of our birth!' The lens creates an uncontainable movement. The film is suffused with patriotic pathos, articulated very strongly in its songs. Particularly dynamic, is the impact of the last chorus, which unlike other song sequences does not end with the film.

Song sequences are an integral part of all these films. Well composed songs, guaranteed success with an audience unable to conceive of a film without 'filmi songs'. These songs helped to depict and intensify, the emotional aspect of a conflict, and often contained an aphoristic commentary of the happenings. In comparison to the early Indian sound movies, marked by an excessive use of songs, ranging up to twenty per film, the Bombay Talkies' movies with their ten songs appeared modest. One can't overlook the fact, that very long song sequences posed, at times, great problems for Franz Osten. His approach to them sometimes appears more schematic than innovative. Only in one film does he try to break the pattern with an unexpected gag. In the film *Jeevan Prabhat* (1937) a young married couple is shown singing a song while rowing in a lake full of lotus flowers. This romantic mood is broken by a visual of a gramophone playing the same song. The use of this device is surprising, since there is no attempt made throughout the film to achieve a distancing effect. Unlike modern Hindi film music, which leans heavily towards

Western disco music, the song compositions were inspired by North Indian classical music, a highly developed form meant for the connoisseur. To achieve congruity with the rural and cater to popular tastes, the highly classical style was simplified to a semi-classical form.

This tendency towards simplification can also be discerned in the language of the Bombay Talkie films. In India, a land of many languages and dialects, the marketability of a film even now depends on the language used. Since Hindi gives access to the majority of the viewers, more than 60 per cent of all Indian films even in the mid-thirties were made in this language. For many the term 'sound film' was synonymous with the term 'Hindi film'. Himanshu Ray shows Hindi (Hindustani, a mixture of Hindi and Urdu) to be the language of his sound films, in order to increase their sales. The Bengali film producer, who did not enjoy a command on the Hindi language, would not pass any script till he had understood every word of it. This practice, resulted in the evolution of a simplified language, which could even guarantee success in the non-Hindi speaking regions of the country. The other films of the Bombay Talkies, were based largely on variations of the films mentioned and described earlier. Characters, who had to incorporate progressive and reactionary forces, were reduced very often to cliched images which could be applied to every village love story. One exception was the film *Bhabi* (1938) which portrays three prevalent images of Indian women. *Savitri* (1937), a film apparently lost, is the only one based on a mythological theme, a variant of the Orpheus myth. Osten was not in a position to influence the choice of the films' themes. He merely directed the scripts, thoroughly worked upon by Himanshu Ray and the script writer Niranjan Pal.

In August 1939, Osten started shooting his last film, *Kangan*. On 3 September, the day England declared war against Germany, Osten and Wirsching were arrested and interned. Karl von Spreti had already returned to Germany in 1938. After seven months of internment, Osten was released on grounds of old age according to the rules of the Geneva Convention. In April 1940, he returned to Germany to take up the post of casting director of the Bavaria Filmkunst in Munich.

Kangan was completed as per schedule by the Indians. The exodus of the Germans, did not affect the quality of the film in any way, wrote Film India with admiration. One hoped to get new creative inputs from the succesors. A year later, Himanshu Ray died. Though the studio established by him, remained successful till 1953, his sudden death in 1940 marked the beginning of the end of this institution, all important in the history of Indian cinema. The next phase was marked by the disintegration of the production team into rival factions and a frequently changing ownership. The spirit of reform was increasingly replaced by that of commerce. After the end of the Second World War, Fŗanz Osten applied his organizational skills in a totally different direction. From 1946 till his death in 1956, the erstwhile director of the Bombay Talkies Studio was employed as the director of the Spa, Bad Aibling.

UFA : (Universum Film AG) One of the biggest German film concerns and importand film production centres of the world. Founded in May 1917, it controlled the destiny of German Gnevna for a few decades thereafter.

CHRONOLOGY OF FRANZ OSTEN'S CINEMATOGRAPHY

Silent Films

1925	*The Light of Asia* (*Prem Sanyas*)
1928	*Shiraz* (*Monument of Great Love*)
1929	*A Throw of Dice* (*Prapancha Pash, Dice of Destiny*)

Talkies

1935	*Jawani Ki Hawa* (*The exuberance of Younth*)
1935/36	*Mamta* (*Maternal Love*)
1935/36	*Always tell your wife*
1936	*Jeevan Nayya* (*The Boad of Love*)
1936	*Achhut Kanya* (*The Untouchable*)
1936	*Janma Bhoomi* (*Homeland*)
1936/37	*Izzat* (*Honour*)
1937	*Prem Kahani* (*Love Story*)
1937	*Savitri*
1937	*Jeevan Prabat* (*The Dawn of Life*)
1938	*Nirmala*
1938	*Vachan* (*Word of Honour*)
1938	*Bhabi* (*Sister-in-law*)
1939	*Nav Jeevan* (*New Life*)
1939	*Durga*
1939	*Kangan* (*The Bracelet*)

BRIGITTE SCHULZE

Subjected Non-Subjects: "Indians" of German Cinema and TV Screens

India has never had full justice done to it, and when I say this I think not only of ancient, but of modern India also. And though it can easily be seen that my chief interest lies with ancient India, it should be remembered that in no other country is the past still so visibly present as in that southernmost home of the ancient family of Aryan speech ..... In India .... the religion of the Veda is by no means entirely extinct. ... I can truly say that there is behind that warm and almost Italian colour of the Aryans of India, the same warm heart, the same trust, and the same love as under the white skin of Europeans. (Max Müller 1899)

Max Müller's well-meaning acknowledgement of "Indians" actually doesn't accept *their* distinctness but their assumed 'aryan' likeness. As non-existent 'they', come to life only through "us", and "we" admire our reflections in/ on "them".

I am carrying out this study of the cinematic iconography and meaning of "Indians" in German cinema and television since last ten years, and it is based on regular videorecordings of the respective television programmes and viewing of most of the films during festivals and/or at archives. Special mention and thanks for a steady and sympathizing support I owe to the present and the former director of the Filmuseum München, Jan-Christopher Horak and Enno Patalas, and to the cinematographic sensitivity of Gerhard Ullmann and Klaus Volkmer.

In most of the films and features viewed by us "Indians" are visually viewed and orally contextualised in manners that are strikingly similar to those of "women". The most important theme is *challenge*. Challenge to the rational world, which has a social and technological order of capitalist civil society along with an uncontrollable and undisciplined psyche and body. Therefore this challenge is posed to imperialists/males in order to act in the name of 'suppressed victims'. The most prominent images of the theme are: spirituality, magic, madness and fanaticism, luring natural beauties, threats to German manliness and establishment of 'order'. These visualised, constantly simmering physical and psychological conflicts are mostly resolved by decisive (male/metropolitan) action and/or by a physical extermination through the self-sacrifice of the ideal 'victim' (preferably female "Indian") and/or by the self-negation through penitential renunciation (preferably male "Indian").

Thus "Indians/women" are catering to the psychological and moral well-being of German societies. "Indian" icons and stereotypes are therefore more than just exotic images and entertaining fantasies. As such they would be amorph, exchangeable and vanishing. But the "Indians" of German silver and TV-screens are a distorted sturdy matter for decades.

I identified a complex mixture of a supposedly widely felt ***need*** for the "Indian" myth rooted in German "Lebenswelten" (outlooks in life) and a specific ***attitude*** to "the Indians" different from other chiffres - consisting of the ambiguous gendered imagery. I start to exemplify this point by looking at oral and visual informations of German television news on the 1996 Lok Sabha elections in India which - as will become clear from the whole analysis - are as ficticional as the fiction films that I will discuss subsequent to the paragraph on TV.

German viewers would understand from the news of April 27, 1996, that India was about to demonstrate to the world what are superlatives in democracy within a timespan of five weeks when about 590 millions would be called to the election booths. The end of the "Nehru-Gandhi Dynasty" and finally of the "Congress (I) era" was discussed, the BJP was introduced as either "fundamentalist Hindu", "fundamentalist" or "nationalist" party. Phoolan Devi, "named as Bandit Queen", was the only candidate out of 14,200 who was given a special coverage.

On April 28 the well-known and supposedly oldest weekly news-magazine of the national first channel (ARD), DER WELTSPIEGEL ('World-Mirror') reported in one of its usual 5 -10 minutes' features on India's elections. The ARD-correspondent to India and his team followed Phoolan Devi, the "Goddess of Flowers" during her election campaign and presented following reports and images: "An air of caste-struggle and violence ... a violence which is centuries old ... and which only rarely someone opposes. In the Mirzapur-Badoi region the myth of Phoolan Devi originated ...The TV-viewer testifies with his/her own eyes sexual harrassments and continuous rapes, "Phoolan Devi" being paraded naked in a village, her return to this place of humiliation and her cruel revenge" .... These images are taken from the highly acclaimed film ***Bandit Queen*** of Shekhar Kapur.

The second channel ZDF followed suit and also topped its visual material with sequences of oppression and sexual harrassment from Kapur's fiction film. The ZDF correspondent Claus Richter knows that "in the eyes of her followers she is the incarnation of Kali, the Goddess of revenge ... Phoolan Devi comes from the Mirzapur Badoi region where women are treated as property of men." Until May 8 to 10 the main public and private channels and ARD, ZDF, VOX, 3 sat, arte, ntv just kept their public informed about what happened on the state's political plain. No background analyses, let alone additional portrayals of any of the other candidates, or of daily lives and ideas of the voters. Finally it was hard to even understand who actually won, and why, and what were the reactions in India.

From the reports' focus on the mythical aspects of Phoolan Devi, it became clear that the sympathies of journalists were with her, but hardly out of solidarity. A self-satisfied 'utterly democratic' (German) viewpoint used Phoolan Devi for presenting her as a paradigmatic *victim* - 'woman', 'low-caste' and 'Indian' - and serve as a witness to an undisputable quality of German democracy. Interestingly enough her oppression is not only put into fitting words, but it is made manifest with the help of highly suggestive images. According to these her oppression is essentially caused by an extremely violent "chauvinism" and by "feudalism". That she had and still has a cause to fight for, at the end, comes under question mark when the correspondent of the ARD points out that she is merely an electoral instrument of Mulayam Singh Yadav.

These oral and visual re-presentations of "Indians" as political subjects who are actually known not as being the 'real' subjects, show a peculiar patronizing attitude. In many cases it is coupled with a widely cultivated air of "our" selflessness and the most selfless advocates of truthful re-presentations of Indians outside India since the Romantics and Max Müller, are the German intellectuals. Today, when the wider German public's curiosity for India and Indians is largely left to the habitual consumption of diverse television programmes, opinions and meanings are largely formed here. The recent agitated debate about Prof. Annemarie Schimmel's understanding of the *fatwa* against Salaman Rushdie is an instructive example of how an (anglicized) Indian is made the object of German public's attention. Schimmel and her critics both argued for an imagined point of view of "Indians" without any real concern for 'them'. A preliminary thesis could identify a peculiar feature of media-ted German attitudes towards Indians as being a patriarchal, self-assuring benevolence, based on the good consciousness of non-materialistic aspirations unspoiled by colonialism. "Indians" as imagined by Germans are preferably populous, immaterial, always caught in contradictory worlds of desires and spirituality and are damned to a self-assertion through self-negation as subservient creatures, revengers or ascetics.

The well known orientalist Schimmel attracted an open-minded and benevolent attention to her statements in the national press and in television.

Her answer to critics, titled "Der unverstandene Islam" ('Misunderstood Islam'), was published in *Frankfurther Allgemeine Zeitung* May 24, 1995, and a 28 minutes' feature of the same title was screened in one of the tv-channels (under public law) shortly before Annemarie Schimmel whould receive the disputed "Friedenspreis des Deutschen Buchhandels" ('Peace-prize of the German book trade') in mid October.

Impressively she manages during the tv feature, which is in fact a telecast portrayal of herself, to propagate an understanding of the diversity of Islamic sects, stressing the shock that especially "Indian Muslims" must have suffered by *The Satanic Verses*. Salman Rushdie as a concrete person dissolves into the offence he allegedly caused to certain religious feelings in Oriental/Islamic worlds, which he is expected to regret.

Usually critical studies on representations of "India/Indians" do accuse the hegemonic media of *"misrepresenting"* India and Indians, transforming them into pervasive ideas, constructs and creatures of dominant histories.

Misrepresentations of that kind are my starting point too, but I won't charge them with not showing realities. Cinema's main concern and purpose is determined by the necessity to realize the invested capital, and its narratives and images often cater to the recreational needs of the audience. I discuss cinema as part of the "Kulturindustrie", and such a discussion can offer instructive insights into the socially important problem of "myth exchange" that it perpetuates: Which images/imaginations are valued on which scale, and why are these so? The cinematic myths are consequently not seen by me as "collective unconsciousness" but, as fitting conscious constructs of a cultural production context—where one side cashes in on the pure lust to see or on existent psychological desires, and the other side longs for entertainment to bear daily chores better, find moral reinforcement, or just have fun.

Accordingly I will analyse features of German cinematic and televisional re-creations of "Indians" since the first decade of this century, and deduce the *necessity of misrepresentation* within the complexities of the emerging modern public sphere of today. To understand the historical beginnings when essential characteristics of how 'Indians' are used as icons of cinematic meanings were shaped, is my main concern here. Those remain the essentials even in today's television, as can be seen from the attitudes towards Indian elections via a mythical Phoolan Devi and political Islam via a mythical Salman Rushdie. In both the cases *the point of view* how one wants to see "it" not only 'kills' the concrete person involved but also distorts the conceptual understanding.

Indische Grabmal, 1921–The pensive "German" heroine
(Courtesy: Filmmuseum München)

The secluded "Indian" woman, 1921
(Courtesy: Filmmuseum München)

Advt. in *Der Kinematograph*, 1917: "India is Trumps"

Advt. in *Der Kinematograph* (27/9/1916)

Responding to the question posed by the editor of *germinal* whether and how representational images of India have reacted to India's definitely different political role after 1947, I would thus state that the objective essence of "Indians" as a chiffre on German silver and tv screens does not show a major shift, but the way these representations cater to subjective moral 'needs' of the public changed according to their respective, historical outlook in life ('Weltbilder'). Consistently the point of reference for "Indian images" was not and is not India but Germany.

A SKETCH OF THE MATERIAL AND MORAL WORLD OF CINEMATIC REPRESENTATIONS OF INDIANS. GERMANY'S SCREENED "INDIANS" ARE PART OF THE HISTORY OF "SENSTATIONAL FILMS" AS A SELF-ASSERTIVE NATIONAL CINEMA

European photography, one of the decisive technoglocial preconditions of the age of mechanical reproduction and the "industrialisation of the gaze" (Scheurer 1987), started around the mid 19th century with a view to explore India's fascinating pictorial richness.

"Benares, the holy city of the Hindus, an excellent documentary, splendid scenes of Indian practices and hitherto unknown customs. First-rate photography—no theatre should miss it!" were the luring words of an advertisement for Raleigh & Roberts' "Pictures from India" in 1911. Those and others on : Delhi, Kashmir, the Maharaja of Baroda's elephant fights, on the fishing grounds of the Maharaja of Kapurthala etc. were a rage until about 1914 (*Der Kinematograph*, September 27, 1911). A variety kind of film programmes, consisting mostly of 'travelogues', 'scientific' piece, 'topicals', one or two 'dramas' and necessarily 'comic', were shown, through which public could even develop a broader outlook in life, watching their Crown prince during his boat-trip along the ghats of Benares (*Der Kinematograph*, April 5, 1911). By 1912 "moving pictures" already mediated decisively between an abstract ruling power and the vast masses and thus helped to develop a subjective spirit of 'citizenship'.

As a result of new technological possibilities, with additional capital willing to be invested into cinema, additional money to be spent on this form of entertainment, and a fierce competition, the short pieces of reproductive or slap-stick nature slowly gave way to more sophisticated narrative forms. But before the long film with its physically and ethically "disciplining effects" (Hiley 1993; Schlüpmann 1996), long 'topicals' played an important role in mobilizing suitable social and political morals while offering a grand spectacle.

In the context of the representation of "Indians" in metropolitan societies one of the most paradigmatic films in displaying imperialist power (Chanan 1980/96, p. 237) to the 'mass' of peoples around the world, were surely those on the great Delhi Durbar of 1911/12.

At first sight its filmic portrayals by Urban, Gaumont, Royal Bioscope (Hiralal Sen) and others, which were appreciated enthusiastically by a world public, were similar to the cranked "moving images" of Curzon's Durbar of 1902/03, an exotic spectacle of "an amazing quarter mile of moving gold, gems and genealogy" (Bottomore 1995).

But the Delhi Durbar 1911/12 taught even a wider public a lesson in the power of cinema as a matured means of propaganda. Urban being His Majesty's, King George V' official cinematographer, offered most splendid (world-) views even in brilliant "Kinemacolor":

> Mr. Urban will certainly bring back to England a pictorial history of the unexampled splendors of the King-Emperor's visit of great vividness and realism. The pomp and ceremony connected with this function will... have a marked effect in impressing the public mind all the world over ... The Durbar films will serve to bind the Fatherland and its Eastern sons closer together, and arouse and develop good-will between nation and nation. (*The Moving Picture News,* December 6, 1911).

The cinema did supposedly present those hegemonic images as 'life' and made the subalterns willingly accept it as amusement within their very concrete daily chores. But cinema actually gave an even stronger 'reality' to the stage-managed confrontation with Indian rulers, who were in the public mind the incarnation of immense oriental wealth and power, subjugating themselves to George V in a 'free' act of their own will - and a worldwide public viewed it with their own eyes.

The "Kinemacolor" film of Urban, a two and half hours' opus was their biggest success ever (Thomas 1969/83 , p. 18), and what can be concluded from the contemporary debates in German dailies and filmmagazines, the Durbar films even created their own reality: A 'cinematic Gaekwar' of Baroda who had allegedly committed a ceremonial faux pas against the King Emperor, and film audiences from London are reported to boo 'cinematic Gaekwar' off the screen (*Das Lichtbild-Theater,* January 18, 1912).

Before World War I we find narrative films, mostly three-reelers or roughtly of half hours length, establish Germany's peculiar and most successful "Sensationsdrama" ('sensational drama' or 'senstional film'). "Indians" can be identified, male and female already performing their basic roles: servant and temple dancer (*Lotos, Die Tempeltanzerin*; 'Lotos, the temple dancer', by Continental Kunstfilm Berlin, 1913; *Das Geschenk*

Des Inders, 'A gift by the Indian', by Karl Werner Berlin/Köln, 1914). The ambience is seldom explicitly "Indian", "India" being an unspecific amalgam of the "Oriental" as in *Lotos, Die Tempeltanzerin*. Here it is the studio decor as a bold borrowing from Greek, Egyptian, Persian and Indian sources that suggests mainly "Oriental" beauty. The temple dancer named Lotos, follows the European who stole a precious jewel (an archetypal theme) from the temple where she serves as dancer. In Europe she fell in love with him, but back in "India", at the end she has to die a suggestively stylized sacrificial death. The conspicuously strong sexual overtones of the celluloid "Indians" have to be interpreted within the broader representation of a gendered imagery and its cinematic treatment. Studying *Die Schwarze Natter* ('The Black Viper'), a "Sensationsdrama" of 1913, reveals clearly that "images" and "characters" which became "stereotypes" as "the wicked woman" or "the virtuous woman" are more often than not enigmatic, and that in concrete films this enigmatic character is highlighted by other "stereotypes" as for example that of "Indianness". I could identify strikingly broad overlapping contexts of meanings for cinematic "woman" and "Indian" as opposed to 'the' German as a would-be citizen and moral individuality, self-assuring him - or herself within the contradictions of the Wilhelminian monarchy. Characteristic strokes of German cinema's "Indians" can clearly be identified before 1914, which are brought to perfection 1916/ 17 to 1921, and are influential with the one or the other alteration until today.

THE PRIVATE AS PUBLIC, AND THE PUBLIC AS PRIVATE: SENSATIONS OF "FEMININITY" AND OTHER "OBJECTS OF PLEASURE"

Heide Schlüpmann, professor of film theory and history at Frankfurt University, unfolds many layers in pre-World War I German cinema, holding hidden life-stories of socially, politically and historically suppressed femininity. Wilhelminian cinema offered thus in a contradictory and ambiguous manner spaces for women contrasting their real existence. As heroines they mastered their actions and of course challenged male spaces. But Schlüpmann observes that those are nontheless still essentially male projections, and in the common plot constructions daring females usually paid their 'coming-out' with their exposure to the male gaze and also to death (Schlüpmann 1990).

Searching for a new access to understand the philosophical subject as formulated by Horkheimer and Adorno in *Dialektik der Aufklärung* ('Dialectic of Enlightenment') Schlüpmann paves the way for reading cinema as potentially unravelling socially subjugated philosophical/

historical (female) subjectivity since their formerly totally 'privatized' existence gains a (contradictory) space in the projections of the public sphere of cinema.

Die Schwarze Natter (1913, 'The Black Viper') by Franz Hofer was an unusual film since the determing polarities of rational and mythic are both female, and the whole driving force of action is controlled by women including sexuality. This "Sensationsdrama" was the newest rage of a dramatic film type during those days of shorter films. This one was about 36 minutes long, and was screened as part of the composite variety kind of programme.

Playing in a circus milieu, and densely packed with sensational events, hunts etc the main theme of the film is, according to Schlüpmann the idea of the mythical being confronted by the rational, both represented by female characters struggling for the love of the same man. At the end the passionate, 'archaic' and destructive Ladya with her "oriental" features the "Black Viper", has to succumb to the enlightened, rational and blonde Blanche d'Estree. Heide Schlüpmann suggests, with reference to conspicuous mirror and gazing-into-the-camera sequences with *Die Schwarze Natter*, and comparing it to contradictory developments in the equally popular 'social drama', that *Die Schwarze Natter* is able to respond to the numerous female gazes in the public well as it could reflect a more hidden wish for a female photography. Heide Schlüpmann interprets this as a prevalent mood of the German silent screen of 1912/13. It celebrates as its topical themes love, passion, family and female lifestories, where even a (contested) liberation of female gazes could happen, even if they seize the male (body). The overlapping between this iconography and photography of female urging for a wider space to unfold her subjectivity and imaginations of "Indians" happens here in the form of a 'doubled' feminity which owns all the possible traits of contesting characters in the competitive world: the sinister, the upright, the sly, the true, the mythic, the rational, the archaic and the modern. Thus "femininity" as it is here coupled with "Indianness" reinforces an image/ imagination of outdated and overcame "forces" of a society in transition.

1914 was a decisive break for the film industry as well. Besides material constraints the films shown demonstrated an open patriotism and wanted to contribute to the moral war effort. But this patriotic euphoria ceased within two years.

From 1916 onwards war-weariness can be felt at the 'cinematic front' when one reads through issues of the most influential film-trade magazines *Der Kinematograph* and *Lichtbildbühne*. They promote an offensive turing away from stirring patriotic feelings and the ongoing war was (especially after the U.S. entry) seen as a lost cause, anyway.

The film market is under the constrains of war economy, and since 1916 a list of dispensable goods has all foreign films in it besides Nordisk's productions, the huge Danish concern (Thompson 1985, S. 84). The German branch of Nordish is merged into what was the state-masterminded foundation of a film-trust, the "Universumfilm Aktiengesellschaft", the legendary UFA at Berlin in late 1917. Whereas the British government was the leading power to advocate a direct state propaganda with cinematography and had even before the UFA foundation established its Ministry of Information, it actually was the German cinema that flourished as a privately organised production and trade already before the end of World War I well into 1923/24 (Thompson 1985, S. 106). Different from the weakened national cinemas in other European countries, German cinema even challenged with "sensationals", and later "monumental films" for a short period the US-Market:

> If you want to 'start' something 'mention *Caligari*.' This astounding product of the motion-picture art has jolted the average American motion-picture mind more than all the other foreign pictures combinded. No American Producer would have dared it... Then there came ***Deception, Passion, The Golem** .... **The Lovers of a Pharaoh, The Mistress of the World*** - an imaginative thriller that outdoes, anything ever done over here-with great spectacles and plays like *The Indian Tomb* ... And it is just here that pictures like ... *The Indian Tomb* are having their effect on American producers and directors. We need better and greater stories and more imagination in their treatment. We need more the bizarre, the grotesque, the exotic in our productions... (New York Times, March 26, 1922)

It is in 1916/17 that Germany's first extensive range of "Indian films" starts. The trade is enthusiastic, and in *Die Lichtbildbühne* of November 24, 1917, there was a question "Why don't you play a real Indian Film? Which shows this wonderland, her fantastically huge temples and palaces truthfully?" This was not an advertisement for Dhundiraj Govind Phalke's films, but for a film, made by the explorer Heinz Karl Heiland *Die Dewadasi* ('The Dewadasis), a tragedy of an Indian temple dancer. Heiland actually travelled with his whole cine-equipment between 1915-17 through the length and breadth of India to shoot "Indian films" with local people acting. His films "on location" were definitely different from the bulk of the other spectacles. Until Franz Osten and Himanshu Rai made the *Light of Asia* (1925) acclaimed for its "authenticity", hardly anyone went to India to make "Indian films". "India", its temples, palaces and splendours of natural and human resources were recreated (much cheaper and equally convincing) in and around Berlin. This was "the bizarre, the grotesque, the exotique" which the New York Times attributed to German productions - but it was only one of aspects of "Indianness" in German cinema. The "Indian films" are a legion and unfold their favourite themes as:

Der Joghi ('The Yogi') by Paul Wegener Film, 1916; *Das Ratsel Von Bangalor* ('The Enigma of Bangalore') by Pax Film with the script written by Paul Leni, 1917; *Der Ring Des Schicksals* ('The Fatal Ring') by Eichberg Production, 1916; *Der Tempelrauber* ('The Temple Plunderer') by Nordfilm/ Heinz K. Heiland, 1919; *Der Thug* ('The Thug' or 'In the Service of the Deadly Goddess') by Decla/Heinz K. Heiland, 1916; *Die Entschleierte Maja* ('The un-veiled Maya') by Münchner Kunstfilm Ostermayr (Franz Osten's brother), 1917; *Die Königstochter Von Travancore* ('The Princess of Travancore') by Decla/Otto Rippert; and many more others.

The next peak of "Indian" presence on the German silver screens was in the early 20s, a time that correlates again with a peculiar economic offensive of German film industry based on the quick devaluation of their currency on highly competitive world film markets.

The three cooperative efforts which Himansu Rai undertook after 1925 (*Light of Aisa/ Prem Sanyas*, *Shiraz* of 1928 and *A Throw of Dice/ Prapancha Pash*, 1929) in collaboration with the German director Franz Osten, Niranjan Pal as scriptwriter and prolific German cameramen and set architects as Josef Wirshing, Emil Schunemann and Carl von Spreti, are exceptional in many respects. Its economics, the motivations the persons involved and the consumption context, reflect an "Indianness" that I understand as essentially different from the other films and I therefore exclude them here from my analysis to avoid oversimplification or an unmanageable length of this article.

With the end of the silent era the common and systematic exploitation of "Indian" themes dispersed, but one can find interesting characteristics of later ideological and iconographical representations up to 1958/59, since a clear-cut continuity is maintained by the three successive film versions, each in two parts, of a popular novel on an "Indian" theme. It was Thea von Harbou's *Das Indische Grabmal* ('*The Indian Tomb*') written in 1917 and soon made into a script by the author herself and her then fiancé Fritz Lang (Czerlinski 1995). From this source sprang Joe May's *Die Sendung Des Yoghi* ('The Yoghi's Mission') and *Der Tiger Von Eschnapur* ('The Tiger of Eschnapur') in 1921; Richard Eichberg's *Der Tiger Von Eschnapur* and *Das Indische Grabmal* in 1938 and finally Fritz Lang's monumental films with the same titles in 1958.

Fritz Lang's film, mostly unfavourably received by critics and disillusioned admirers (Jansen, Schütte 1976), but celebrated by the general public, was like May's and Eichberg's productions launched as an economic offensive against the supremacy of the US productions, and I think it remained the last decisive grand feature produced in Germany till date. There have been several co-productions in the 60s between Germany, Italy and France mainly, trying to pick up the thread

Advt. in *Lichtbildbühne* No 16, 1917

Advt. in Fritz Lang's Film, 1958

The Goddess of Sita, the temple dancer in *Das Indische Grabmal*

The German Heroine and Indian Maharaja; Conrad Veidt in *Das Indische Grabmal,* 1921

Set constructions for *Das Indische Grabmal,* 1921

of the golden silent "sensational" and "monumental" films, among others *Kali Yug: Die Göttin Der Rache* ('Kali Yug, The Goddess of Revenge, 1963) directed by the Italian M. Camerini, and Richard Eichberg being one of the producers. It recycles without any major innovations possibly with a slightly stronger accent than in the earlier films on "religious fanaticism" - the old images and meanings—and has to be seen within the context of the last upheaval of the 'big screen' against television.

But instead of cinema being able to reassure its position as the dominant mass medium, television became the location where the old celluloid myths were revived on another scale. As the grand old dame of the German silent screen, Lil Dagover, had once put it, India lost her peculiar luring charm which had made her an excellent theme for the big screen, due to mass tourism and television (Dürrenmatt 1982, p. 169). Henceforth one could watch *Das Indische Grabmal* (Eichberg, Lang) at least once a year (preferably around Christmas and Easter) on one of the channels, the newest *Indiana Jones'* adventure in an "Indian" *Temple of Doom* or switch over to the more intellectually refined French films like *India Song* (1975) by Marguerite Duras or to James Ivory's *Heat and Dust* of 1982.

Unlike the cinematic revival of the Raj during Thatcherism or the constant attention that French filmmakers pay to "India"/ "Indians", German filmmakers seem to shy away from fiction film and search to interpret "Indians" more via the non-fiction. I remember Reinhard Hauff's portrayal of Mrinal Sen *Ten Days in Calcutta* in 1984, and Mirjam Quinte's and Pepe Danquart's recent *Phoolan Devi*, *Rebellion Einer Banditin* ('.... rebellion of a female bandit', 1994).

"INDIANS" AS SPACES OF MEANING AT THE CUTTING LINES OF RE-PRESENTATION OF GENDER, RACE AND THE MORALITY OF A DEVELOPING CIVIL SOCIETY

As we have seen, one material aspect of cinematically imagined "Indians" has always been the keen eye, absorbing the visual richness of attractive images. Those are, irrespective whether seen in non-fiction or fiction films, transposed into imaginations and meanings. It is the necessary, more or less conscious act of the spectator. Within the reign of the perfecting "Kulturindustrie" feature films have become ideal foils of mass-produced and - consumed images of the macro-and the micro cosmos of the outer and inner worlds, and cinema's curiosity to explore them knows hardly any limits.

Concrete human beings and things are *used*/ borrowed only to be transformed according to the dominant moral/psychological struggles fought in the social subject's "Lebenswelt". The screen thus, becomes an externalised terrain of contesting moralities (Schlüpmann 1995).

Siegfried Kracauer (1947/70, S. 56/57) wrote on Joe May's *Das Indische Grambal* comparing it to the then highly successful "serials" with their "sensational adventures encountered at every known or unknown spot on earth" and concludes:

> Even though Joe May's 20-million-mark film *Das Indische Grabmal* (*The Indian Tomb*) modestly confined itself to India and normal footage, it outdid the serials in thrilling episodes. This superproduction, which imparted the same sinister moral as the Lubitsch pageants, not only adapted the miraculous practices of yoga to the screen, but showed rats gnawing the fetters of its captive hero, elephants forming a gigantic lane and an all-out fight against tigers .... The whole group of films [sensationals, serials, B.S.], with its craving for exotic sceneries, resembled a prisoner's daydream. The prison was of course the mutilated and blockaded fatherland; at least, this world mission had been thwarted, and now all exits seemed barred. These space-devouring films reveal how bitterly the average German resented his involutary seclusion. They functioned as substitutes; they naively satisfied his suppressed desire for expansion through pictures that enabled his imagination to reannexe the world.

Kracauer's arguments are founded on the premise that "the average German" is an out and out nationalist. How does Kracauer paint nationalism? As an outward lust of every German to expand, which could not happen after Versailles and the overall expansion of the 'other' imperialist nations. Consequently 'the' German sates his thirst imaginatively in the cinema - a statement that would verify the advertisments of those days praising the serial "Sensationsdrama" for it makes the whole world the spectator's stage. But the peculiar attraction of pictures as *Das Indische Grabmal* results to my understanding from a more complex communication in cinema than the one Kracauer suggests. From the many contemporary voices one can easily make out the "average" spectator's emotional attraction to certain films and that patriotism was an important ingredient to it. But what I suggest is to attribute other aspects to the moral subjectivity of the then freshly democratized citizens, too.

What I tried to show by discussing actual consumptive features of 'topicals' like the Delhi Durbar (whether shown in England, France or in Germany) which later developed into the newsreels and finally into 'news', is that cinema developed at quite an early stage the potentials to communicate ethically, morally and politically contested values and contributes to an ideological conflict management. One aspect would be the stipulation of the 'right' patriotic/ nationalistic attitudes. MacKenzie (1984, p. 72) adds to it the propagandistic force of W.G. Barker's contribution to a suitable reception of the proclamation of King George V as "Emperor of India" in British proletarian music halls in 1912.

I argue here that German cinema's public exposure of moral 'battlefields' knew already before the war "Indianness" as a specifically ambivalent chiffre as can be studied from *Die Schwarze Natter*, 'The black viper', 1913. A sexually attractive and pleasant (imaginative) playground for 'the' constrained and checked German, his or her lust could by times be 'liberated' if its object of desire is not German - and in 1917: not French, English, Russian, American etc. pp. - thus finding its partner in the "exotic" (but preferably 'Aryan').

German females desiring an "Indian" and staying with him out of their own free will as shown in the film *Die Lieblingsfrau Des Maharaja* of 1917 ('The favourite Wife of the Maharaja') remained a disputed/ scandalous escapade soon being channelled back into the homely haven of one's 'own' race and nation. I have not seen *Die Lieblingsfrau Des Maharaja*, and as far as one can be sure about what filmstock is still existing in the archives, this film is at least not available in the main German archives. The plot as described in the contemporary film magazines is built around European woman and an Indian Prince who fell in love and married in India. Her seclusion and the polygamy of her husband are constant threats to their love and finally she is offered the opportunity to leave the harem and return to Europe. After highly dramatic inner struggles she stays on, and both reunite in their true love.

Die Lieblingsfrau Des Maharaja produced by the Danish Nordisk was one of the most successful films of 1917 and the following years. Even in 1924 the German film magazine *Film-Kurier* (August 12, 1924) reports about the film's "triumphal march" around the world, and refers to it as just having been screened in India, too. The 'star' of this film is "Scher Sardar, Maharaja of Blagalpur, with his royal dignity, his tall and slim build and his noble, prominent face, a true Indian Prince" as an advertisement in *Der Kinematograph* (December 27, 1916) described him. The Danish actor Gunnar Tolnaes was since then synonym with the Indian Maharaja and a favourite heart-throb of German woman of all classes, as well as a definte box-office draw. The film's success was a disputed theme because it was not a German one, neither in terms of production and income and nor in terms of its widely adored hero. Contemporary arguments indicate also what I have criticized of Kracauer's statement: to understand 'the' spectator not as nationalist in the sense of a premordial agreement between "him" and official nationalism but as a social and political subjectivity who forms nationalist attitudes according to individually felt (psychological) needs. Within this process of cognitive activity deviations from the 'official' line are logically consistent and make it possible for the individuum not only to consciously differ (say as an outspoken opponent) but also to cultivate his 'own' nationalist attitude. Within this context, widely felt likings of "Indians" therefore result from a more complex, and not a mere reproductive and stable, but an active and dialectical emotional and mental consciousness which seems to 'need' what stimulations it gets from cinematical representations.

Ironically enough the film magazine *Lichtbildbühne* (No. 15, 1917) where the discussion of *Die Lieblingsfrau Des Maharaja* is also the cause for an agitated long article, this voice of Germany's exhibitors in 1917 misses badly within the German film industry what the *New York Times* in 1922 found a challenging characteristic of German flims: inventiveness and creativity.

And the ultimate secret of the success of Nordisk's *Die Lieblingsfrau Des Maharajas* according to *Lichtbildbühne* is its definite "foreigness", "exotism and unusualness" which attributes are identified as a mania of the (famale) German spectators. Those are with their alleged 'straying' taste held responsible for a struggling German film industry without any big hit as *Die Lieblingsfrau Des Maharaja*.

Openly rassistic and agitating for a clear cut fundamental consciousness of who the enemies are, is an article by Erich Röhrer in 1917 who castigates in the daily press Germany's "female population" of not having understood the "irriconcilable polarity between the White and the Coloured". *Die Lieblingsfrau Des Maharaja* helped to his opinion in an unprecedented way to "alluringly describe to our girls the beauties of marriage with noble Gurkhas, whose Indian way of killing left with our heroes at the Western front less pleasant memories."

This example illustrates again my point that "Indians" on the German screens performed roles of 'mirroring' or 'contrasting' the German 'self' in the broader context of a developing civil society, that was not only materially but also morally laden with conflicts and contradictions, which a free subjectivity had to tackle.

Consequently, this analysis has to sooner or later again ask why then essentials, as I state here, of the representations of "Indians" on German cinema and television screens have not decisively changed. Firstly because the material conditions of entertainment and information industries have today even perfected competitiveness and commerical orientation as against fostering an understainding of the re-presented *on its own* essential terms. Secondly because the function of cinema and television is only exclusively *presentation and recognition* of a piece of art, usually it is a compensating consumptive act for constant physical and psychological struggles to be fought.

After 1918 the desired screen - "Indians" have to be and are actually female, being harrassed in most of the cases by an "Indian" male. Especially when one studies the shifts in the construction of characters

A typical scene: The Indian temple dancer had to sacrifice herself in *Die Kaiserin Von Indien,* 1917 (The Empress of India)

Die Lieblingsfrau des Maharadscha

NORDISKFILM

NORDISKFILM

Im Harem

Ein indischer Liebesroman in 4 Akten

Bilder von märchenhafter Schönheit aus dem Orient

Gunnar Tolnaes

als Scher Sardar, Maharadscha von Blagalpur, ist mit seiner königlichen Würde, seiner hohen, schlanken Gestalt und seinem edlen, markanten Gesicht ein wirklicher indischer Fürst.

Der fünfte Film **der Siegerklasse**

NORDISCHE FILM Co. G. M. B. H.

BERLIN BRESLAU DÜSSELDORF HAMBURG
LEIPZIG MÜNCHEN AMSTERDAM ZÜRICH

Advt. in *Der Kinematograph* (27/12/1916)

and erotic relationships between the protagonists from the three versions of *Das Indische Grabmal* one finds a progressively growing gulf between male and female "Indian", symbolizing what each of the film has as an important message. That "India" is a 'double'. It is the female against the male, the weak against the strong, light against darkness, the spiritual against the sinister, the rich against the poor etc. The final polarities bearing all the contradictions, are: "India" which the European understands and "India" which the European does not and cannot understand. Consequently all the dominant narratives construct their stories, images and the suspense as a jointly fought struggle of the European and the (female) "good India" against its "drak" side. Fritz Lang's interpretation is the closest perfection of this viewpoint, and his films tear also the deepest rift between "Indian" man and woman.

This polarisation is omnipresent in the outer and the inner worlds. "Indian He" incarnates (sexual, emotional) perversion and fanatism, irrespective whether directing his lust to his 'own race' or to "Germans" (all the Maharajas of the three *Das Indische Grabmal*). Staying with "him" means physical and psychological imprisonment and a deadly threat. Whether it is one of the notorious "India servants", intriguing against their European patrons (and their wives), or the Maharajas.

Conrad Veidt in Joe May's version of *Das Indische Grabmal* is physically extremely attractive, a tribute to Gunnar Tolnaes, and his character is allowed to display certain nuances, disappearing in the later versions of Eichberg and Lang. Veidt plays fascinatingly his emotional confusion, and reveals by times traits of a hu-/ manly loving being. But he *madly* loves his Maharani, who deceived him with a European (again this is the case in all the three films). To punish her he lets German/ European architects built the marbled tomb where she should be burried alive-after an "Indian custom". "She" has to suffer from the destructive love of "Indians" (the Maharaja, and in Eichberg's film his brother), is damned to her "Indian" prison, but - except for Lang's interpretation where her liberation is her happy-ending as half-European at the German architect's side-she is only allowed a liberation by sacrificing her physical being for 'others'. May's version claims her life to rescue the German woman, and Eichberg wants "her" to die for the Maharaja in the grand finale of the respective films. The broken Maharaja ekes out a miserable existence as a penitent in all the three films.

Since my reading into the German cinematic representation of "Indians" of the last eight decades tries to carve out "images" and "stereotypes" as *contextualized spaces of meanings,* instead of enumerating "images" and "stereotypes", I leave out many interesting details about each of the mentioned films. Resuming my findings at this point the iconic "Indian" images and themes as the 'doubled India' and "the Indians" only being at 'their own' if subjugated to Europeans as the acting forces or to values set by them, the "servant", "yogi", "maharaja", "dancer/princess" are icons to be watched and to be displayed for enchantment, fascination or chill, and the same time those icons are only the outer form of meanings which have their roots within the moral/ psychological framework of the respective German society. Another quite interesting aspect which I won't follow up here in detail, is that those striking similarities between cinematic imaginations of "India" and the dominant indological constructs (Inden 1990/ 94) seem to establish a link between the scientific and the popular. It not only creates hisorical continuity, but the cinema also lends a broad visual and emotional experience to scientific assumptions about "India". Thus, unfortunately, no influential counter-forces exist even today to the re-presentation of the "India".

NOTES

1. Ahmad, Aijaz (1992), *In Theory. Classes, Nations, Literatures,* London & New York: Verso
2. Bottomore, Stephen (1995), "'An Amazing Quarter Mile of Moving Gold, Gems and Genealogy': filming India's 1902/03 Delhi Durbar", in: *Historcal Journal of Film, Radio and Television,* Vol 15, Nr. 4. October, p. 495-515
3. Chanan, Michael (1980/ 96), *The Dream that Kicks. The Prehistory and Early Years of Cinema in Britain,* London & New York: Routledge
4. Czerlinski, Ursula (1995), *Leben und Werk von Joe May unter besonderer Berücksichtigung der "Filmstadt" Woltersdorf und des dort gedrehten Filmes DAS INDISCHE GRABMAL (1921),* unpublished M.A. dissertation, Berlin
5. Dürrenmatt, Dieter (1982), *Fritz Lang, Leben und Werk,* Basel: Museum des Films
6. Hiley, Nicholas (1993b), "A Proletarian Public Sphere. The British Cinema Auditorium in the First World War, paper presented at the International IAMHIST Conference Amsterdam, July 5-11, 1993
7. Inden, Ronald (1990/ 94), *Imagining India,* Cambridge/Mass. & Oxford: Blackwell Publishers
8. Jansen, Peter U. and Wolfram Schütte (1976), *Fritz Lang,* München Wiem: Carl Hanser Verlag
9. Kracauer, Siegfried (1947/ 70), *From Caligari to Hitler. A Psychological History of the German Film,* Princeton: Princeton University Press
10. MacKenzie, John M. (1984), *Propaganda and Empire. The Manipulation of British Public Opinion, 1880-1960,* Manchester University Press

11. Mookerjee, Nanda (1970) (ed.), *I Point to India. Selected Writings of Max Müller (1823 to 1900)*, Bombay: Shakuntala Publishing House.
12. Müller, Max (1899), *Auld Lang Syne* (My India Friends - Second Series) as cited by Mookerjee (1970), S. 4
13. Said, Edward W. (1979), *Orientalism,* New York and others: Vintage Books
14. Scheurer, Hans J. (1987), *Zur Kultur - und Mediengeschichte der Fotografie. Die Industrialisierung des Blicks,* Köln: DuMont
15. Schlüpmann, Heide (1990), *Unheimlichkeit des Blicks: Das Drama des Frühen deutschen Kinos,* Frankfurt am Main: Stroemfeld/Roter Stern
16. Schlüpmann, Heide (1995), "Die Widerkehr des Verdrägten. Überlegungen zu einer Philosophie der Filmgeschichte aus feministischer Perspektive", in: *Frauen und Film,* Nr. 56/57, Frankfurt am Main, p. 41-58
17. Schlüpmann, Heide (1996) (forthcoming), "'Die Erziehung des Publikums' - auch eine Vorgeschichte des Weimarer Kinos", in: *KINtop* (1996), No. 5, Frankfurt a.M.: Stroemfeld/Roter Stern
18. Thomas, D.B. (1969/ 83), *The First Colour Motion Pictures,* London: Her Majesty's Stationary Office
19. Thompson, Kristin (1985), *Exporting Entertainment. America in the World Film market 1907-34, London: British Film Institute.*
20. Weinberger-Thomas, Catherine (1988), "Le Tigre mis au Tombeau: L' Inde-Objet de Fritz Lang", in: Purushartha, *L'Inde et L'Imaginaire/India in Western Imagination,* Paris: Editions de l' Ecole des Hautes Etudes en Sciences Sociales

VIBHA MAURYA

Oriental Images in Contemporary Spanish Writings and the Politics of Publication

Conferring awards for literature, by the state or by private publishing houses, has always called for widespread debate in Spain. Usually after the award is announced the media, especially the electronic media (radio, television) organises rounds of discussion mainly to criticise the decision of the jury. The question central to the debate is whether there is any relationship between these literary awards and the kind of literature written.[1]

In 1994, when the Nobel Laureate for literature, Camilo José Cela was awarded the *Premio Planeta* (Planeta Award) a similar debate took the nation over. Most of the literary personalities and major critics were engaged in approving or disapproving the award to Cela.[2] Part of the controversy was that, some publishing houses had been, for some years, 'placing orders' to leading novelists to write for them with a clear understanding that his/her novel would definitely be awarded. Many eminent writers like Miguel Delibes and Soledad Puértolas have confirmed the fact that some publishing houses contacted them in earlier years and they had turned down the offer. Undoubtedly, a nomination for such awards itself ensures that the book would gain one of the top places amongst the best sellers of the year.

The above reference to the politics of award for literature in Spain has an interesting relation to the subject of my essay. Many of the narrative texts that will be discussed in the following pages were actually written with India as a theme 'on order'. Two of the texts of Fernando Sánchez Dragó *El Camino del Corazón* (The Way to the Heart) and *La Prueba del Laberinto* (The Test of the Labyrinth) were part of the 1991, 1992 *Planeta* contest respectively. While the former was the finalist in 1991, the latter got the 1992 award. The narrators of the two novels do mention that they were persuaded by a friend to write such a book. It could be a strange coincidence, nevertheless, both the books were on the best-sellers list for three years. The Indian subcontinent is the main subject matter of both the texts. One could say, that for a few years now, the East in general and India in particular are 'fashionable themes' in Spain.

A fascination with 'the idea of the Orient' is not a new phenomenon. Curious travellers, intellectuals and writers have been from time to time constructing their discourses around it. 'East is a careerr'[3] was honestly declared by Disraeli (1804-1881, novelist and the leader of the Tory party) in his novel *Trancred*. Numerous twentieth century projects, whose dimensions take the most disparate realms of representations, have proved beyond doubt that Disraeli's idea about the Orient has been gaining prevalence. In the present essay I study the representation of India in contemporary Spanish writings in the backdrop of the increasing commercialization of the publishing industry and thus, examine if certain aspects of this discourse could be defined as Neo-Orientalist elements of the pop variety.

I

Indology, Oriental studies, Area Studies, etc., have not really constituted any major discipline of the social sciences or humanities in Spain. In fact, even today, in most of the universities of Spain there is a complete absence of such departments or schools. The teaching of Sanskrit is carried out at a very small scale as part of Indo- European Linguistic studies together with Greek and Latin. Since Spain was not a part of the imperial formation in the East, it did not engage in producing discursive knowledge about India which could help it in establishing its leadership in this part of the world. On the contrary, Spanish and Portuguese exercise of colonial power in the earlier periods (fifteenth century) were entirely different, as theological discourses were central to the imperial practices in the Americas. Thus, the deployers of this knowledge were those agents who had direct relations with the clergy, missionaries and the church itself. These agents also formed part of the colonial polity and the discourses produced by them acquired a certain authority. Although, the Spanish idea of India should be studied as a distinct phenomenon, India as an Asian land 'governed by a disorderly imagination instead of a world-ordering rationality'[4] constitutes the main thesis of all those who may be considered Spanish Orientalists of the nineteenth — twentieth centuries. The objects of study which constituted the core of Spanish discourse are 'classical language', history of religions, philosophy and philology (literature and some ancient Indian languages). Thus, it is a relatively limited area of study though seemingly diverse.

The distinctness of Spanish discourse on India is that it is primarily about the 'civilized', 'erudite' India and not the 'primitive', 'miserable', 'poverty-stricken' India. It is important to note that approaches to the study of India in Spain have never been anthropological. Interestingly, the way the Indian Other is constructed draws a sharp contrast with the way the Islamic Other has been depicted all along by Spanish intellectuals. We shall, in the later part of the essay, briefly dwell upon Arabigo - Spanish relations.

The Spanish scholarship on the Orient and particularly on India should also be examined in the light of the Saidian thesis on the question of knowledge and its multiple relations to power in the representation of Asia. Except for the Philippines, Spanish imperial interest was not perceived anywhere in Asia, nevertheless, the Spanish representations of India do not reflect a 'real' Orient. Spain also produces images that would define India/Indian as irredeemably different/strange and therefore, inferior to the West. Thus, a set of polarities is established in which the stereotypification of India is not avoided. My critique of Spanish writings does not revolve around the question of like or dislike, prejudice and bias or lack of objectivity or empathy. Because the issue before us is not of 'rectification of attitude' towards the Other.[5] I would discuss the motivated, intentional and monolithic Spanish discourses on India and relate it to the Spanish reader- consumer because as in France, England and Germany even in Spain the image of India is constructed on the basis of a series of signs whose meaning lies more in the consolidation of the West's self image than in any truth about India and Indians. As Said says: 'the Orientalist, poet or scholar makes the Orient speak, describes the Orient, renders its mysteries plain for and to the West. He is never concerned with the Orient except as the first cause of what he says.'[6]

In the late nineteenth and early twentieth centuries literary critics, fiction writers and philosophers like Menendez y Pelayo, Juan Valera, Menendez Pidal took a very keen interest in the Orient. Much under the influence of other European Romantics (like Joseph Campbell, 1904) of the period, Spanish romantic writers and philosophers also assumed that there was a single (maybe not a fixed one) humanity and a universal human nature. The idea is that humanity is like a single tree[7] - a metaphor for universal ethnic and linguistic history- therefore anyone can become a whole person by reuniting in him/herself the best of both worlds. India, being one of the leading sites for such teachings acquires a lot of importance for the Romantics:

A person can somehow look into him or herself and step mentally outside his or her social world in order to create for himself or herself a new person. India here becomes a living museum (and a keen marketplace) of religious humanism, of New Age psychic phenomenon, yogic health practices, and ultimate experiences.[8]

References to India by all these scholars have embodied these essences. Being engaged in literary criticism and the history of religion, they located their knowledge in the origins of literary genres from India while strongly recommending their adoption in Spain. Commenting on the origin of the novel, Menendez y Pelayo not only discusses the great tradition of fables, parables, allegories, legends and myths of India and other Asian countries but also suggests that India is the creator of the shorter narrative genre which in turn gave birth to the novel. 'Origin of the Novel' was the topic of his doctoral thesis in which he says:

> It is true that the novel was born in the East for the simple reason that land is the cradle of human genres. The Orientals are interested in all that is marvellous, and it is a known fact, this interest gives birth to the stories, which is a primitive and rudimentary form of novel. The Arab stories, for example, all originate in India and later travel triumphantly through Europe.[9]

Thus, the author goes on to trace the route and source of many Spanish stories which have some link with the *Panchatantra* and stories from the *Hitopadesh*. Similarly, Juan Valera, novelist, literary critic and philosopher decided to bring out an edition of *Legends from the Ancient Orient* in 1863. In the introduction to the collection, Valera argues at length for the need for such a collection in Spain. One of the reasons according to him was the absence of any Indological studies in his country. He says:

> There is another reason that pushes me to write these legends. We wish to popularise a bit the ancient oriental literature and begin to use it in our modern Spanish literature. In France, England and Germany the Oriental renaissance as I spoke earlier, had taken place long ago, and has left its impact on art and poetry. In Spain, nothing of this sort is noted yet.[10]

Valera, in the same introduction goes on to compare Oriental Studies in Germany, France and in Spain. He is well informed about different translations of the *Mahabharata*, the *Ramayana,* the *Vedas* and the *Shah-Named* in Germany and various verses and poems which were inspired by Indian/oriental ones. The same is true of France. Valera, almost with a sense of envy and a spirit of competition, calls upon his countrymen to fill this void in knowledge in order to be at par with other Europeans:

> We have already explained as to what we understand by progress. We understand by it the total inherited wealth of knowledge and morality, its diffusion amongst large numbers of peoples, families, tribes and nations.[11]

The body of knowledge produced by the Orientals for Valera had a great significance. The Asians were gifted with 'exclusive faculties and powerful initiatives' which facilitated the creation of 'infinite legends'[12] and stories. He also contrasts the Spanish/Europeans with the Orientals and calls them 'sterile and lazy'. However, this is only limited to the creative writings in the ancient period. Juan Valera, in the same introduction also touches upon the degradation and the fall of the Indian/ Egyptian race and the ascendance of the European as rooted in the ideas of humanism and rationality.

Ramon Menendez Pidal, the founder of modern Spanish thought, a erudite literary critic has also attributed to Indian religion and philosophy various spiritual and ethical practices in Spain. While analysing in detail the renowned seventeenth century play *El condenado por desconfiado* by Tirso de Molina, Menedez Pidal discusses the issues of morality, faith and the good and evil dichotomy. By using different aspects of Hindu religion, he bitterly criticises the fundamentalist politics of Spanish Catholicism of both Franciscan and Dominican streams. As the play is based on a legend from the *Mahabharata*[13] Pidal not only traces the route by which the story could have travelled to the far end of the Western land but he also shows the changes which the original story went through while undertaking the journey, i.e. the Pelvi, Persian court, the Muslim invasion which brought it to the Jews and the Christians. At each stage the story was adapted according to the individual religious practices and social norms of the community. Thus, the original story of a Brahmin and a butcher is converted into a story of a hermit and a criminal. Tirso de Molina, himself a priest, in what was one of his most controversial plays, depicts Paulo as a 'true, practising religious activist' who loses God's favour as he lacks absolute faith in him and because he always desires to know his destiny/fate in anticipation. Whereas the thief and assassin, Enrico, although a hard-core criminal receives the highest favour from God for his blind and absolute faith in him till the end of his life'. Pidal agreed to more than one interpretation of the play - the theological and the social. Dogmatic views, according to him, were detrimental to the reader, therefore he preferred to take his cue from the 'Hindu ethical practices' (whatever he understood of it) in order to emphasise the human values in the plot. He underlined the following:

Great plays are not exclusively invented by their authors; *the Condenado* ... is also based on a very ancient legend of the Orient, which had its deep roots in far-away lands and remote centuries before it reached the extreme end of the West. Here, in Spanish theatre, it sprung up in a most splendid bud; it is only natural that we do not appreciate just the last blossoming as an artificial and isolated product, but we admire it together with its branches, trunks and roots which actually made it sprout and gave it nectar. It is even more interesting to see how one of the most appreciated productions of Christian theatre, which seems to have been created in one stroke by a Catholic theologian, and very concretely depicts the pious exaltation of seventeenth century Spain, has its ancient root/ antecedent in an Indian story. The Spanish drama is as penetrated with deep dogmatism as the Indian one, which is not touched by any faith or hope but only trusts the transmigration of the human soul and high brahmanical castes. Nevertheless, besides this religious technique (used in the Indian story) its simplicity and its soft moral sensibility recreated and instructed the Jews, the Muslims and the Christians.[14]

Spanish interest in India didn't project any imperialist design, but the early writings (all the above mentioned scholars were engaged in academics till the middle of the 1920s) were no different from their English and French counterparts. Historians of religion and philosophers took only Hinduism to be the core religion of India and considered it an example of the Indian mind. Ronald Inden very correctly writes:

The essence of that mind was its feminine imagination, source of the dream- like worldview of the Indians. She was an inferior substitute of the West's masculine, world- ordering rationality. So the Indians were seen as concerned more with the renunciatory quest of the individual for mystic absorption....[15]

II

Although Spanish scholars, due to the political and socio- religious tensions within the country, didn't reject the Indian 'way of life' altogether. Nevertheless, the perceived constraints and excesses of the Hindu caste divide did bring the debate back to the central issue of the 'freedom and moderation of Western civil-society' as opposed to the rigid Indian system. The main reason for such similarities between Spanish and other European discourses was that the entire Spanish knowledge on India of the earlier period (the late nineteenth and early twentieth centuries) was based on the experiences of alien studies and research rather than their own. One more foreign source of information about ancient India, as mentioned earlier, was the Muslim world. India became accessible to Spain through Muslim travellers and traders. Islam had occupied a prominent place in Spanish culture for more than ten centuries. The Moors, Saracens, Turks and Moroccans had inspired and influenced Spanish theatre, legends, poetry and songs by stimulating the imagination and fantasy of its creative artists over several centuries. This fascination for the Arab grew in specific historical circumstances. From the time of the Arab invasion of Spain in eighth century till the present, Spanish life is centred around the Moor/ Christian dichotomy wherein the 'Other' is both Muslim and foreigner and the 'Self' is Spanish and Christian. Thus, Catholicism and Hispanism have been placed in opposition to the religion and nation of the 'intruder'.

The image of this 'Other' is unfolded by experimenting with a process of idealization and positive depiction at some stages and a negation of all this at other stages. Until the fifteenth century warring rivalries between the Moors and the Christians had symbiotic manifestations at the level of culture and society. While on one hand intolerance and repulsive attitudes sharpened, on the other, the mythical exaltation of the Arab in literature gained prominence corresponding to the image of a 'noble savage' of the Ibero-American type. Menéndez y Pidal in his famous article 'Spain between Christianity and Islam' had described the above 'attitude':

> Just as the military threat of the Saracens ceased, the Spaniards felt attracted to that exotic civilization the luxurious costumes, the ornamentation of their architecture, that strange way of living...[16]

However, technological advancement and accumulation of knowledge about this 'Other' gradually changed the image of the Moor/Saracens/ Marrocan, etc., in Spanish texts. Thus, the relationship of power and knowledge in the Arabigo-Spanish context influenced the representational practice. Juan Goytisolo, a contemporary writer and an expert on Arab culture and society, in his *Chronicles of Saracens* has aptly described the Spanish 'Arabist concerns':

> From the very inception in our language, the Muslim has always been a mirror in which, somehow, we have seen our reflection, our external image that interrogates and troubles us. Sometimes it would be our negative: which questions as to how much we inwardly censure ourselves and thus become an object of envy and detestation.[17]

Arabigo-Spanish relations went through very turbulent phases and this was clearly perceived in literary texts and political statements. The Spanish links with India through the Arab world were also affected by the ups and downs in their relations. However, whereas the construction of the Arabic/ Moorish Other was dictated by the multiple relations between power and knowledge, the Indian Other carried with itself the indelible mark of the place and time of its originator which also determined its character, i.e. as a 'civilized' India. Spanish scholarly access to India at least till the mid-1940s was mostly mediated by European/ Arabic interests. To a large extent, Spanish writings of earlier times are found to be based on borrowed information, therefore, they could be called mimetic. Even though the writings of such luminaries as Valera, Pidal and Menendez y Pelayo may not be considered purely reader-consumer oriented, nevertheless they did, consciously or unconsciously, serve in popularising such literatures.

III

Spanish knowledge of India, due to the mimetic and indirect nature of its construction, remained empirical, unsystematic and dispersed rather than being cohesive, ontological and organized. This is the reason why it is difficult to canonise this discourse unlike other European ones as corresponding to romantic, modernist or even post-modernist discourses. Though, I have drawn a parallel between Spanish and European romantics this may be more of a coincidence in terms of time/period. It is important to note the anachronic element in these writings on India, because even the texts produced after the war (1945 onwards) carry in them a certain romantic idealization of our space on the one hand and a mythical, exotic and ornamental exaltation on the other. Both, incidentally are important aspects of a market-oriented product, which has gained unprecedented prevalence in the last decade and a half and has led to the commercialization of the publishing industry.

Commercial concerns and market orientation are very obvious in the discourses, which are based on so-called first hand knowledge of India (as opposed to the earlier period). However, before discussing these writings (written in the 1980s and 90s) it is very important to briefly mention here two texts of major contemporary literary personalities- ***Imagen de la India*** by Julian Marias and ***Vislumbres de la India*** by Octavio Paz.

The first text entitled ***Imagen de la India*** (Image of India) was published in 1960 in the form of a small book. It is written by Julian Marías, a leading social scientist, philosopher and a disciple of José Ortega y Gasset. Presently he is a member of the Royal Academy of Spanish language. The text is a journalistic essay of an impressionistic kind, therefore it does not analyse events or issues, and rather it gives an account of his personal experiences and perceptions. It is important to note that the author has a well-developed faculty of observation and has creatively used it to write a text that is informative as well as interesting. The philosopher in Marías is very much present in it through his philosophical rhetoric. However, he is sincere and inquisitive. It is an account of the author's experience in India during his very short visit to Bangalore to the International Philosophy Congress. Julian Marías belongs to that generation of writers who lived through the Spanish Civil War (1936-39), the Second World War and the long years of Franco's fascist regime (1939-75). However, his political interventions, ideological inclinations and philosophical discourses are not directed against the establishment. Being an erudite scholar and a leading philosopher, Marías has an important place in Spanish intellectual life, though he does not belong to present-day Spain. That is why his essay on India could be read as a romantic text, which idealises India and it serves in breaking the canon as mentioned earlier. His involvement with India is different. He looks for specific signs, as he is more interested in representing the cultural imagery of India. In the ultimate analysis, these signs consolidate more the image of the self, i.e. Spain/ Europe. The text has signs such as figures of villagers, eyes, crows, etc., whose imagery is constructed to indicate a 'strange living' based on ancient beliefs and customs which for a European may signify something inferior both socially and economically. The author tries to forward philosophical explanations, which makes the text less 'hermetically sealed' and therefore, leaves some scope for interpretations. Therefore, we find here a positive, well-disposed European writer whose narration is not only beautiful but is also seemingly objective, though in no way could it be viewed other than as a Eurocentric one.

The text - an essay - adopts a monological form that disallows the Indians an active participation. Thus the writer remains outside that space both as 'an existential as well as a moral fact.' Due to this exteriority his representation of the Indian Other runs into problems.[18] Indian landscape and human figures that appear on that landscape are compared with European ones:

Poverty here is not an accident, it is a condition of India.... This poverty seems to be necessary.... The extreme poverty of the West - the one in Spain if it is there, for example - would appear to be 'infra human'; but here it never gives this impression....

Hunger itself is routine like the heat which oppresses, like the rain which drenches, like the flood or old age which makes one bend and go grey or like death which comes one day.[19]

The depressed conditions of the Indians, a stagnant, still and monological whole is constructed as if to justify the author's views on India which he had already formed on the basis of his study of Indian (Hindu) religion and philosophy, i.e. a renunciatory, destiny oriented, fatalist thinking of all the Indians:

This poverty does not in anyway hamper the dignified and beautiful gesture, the two hands folded on the chest to greet, the paused pleats of the sari, the back and forth movement of the plate near the neck, the smile...[20]

The entire text, though written with respect and love for India and the Indians, represents them as a 'manifestation of an alien mentality'.[21]

The titles of the chapters would give an idea as to how Julian Marías builds his discourse around the metaphors already existing in the European body of knowledge on India. 'Open Doors', 'The Eyes', 'Landscape with Figures', 'The Vice-President and the Crows', 'Meditation of Time', 'India as a circumstance', 'Happiness and Discontent', etc. All indicate at the age-old 'dreamland' metaphors which are mystical in some way, self-denunciatory in other and precludes any relationship between external reality 'out there' and human knowledge. The writer, therefore prefers to 'represent', 'copy' or 'mirror' that reality rather than rationally interpret it by giving a scientific explanation. In fact, the 'impenetrable India' in all respects is the main concern of the Spanish philosopher.

Vislumbres de la India- un diálogo con la condición humana (1995) - *In Light of India* - a dialogue with Human Condition[22] is the title of the book written by the eminent Mexican poet, writer and essayist Octavio Paz. Though the present essay includes only the texts by Spanish writers, however, I feel that Paz's latest long essay on India could be characterized more as a European view of India than any other. Octavio Paz is not only well known to Indians but he is also an India-expert in his own right. The book has constructed an image of India, which is seemingly based on his personal experiences, long research and study. However, it is notable that despite his long association with and stay in India, Paz has used only European sources on Indian culture and society.[23]

In Light of India has the main objective of informing the Western reader (more the European, North American than the African or South American) about this 'enigmatic land'. With a full sense of authority and as a responsible scholar Paz takes on the task of examining - as the blurb of the book says - 'an India, full of its national, religious and historical complexities'. The narration in first person and the autobiographical style makes it perhaps more accessible to the general reader and gives it a personal tone, but the major part of the text is based on information which is already available in history books, encyclopaedia, etc. Therefore, it cannot be said that it includes any new or original interpretation of Indian space based only on personal experiences. The discourse is rooted in stereotypical enquiry on India - Religions, Castes, languages, the national project, the plenty and the scarce, etc. The caste system, as in other cases, becomes an important issue even in this book. Paz, while explaining the system once again uses European sources though Romila Thapar was one of his close friends during his stay in Delhi as Ambassador of Mexico (Agyeya, J. Swaminathan, Shamlal, Krishan Khanna, Ruth Jhabwala, Romesh and Romila Thapar, Khushwant Singh are amongst the group of friends mentioned in the book). He explains:

To all this I must add something essential: unlike the Greeks, Romans or Chinese, Ancient India had no notion of history. Time is a dream of Brahma. It is maya: an illusion. Therefore, the origin and model of social institutions is not, as among the Chinese or the Greeks, in the past.

The caste system was not founded by a mythical hero like the Yellow Emperor or by a legendary legislator like Lycurgus. It was born by itself, although by divine, cosmic will, from the soil and subsoil of the society, like a plant...

In the *Bhagwad Gita*, the god Krishna tells the hero Arjuna that caste is one of the spokes of the cosmic wheel.[24]

There are innumerable instances in the book, which are no different from any Orientalist discourses of the past or present century. The subtitle: 'A Dialogue with Human Condition' is very symptomatic, as it once again hints at old metaphors used to depict India, e.g. 'The dreamland', and 'The Salvation of the Human Soul', 'Neurotic', etc. Octavio Paz makes brief references to some of the socio-political conditions of Mexico and of India and has drawn a parallel, which I consider very interesting and original aspect of the book.

IV

Commercialization and the process of commodification of all goods whereby there occurs a shift in the concerns of industry - to production for sale - is not a new phenomenon. This radical shift is witnessed in the early nineteenth century itself. The printing and publishing industry could not remain unaffected by this change. The huge increase in population and literacy during the last century influenced market conditions which in turn dictated higher output and faster turnover of products (books and journals in this case). It got an additional boost from the advances in technology and transport:

More than at any time since the invention of printing and the beginnings of the first comodified literary genre, the novel, printed matter in general was becoming just another 'novelty' to be devoured or consumed as fast as fashions changed. Production might in extreme cases be systematized to the extent of New York's 'literary factories'[25] which produced a regular quota of 'written-by-the-yard' novels commissioned from a list of competent workers. In general, the rationalization of the publishing industry radically modified the status of writers, now generally increased in number in proportion to the rise in output.[26]

Rachel Bowlby makes this observation in her remarkable book entitled *Just Looking: Consumer Culture in Dreiser, Gissing and Zola*. Undoubtedly, commercial concerns immediately catch on with the concerns of the period. Reading, during the last century, became a private and domestic affair mainly involving short-term rather than long-term durable goods. A predominance of signs, images, pleasure elements and aesthetic value are some of the aspects that commerce shared not only with the practices of industrial production but with that of arts. However, this interaction between art and industry over the century, brought to the fore an interesting issue, i.e. if industry, through its selling techniques became more like art, art too was adopting the 'rationalized structures of industry'. This mutually benefiting relationship resulted in the commercialization of literatures.

This was the background in which the major Orientalist of the nineteenth century Europe were engaged in the production of their work. Therefore it is not surprising that we come across statements such as made by Byron in 1813 to his friend Tom Moore:

> Stick to the East; - the oracle, Staël (Madame De Staël) told me it was the only poetic policy (...). The little I have done in that way is merely a 'voice in the wilderness' for you; and, if it has had any success, that also will prove that the public are Orientalizing, and pave the path for you.[27]

After quoting Byron's letter to Moor Nigel Leask goes on to comment that

> Byron speaks like a Levantine or East Indian merchant who has tapped a lucrative source of raw material in a newly opened up Orient (. . .). He offers Moore partnership in his business venture which, he has been assured by Europe's leading consultant in cultural capital, cannot fail as long as the exotic imported commodities are somewhat tailored to domestic tastes.[28]

Byron certainly had a feel for the market. He was encouraged by his publisher to make his poems with an 'Oriental Flavour' thus the series of ***Eastern Tales*** written between 1813 and 1816 made him the most popular poet so much so that a 'Byron Myth' was created.[29]

This long reference to the publishing politics of nineteenth century writers, I feel, is necessary and important, as there is an unmitigated occurrence of the same phenomenon in our times. Spanish texts on India, produced during the 1980s and 1990s are the most ardent examples of the commercialization of the publishing industry. In the following pages I shall be looking at the varied discourses produced by the Spanish writers in the 1980s and 90s and examine whether these discourses can be categorized as 'neo-Oriental discourses' since they are replete with such elements which not only represent the age-old static, dogmatic India and thus, are reduced to representing something that can only be called Orientalism of Pop variety. It is unnecessary to repeat that the approach of these writers to India is very similar to that of Byron's:

'exotic, imported commodities are somewhat tailored to domestic tastes'.

The two novels of Fernando Sánchez Dragó *El camino del corazon* (The Way of the Heart, 1991) and *La prueba del laberinto* (The Test of the Labyrinth, 1992) were also best-sellers in their respective years of publication. The novels certainly have hidden commercial motives, which are an inherent aspect of the best-seller genre.

The two books form a series, as the hero of both the texts is the same person. Dragó takes his confused, sad, sensitive and emotional hero - Dionisio - on a tour through Palestine, Egypt and India between the spring and the summer of the year 1991. *La prueba del labrinto* is structured around the existentialist concerns of the narrator and the first part is composed of dialogues and monologues. The author, through a description of the mental and physical state of his hero, his family conditions, and his philosophical bent of mind, predicts the forthcoming journey to the far-eastern lands. Within this personal discourse are built in the justification of imminent travels and the acceptance of a publisher's proposal to write a book on the East. This text comes as a continuation of the earlier one *El Camino del Corazón*. The novels are autobiographical in character and the plot revolves around the theme:

A man decides to go on a long journey to the Orient with the aim of finding there knowledge, delight, spirituality and Happiness, all that the Occident has denied him.[30] Thus, if in *La Prueba* the objective of the journey is 'to search the Jesus de Galilia', then in *El Camino* it is 'Happiness'. Nevertheless, religion is an integral part of the discourse. The use of the name 'Jesus' is deliberate and symbolic. There are extensive quotes from *I Ching, the Bhagvad Gita* and the *Bible* and other ancient European and non-European texts. In the first text we are informed of the process of familiarization and acquisition of knowledge of the Orient by the narrator while in the second text, the narrator projects himself as an authority on Oriental space, its philosophy and religion. Though both the texts are located in the 1990s an indelible mark of 'hippieism' (of the 1960s) is perceived, for example, in the search for happiness, spirituality, the escape from one's own milieu, *hashis* - all these are associations with the hippie movement. In real life too, Sánchez Dragó came into contact with India for the first time in the 1960s. Therefore, the personal experiences of the author are used to construct the texts. The short visits to the East at different periods of time seem to give the author a confidence in his knowledge of India which is why he engages in comparing, differentiating, and interpreting human existence in different parts of the world. The texts themselves are confused, hybrid and crafty constructions. They develop a rhetoric of philosophic, moralistic and satiric nature which, in turn, help him to comment on European, particularly Spanish manners/ philosophy/ way of life. The blurb of *La Prueba* contains the following text, which, in my opinion, is very symbolic:

> In his life, there are mysteries, journeys, tensions, uncertainties, ambushes, good and evil, beautiful women and kind women, traitors, exotics, occultism, tyrants, political and religious struggles, clashing of swords, conspiracies, the three wise men, lepers, prostitutes, adultery, love, pain, death and even a resurrection - what more does one need?[31]

Perhaps the question 'what more does one need?' defines the objective of the texts. The predetermined expectation of the targeted reader, whose involvement with Oriental space is superficial in nature, finds all the (pop) elements in the novel; therefore what more is needed?

The elements that could be categorized as pop elements are related not only to the so-called luxurious/peaceful/exotic/sublime ambience of the Orient but also to the specific imagery and signs which have mercantalistic objectives. The great stimuli for the newly developed taste of the Orientalized Spanish reader are the signs which are once again derived from civilized/erudite India and are aptly adapted to Spanish conditions. These are mainly the signs belonging to the cultural-religious fields of knowledge. This image of India is sought to be represented as an 'objective reality' but without much success, as the author is located outside the political, productive or social process of that reality. The monological form of the texts helps in emphasising the exteriority factor because as Said says:

> The Orient is less a place than a topos, a set of references, a congeries of characteristics that seem to have its origin in a quotation or a fragment of at text or a citation from someone's work on the Orient...[32]

The 'consumer conscious' Dragó carefully selects these references, as he knows exactly what will appeal to the reader:

> One last thing is left to be done; to transcribe the sentence from the Bhagvatam, which this morning I sent to my mother. It says that just as a bee covets honey from different flowers, the prudent man too accepts the essences of different scriptures and sees only the best of all literatures.[33]

In another context he alludes to Gandhi's *ahimsa*:

> Heraclitus, before Plato could predict, says that those who are awake live in a common world but those who are asleep live in separate worlds.
>
> The second part of this profound sentence is equally important as all the four sectors of inhabitancy, due to religious fanaticism, are breaking into pieces the

old crown of Jerusalem. When will a Christian or a Moorish or a Jewish Gandhi be born here, who will be capable of imposing his *ahimsa* in this crazy situation?[34]

Any number of stances from the text could be cited where Dragó has used such imagery as Gandhi/ Bhagvad Gita/Ahimsa/Karma/ Shiva/ Vishnu/ Brahma/ Devi/ Kali/ Ganga. However, all these devices of a highly encoded language do not describe '*the real thing*' as India, rather they express an idea of India, which is out of context. A-historical, non-contextual reference serve to consolidate the image of the lost/ unfortunate/ materialistic/ unhappy/ disturbed Dionisio, meaning therefore, a European 'self':

Yes, I tried to do that when I had the Communist fever, during my youth and also later in 1969, then Brahma, Shiva, Vishnu knocked me down from the Western horse straight onto the steps of the Ganges passing through Benaras.[35]

As the journey of the protagonist is planned out as a pilgrimage it relapses into a series of prayers and recitations which are taken more from the scriptures and ancient texts than from any perceptible physical experiences. Thus, the actual identity of India vanishes and a set of fragments appear. The texts are not very substantial, their geo-political and social reality is overlaid with exaggerated valorization, exalted sympathy and extreme generalizations. Therefore, it is important to differentiate between the writers who absorb Oriental material into the special structures of their discourses with a view to create a fabulous, exotic impression and those who use Oriental material to develop consumerist consciousness in the reader for whom these texts are also a product. Like the pop Art of the 1960s the 'neo- Orientalist' texts also seek to celebrate the wonders of consumerism and the glamorous pop images of the Indian 'Other'. However, one can argue that this literature adequately responds to contemporary pop culture, which is indeed lively and entertaining.

V

The zeal with which the contemporary Spanish reader is being instructed on Oriental matters itself is a reflection of the commercial concerns of publishers. In fact, the Orientalizing process of the European public in general has taken a new but trivial form. In an interesting article in The *Times of India*, Jug Suraiya rightly points out that journalistic pieces on India are most varied:

. . . from inspiring first hand accounts in London's Sunday papers of top flight New York fashion models who spent a sabbatical season bandaging lepers in

Mother Teresa's home for the dying destitute in Calcutta; from German tourists extolling the virtues of bidis over cigarettes, to American sociologists upholding the practice of sati as a supreme example of spontaneous spiritual combustion.[36]

Such an endorsement of Indian values by the West could be interpreted as the rebirth of old Orientalism in a more degenerate form. Oriental characteristics such as fatalism, quest for spiritual salvation, indolence and tolerance are now posited against all the Western 'materialist' values and are being valorized. This, however, does not indicate that the West has come of age in its approach to India. The keywords still remain Pundit, Brahmin, Maharajas, beggars, Harijans, Ganga, spirituality, etc. Therefore, the main focus is on the age-old mystic/ mythical impermeable India.

One more fiction in this series is that of Alvaro Bermejo's *Benarés* (1995). The narration begins in Spain (San Sebastian, Barcelona, Madrid) and ends in Benaras. No doubt, the above sentence is more than sufficient to imagine the entire plot of the novel. The theme (if any) revolves around the question of death and how to confront its imminent arrival. The main character, a publisher and writer himself, decides to transport his beloved to India (to Banaras) so that she could peacefully die of cancer and subsequently he also vanishes in the burning ghats of Benaras at the bank of the Ganges. Paradoxically most Europeans find Benaras to be most disturbing, shocking, repugnant and inhuman of all places. But it is still equated with a location of tranquillity and peace. Bermejo is also unable to remain outside this space where only 'death lives all the time', still the quest for spirituality and inner strength continues:

> Juan Narbona, that I knew, was also dying together with Elba in the midst of infinite silence of each one of those nights. He was dying to facilitate the birth of a new man, a man purified by the profound magic of India, by her ancient mysticism and by all her mysteries.[37]

Every pilgrim, I think, sees and perceives things in his/her own way, though the experiences of earlier pilgrims are also taken into account. The river Ganges, undoubtedly, has a special place in Indian mythology and tradition and has drawn millions of Indians in the quest for spiritual salvation to her banks. However, there are increasing reports about hundreds of Westerners arriving at the river either to immerse the ashes of their friends and relatives or to die in peace. Bermejo, in his book, perhaps makes an attempt to explain and justify this new engagement of the Europeans with the question of death or more importantly with dealing with death. As explained by the protagonist, there is an increasing realization in Europe that death is not something that comes at an indistinct time in the future. European thought and culture, according to the author does not prepare them to face it. Therefore they turn to India, to Ganges and to Benaras where death is most alive. In the present day global context where incurable diseases like AIDS, terrorism, regional wars, cut-throat competition, etc., are constantly on the rise and due to economic recession, unemployment, etc., a sense of depression and insecurity has set in, one might say (though it is more for psychologists and sociologists to comment) that discourses on salvation and death are natural. If solace is to be found at the banks of river Ganges, what is the harm? My critique is not of people's behaviour in a given situation but that such cross cultural appropriation by writers should be submitted to a serious scrutiny, as the image of India does not undergo any transformation in the European mind, rather it once again consolidates the primeval stereotypes of a nation nestling in mysterious antiquity. Bermejo's fiction represents only this mysterious, incomprehensible India which is an adequate location for escaping from the 'worldly rationality of Europe'. The imagery and metaphors selected by the author are neither original nor different. They are very appropriately packaged for Spanish consumption. It is to be noted that the Spanish readers' response is very satisfying for the author and the publisher of the book as it was awarded the *Pio Baroja* prize by the Basque government - a prize equivalent to the National Award for literature.

Contemporary writings on India by Spanish writers and scholars can not be defined as voluminous, nevertheless, there is a perceptible increase in the production of such texts. In the years 1990-95, one could at a glance find five to six fictional texts and an equal number of philosophical treatise and several volumes of translations of both fiction and non-fiction of Indian authors on the shelves of leading book stores in Madrid. Some of these writings, however significant or insignificant they may be, have been examined above, to some others I will make a brief reference.

In 1995, Javier Moro Lapierre wrote a sentimental text *El Pie de Jaipur*[38] (A Foot from Jaipur) in which, as the title suggests, he narrates the protagonist's journey through Europe to Jaipur where he acquires a foot for those who had been victims of the Wars. The experiences of Phnom Penh, New York, Paris and finally Jaipur form the core material for the plot. The author uses the real life experiences of a Cambodian youth who had lost his leg in a mine explosion. Central to the discourse is the theme of passion for life: courage, valour and unmitigated faith in life rather than in death. Obviously, for dwelling upon such existential questions - the quest for salvation, etc. - India proves to be a suitable location. *The foot from Jaipur* appropriates these aspects by conjuring up images of destiny/ faith and dealing with life as given by fate because he 'was born on the day of his accident.'

A similar text on the 'question of dealing with life/death' was written by an eminent woman writer Soledad Puertolas - *Queda la noche* (1989).[39] It is a disappointing text both in its subject matter as well as in the style, more so as Soledad Puertolas is a leading writer of short stories and novels of certain calibre. The plot situated partly in India, partly in Nepal only revolves around the experience or the experimentation of hashish. The use of the drug is also important as it describes the protagonist's escapism. The novel completely fails to exploit the objective of the theme and ends in a chaotic fashion. The total failure notwithstanding, the text was a grand success in Spain (apart from receiving the *Planeta* award for 1989, 200,000 copies of the first edition were sold). This is a matter of concern as in the name of India/Orient, publishers are selling just anything.

In conclusion, I can only add that the image of India in contemporary Spanish writings project only a rebirth of the old belief of an eternally ancient India with its various essences like religion, caste, spirituality, etc. However, an important point to note about the new Spanish discourse on India is its triviality as the imagery and signs used to represent India can only be characterized as of the pop variety.

I also conclude that though the Spanish discourse represent a 'civilized' India it does not in any way transform, reverse or change the age-old image of India. This is clearly not the objective of writers as consumer consciousness has overtaken all other concerns. Therefore, the carefully selected metaphors and signs only aim at serving commercial purposes.

NOTES

1. Miguel Garcia-Posada in an article entitled 'Contributors and Awards' (Premios y Contribuyentes) published in *El País* dated 28.12.1995, discusses at length the purpose of literary awards, mode of selection and existence of any real relationship between literary awards and literature.
2. Editorial *Planeta*, Barcelona, Spain is a well-known publishing house which brings out a series - 'Colección Autores españoles e hispanoameicanos'. This publishing house has an established annual award for literature, which is conferred to Spanish or Latin American writers after the decision of a jury.

   Camilo José Cela is not only a Nobel laureate but he has also won several other awards for literature. However, it is said that Cela personally took an interest in getting himself nominated for the Planeta Award.

3. As cited by Edward Said in *Orientalism*, London, 1978, p. 5.
4. Ronald Inden, *Imagining India,* Oxford, 1990, p. 49.
5. Ibid., p.3 8.
6. Edward Said, op. cit., pp. 20-21.
7. Ronald Inden, op. cit., p. 81. See also *Culture and Imperialism* by Edward Said, London, 1993.
8. Ibid., p.38.
9. M. Menéndez y Pelayo, *Obras Completas*, Tomo IV, 'Origenes de la novela', ed. Miguel Artigas, Madrid, 1941-1947, pp. 201-12.
10. Juan Valera, *Obras Completas,* Tomo I, Madrid, 1958, pp. 900-1.
11. Ibid., p. 903.
12. Ibid., p. 902.
13. Tirso de Molina, a priest and playwright adapts a story from the *Mahabharata* for his play. The story about a devotee and a butcher is used by Tirso to criticise the fundamentalist and dogmatic views of Catholicism. The Arab and Jewish adaptations are very similar to the original story in the *Mahabharata*. In all the versions a contrast is sought to be drawn between an illustrious, erudite man (a brahmin in the Hindu religion) who leads a sacred life devoted completely to the service of God and a butcher whose main virtue is his unshakeable faith in God. The butcher in the *Mahabharata* is shown to possess high moral values and professional merits and serves as a model to be emulated. Whereas, in order to sharpen the contrast in the Arab and Jewish versions the personal merits and professional skills of the butcher is not highlighted. Pidal uses these differentiations to underline the age-old contradiction between one set of people and another as provided in the Hindu caste system.
14. *El condenado por desconfiado* by Tirso de Molina, Lecture delivered by Ramon Menendez y Pidal in the Royal Spanish Academy on 19.10.1902. (Appears in *Estudios Literarios* by Menéndez Pidal, Atenea S.E, Madrid, 1920, pp. 13-14.)
15. Ronald Inden, op. cit., p. 4.
16. Ramón Menéndez Pidal, 'España entre la Cristianidad y el Islam', in *Mis páginas preferidas* , Madrid, 1957.
17. Juan Goytisolo, *crónicas sarracinas*, Barcelona, 1982, pp. 8-9.
18. Edward Said, op. cit., p. 21.
19. Julian Marías, *Imagen de la India*, Editorial Revista del Occidente, Madrid, 1973, p. 27.
20. Ibid.
21. Ronald Inden, op. cit., p. 39.
22. Octavio Paz, *In Light of India*, Tr. Eliot Weinberger, The Harvill Press, London, 1997.
23. Most of the sources and references mentioned by Paz are either European, e.g. 'Islam in Medieval India' by Peter Hardy in *Sources of Indian Tradition* by A.T. Embree, New York, 1988; *History of India* by Vincent A. Smith, Oxford and New York, 1951; *Homo Hieraricus: The Caste System and Its Implications* by Louis Dumont, Chicago, 1970; (*Ghalib: Life and Letters* by Akeel Bilgrami, Cambridge, 1969; *L'Indie, le pouvoir et la puissance* by Jean-Alphonse Bernard, etc. Except for Romila Thapar and D.D Kosambi

no other Indian references, researches or sources are used by the author, which is strange as Paz had the opportunity of working in Indian libraries.

24. Octavio Paz, op. cit., p. 66.
25. For more information on the subject see E.W.Bok 'Literary Factories', *Publishers' Weekly*, no. 1072, 13 August 1892.
26. Rachel Bowlby, *Just Looking*: *Consumer Culture in Dreiser, Gissing and Zola,* New York and London, 1985, pp. 8-9.
27. Nigel leask, *British Romantic Writers and the East: Anxieties of Empire*, Cambridge University Press, pp. 8-9. (Nigel Leask focuses her study on the 'anxieties and instabilities' in the Romantic discourse on the Orient. We have quoted here from Chapter 1 entitled 'Byron Turns Turk: Orientalism and the Eastern Tales'. This chapter discusses Byron's 'Eastern Tales' in the context of Byron's own approach to empire as also his attitude towards the orient.)
28. Ibid., pp.8-9.
29. Ibid.
30. Fernando Sánchez Dragó, *El camino del corazón*, Editorial Planeta, Barcelona, 1990, see the blurb.
31. Fernando Sánchez Dragó, *La prueba del laberinto*, Editorial planeta, Barcelona, 1992, see the blurb. (In this essay I have been compelled to quote several times from the blurbs of the books as I felt that these project the real intention of the publishers/ writers. Consumer conscious writings and best-seller genres find it necessary to make sensational references to the content of the book.)
32. Edward Said, op. cit., p. 177.
33. Fernando Sánchez Dragó, *La prueba del laberinto*, op. cit., p. 248.
34. Ibid., p. 240.
35. Ibid., p. 223.
36. Jug Suraiya, 'The Fine Balance of Neo-Orientalism' in *The Times of India*, New Delhi, 4 November 1996. (The term Neo-Orientalism used in the present essay is borrowed from the said article. Jug Suraiya has shown how the West is again trying to tell us how to be 'properly Indian'. This round about instruction on how to be ourselves comes in various forms and at various levels: from the so-called 'curry clubs' of Britain where culinary authenticity is measured in direct proportion to the chillies in the food. He goes on to say that unfortunately this West sponsored 'Indian' values are seized upon by ideological opportunists here... What is a matter of great concern is this West sponsored 'Indianization' of India could represent the rebirth of Orientalism. This new discourse with the added elements of the market is effectively Neo-Orientalism.)
37. Alvaro Bermejo, *Benarés*, Ediciones Jucar, Madrid, 1995, p. 155.
38. Javier Moro, *El pie de Jaipur*, Planeta/Seix Barral, Barcelona, 1995.
39. Soledad Puértolas, *Queda la noche*, Planeta, Barcelona, 1989.

Contributors

Chitra Harshvardhan teaches German at the Centre for German Studies, Jawaharlal Nehru University, New Delhi.

Gerhard Koch is Professor at the Fachhochschule, Munich, Germany

Margit Koves was Fellow, ICHR and is presently teaching at the Hungarian Studies Section of the Department of Slavonic and Finno-Ugrian Stuties, University of Delhi.

Vibha Maurya, editor of this volume, is Professor of Hispanic Studies at the Department of Germanic and Romance Studies, University of Delhi.

Ranjani Mazumdar is a documentary filmmaker.

Shashi Raina is Reader in English at Lakshmi Bai College, University of Delhi.

Jyoti Sabharwal is currently teaching German at the Department of Germanic and Romance Studies, University of Delhi.

Brigitte Schulze is a lecturer is Social and Political Sciences at the Fachhochschule, Frankfurt, Germany, and is presently completing her Ph.D on D.G. Phalke.

Radha Sharma teaches French at the Department of Germanic and Romance Studies, University of Delhi.